International Influence Beyond Conditionality

The European Union's (EU) membership conditionality has been perceived as a highly effective means of influence on non-member states in the run-up to the 2004 and 2007 enlargements. According to the main incentive-based explanation that dominates the literature, conditionality has been particularly effective whenever the EU offered a credible membership incentive and when domestic opposition to the terms of conditionality was low.

This book challenges much of the existing work on EU enlargement and postcommunist transition, however, by testing the conditionality thesis in the post-accession setting. Whereas a conditionality hypothesis would predict deteriorating compliance among the newest member states, several chapters find the opposite. Enduring compliance among postcommunist states with the acquis, as well as with less formally institutionalized EU preferences for economic liberalization and minority protection, calls into question the role that conditionality plays in eliciting conformity. However, conditionality's effects have been seen to vary across countries and issues. As the first study to systematically examine the relationship between international institutions and postcommunist states after enlargement, this book provides new insights into how external actors exercise their power in domestic politics.

This book was published as a special issue of the *Journal of European Public Policy*.

Rachel A. Epstein is Associate Professor of Political Economy and European Politics at the Josef Korbel School of International Studies at the University of Denver. She has written widely on the role of international institutions in denationalizing defence and financial policy in Europe and is the author of *In Pursuit of Liberalism: International Institutions in Postcommunist Europe* (Johns Hopkins University Press, 2008).

Ulrich Sedelmeier is Senior Lecturer in International Relations at the London School of Economics and Political Science. He is the author of *Constructing the Path to Eastern Enlargement* (Manchester University Press, 2005) and co-editor of *The Politics of European Union Enlargement: Theoretical Approaches* (Routledge, 2005) and *The Europeanization of Central and Eastern Europe* (Cornell, 2005).

Journal of European Public Policy Series

Series Editor: Jeremy Richardson is a Professor at Nuffield College, Oxford University

This series seeks to bring together some of the finest edited works on European Public Policy. Reprinting from Special Issues of the 'Journal of European Public Policy,' the focus is on using a wide range of social sciences approaches, both qualitative and quantitative, to gain a comprehensive and definitive understanding of Public Policy in Europe.

Towards a Federal Europe
Edited by Alexander H. Trechsel

The Disparity of European Integration
Edited by Tanja A. Börzel

Cross-National Policy Convergence:
Causes Concepts and Empirical Findings
Edited by Christoph Knill

Civilian or Military Power?
European Foreign Policy in Perspective
Edited by Helene Sjursen

The European Union and New Trade Politics
Edited by John Peterson and Alasdair R. Young

Comparative Studies of Policy Agendas
Edited by Frank R. Baumgartner, Christoffer Green-Pedersen and Bryan D. Jones

The Constitutionalization of the European Union
Edited by Berthold Rittberger and Frank Schimmelfenig

Empirical and Theoretical Studies in EU Lobbying
Edited by David Coen

Mutual Recognition as a New Mode of Governance
Edited by Susanne K. Schmidt

France and the European Union
Edited by Emiliano Grossman

Immigration and Integration Policy in Europe
Edited by Tim Bale

Reforming the European Commission
Edited by Michael W. Bauer

International Influence Beyond Conditionality
Postcommunist Europe after EU enlargement
Edited by Rachel A. Epstein and Ulrich Sedelmeier

The Role of Political Parties in the European Union
Edited by Björn Lindberg, Anne Rasmussen and Andreas Warntjen

International Influence Beyond Conditionality

Postcommunist Europe after EU enlargement

Edited by Rachel A. Epstein and
Ulrich Sedelmeier

LONDON AND NEW YORK

First published 2009 by Routledge
2 Park Square, Milton Park, Abingdon, Oxon, OX14 4RN

Simultaneously published in the USA and Canada
by Routledge
711 Third Avenue, New York, NY 10017

Routledge is an imprint of the Taylor & Francis Group, an informa business

© 2009 Edited by Rachel A. Epstein and Ulrich Sedelmeier

First issued in paperback 2013

Typeset in AGaramond by Value Chain, India

All rights reserved. No part of this book may be reprinted or reproduced or utilised in any form or by any electronic, mechanical, or other means, now known or hereafter invented, including photocopying and recording, or in any information storage or retrieval system, without permission in writing from the publishers.

British Library Cataloguing in Publication Data
A catalogue record for this book is available from the British Library

ISBN13: 978-0-415-48648-4 (hbk)
ISBN13: 978-0-415-84525-0 (pbk)

Contents

	Notes on Contributors	vi
1	Beyond conditionality: international institutions in postcommunist Europe after enlargement *Rachel A. Epstein and Ulrich Sedelmeier*	1
2	After conditionality: post-accession compliance with EU law in East Central Europe *Ulrich Sedelmeier*	11
3	The remains of conditionality: the faltering enlargement of the euro zone *Juliet Johnson*	31
4	The politics of EU conditionality: the norm of minority protection during and beyond EU accession *Gwendolyn Sasse*	47
5	Tempered by the EU? Political parties and party systems before and after accession *Milada A. Vachudova*	66
6	The social context in conditionality: internationalizing finance in postcommunist Europe *Rachel A. Epstein*	85
7	Out-liberalizing the EU: pension privatization in Central and Eastern Europe *Mitchell A. Orenstein*	104
8	EU political accession conditionality after the 2004 enlargement: consistency and effectiveness *Frank Schimmelfennig*	123
9	A governance perspective on the European neighbourhood policy: integration beyond conditionality? *Sandra Lavenex*	143
	Index	161

Notes on Contributors

Rachel A. Epstein is Associate Professor of Political Economy and European Politics at the Josef Korbel School of International Studies at the University of Denver, USA.

Juliet Johnson is Associate Professor of Political Science at McGill University, Canada.

Sandra Lavenex is Professor of International Politics at the University of Lucerne, Switzerland.

Mitchell A. Orenstein is the S. Richard Hirsch Associate Professor of European Studies at Johns Hopkins University School of Advanced International Studies, USA.

Gwendolyn Sasse is Professorial Fellow, Nuffield College, and Reader in Comparative Politics, Department of Politics and International Relations, University of Oxford, UK.

Ulrich Sedelmeier is Senior Lecturer in International Relations at the London School of Economics and Political Science, UK.

Frank Schimmelfennig is Professor of European Politics at the Centre for Comparative and International Studies (CIS), ETH Zurich, Switzerland.

Milada A. Vachudova is an Associate Professor in the Department of Political Science at the University of North Carolina at Chapel Hill, USA.

Beyond conditionality: international institutions in postcommunist Europe after enlargement

Rachel A. Epstein and Ulrich Sedelmeier

INTRODUCTION

International institutions use conditionality – the conferral of rewards in exchange for compliance – to direct policy in target states. The use of conditionality has proliferated in recent decades since the 'first wave' of conditionality exercised by the International Monetary Fund (IMF) in the 1950s. A growing range of international institutions has become increasingly engaged in areas of domestic politics the world over. Yet the capacity of such conditionality to elicit its intended response has been notoriously uneven – except in one region – and that is East Central Europe (ECE).

The European Union's (EU's) membership conditionality, employed most intensively in the run-up to the 2004 and 2007 enlargements, has been perceived as a highly effective means of influence. It is widely credited with having brought about an alignment of the ten postcommunist countries' systems of governance, economies and legal structures with the West European member states and the EU's *acquis communautaire*. According to the rationalist, incentive-based explanation that dominates the literature, conditionality has been particularly effective when the EU offered a credible membership incentive and when incumbent governments did not consider the domestic costs of compliance threatening to their hold on power (Kelley 2004; Schimmelfennig 2005; Schimmelfennig and Sedelmeier 2005; Vachudova 2005).

From the perspective of such an incentive-based 'conditionality hypothesis', however, the EU's 2004 and 2007 enlargements might present a turning point for the influence of international institutions in postcommunist Europe. For if the incentive-based explanation were correct in predicting the circumstances under which non-member states comply with the demands of international institutions, we would expect their influence on postcommunist domestic politics to deteriorate after the 2004/07 enlargements. After enlargement, the main conditions that incentive-based explanations regard as critical for the EU's influence through conditionality – a credible membership incentive and non-prohibitive domestic adjustment costs – are no longer as favourable in postcommunist Europe. According to the conditionality hypothesis, the decreasing influence of international institutions should be particularly salient in three different contexts: (i) the new member states *after* accession; (ii) candidate countries in the western Balkans and Turkey; and (iii) the postcommunist countries involved in the EU's European neighbourhood policy (ENP).

This book tests the conditionality hypothesis explicitly in these areas and finds only mixed results for it in the post-enlargement setting, and in some instances reaching back to the pre-enlargement setting, as well. Some contributions find evidence for the incentive-based approach. For example, in certain issue areas compliance with international institutions indeed corresponded to membership conditionality before accession and declined after, particularly with respect to political party platforms and economic and monetary union (EMU). Likewise, the high domestic costs of compliance with international institutions' demands in the western Balkans and Turkey do undermine the power of the EU's membership conditionality in the current period.

But other findings from this book call the conditionality hypothesis into question. Compliance with EU law among postcommunist member states has been strong in the post-enlargement period. Although compliance with EMU has been uneven across states, some postcommunist states are indeed striving hard to join. Compliance with the prescriptions of international organizations (IOs) in the areas of bank privatization and pension reform has remained consistent, despite the absence of EU conditionality, in the pre- *and* post-enlargement periods. Finally, the ENP exercises influence differently without the membership incentive, namely through extending less hierarchical governance structures to non-member states. In what follows, we first derive expectations from the conditionality hypothesis and then compare those predictions to the findings in the book, highlighting where the conditionality hypothesis does and does not get support from the evidence. We conclude by outlining further avenues for research.

THE CONDITIONALITY HYPOTHESIS: EXPECTATIONS

New member states: post-conditionality compliance

After accession, the membership reward is no longer conditional for the EU's new member states. As the incentive structure for the new members changes, post-accession compliance with costly pre-accession demands of international institutions should deteriorate. After all, if it had only been the external incentive of membership that drove compliance, then – having won the ultimate reward – why would the newest EU members not be tempted to roll back reforms that had been the most costly to implement? Of course, dismantling institutions is not always cost free, and domestic actors benefiting from IO demands can raise the costs of non-compliance. However, if domestic costs of compliance remain high, a rationalist perspective would expect the likelihood of continued post-accession compliance to vary across issue areas, according to the extent to which the EU is able to sanction (non)compliance by its members.

We can distinguish four such issue areas: (i) the rules that are part of the *acquis communautaire*; (ii) rules for which EU institutions continue to apply conditionality after accession; (iii) rules that the EU made subject of its political conditionality; and (iv) rules that are neither part of the *acquis* nor were an explicit part of conditionality.

Acquis communautaire
With regard to the *acquis communautaire*, EU institutions can sanction persistent non-compliance in member states through financial penalties imposed by the European Court of Justice (ECJ). Yet despite such leverage, a sanctioning gap should appear compared to the pre-accession phase. The ultimate sanction of withholding membership is no longer available and financial penalties take time to impose. All else being equal, rules that are part of the *acquis* should then see a general deterioration of compliance. However, non-compliance is most likely to be temporary (albeit possibly drawn-out) until the ECJ imposes sanctions, rather than a complete reversal and durable non-compliance.

Continuation of conditionality
Although membership conditionality ends with accession, in a few policy areas conditionality continues. Membership in the Schengen area and in EMU are not automatic with EU membership. In both cases, membership requires a separate decision, which is subject to would-be members meeting certain conditions. An incentive-based explanation would then expect the likelihood of compliance to depend on governments' issue-specific cost/benefit calculations that include the incentive on offer. The decoupling of compliance from EU membership suggests that compliance will vary across the new members.

The new members already had to adopt Schengen rules as part of the EU's accession conditionality. Continued compliance in order to qualify for membership should be more uniform than with the EMU convergence criteria, because although the new members had to accept EMU ultimately, they were not asked to meet the conditions upon accession. Indeed, all new members (except for Cyprus, Bulgaria and Romania) joined Schengen in December 2007, while so far only Slovenia (January 2007), Malta and Cyprus (January 2008) have been accepted into EMU.

Rules of political conditionality
Rules that are not part of the *acquis*, but were part of the EU's political conditionality, include democratic principles, human rights, and minority rights. In these issue areas EU institutions do not have any sanctioning power in full members, except in extreme cases of a 'serious and persistent breach' of democracy and fundamental rights, where they can act under Article 7 of the EU treaty to suspend certain membership rights. An incentive-based approach would then expect a significant loss of influence for international institutions after accession. The new members might not implement pre-accession commitments after accession, or reverse earlier concessions in costly areas – unless domestic beneficiaries of internationally induced reform have veto power.

Rules that are not subject to EU conditionality
Incentive-based approaches expect the influence of international institutions to be weakest in areas in which the EU never applied conditionality. Such areas concern rules that are neither part of the *acquis*, nor explicitly included in its accession conditionality. Post-accession compliance problems could also be expected in issue areas in which other IOs – including the IMF and the World Bank, which supported a similar overall reform agenda as the EU but could not offer similarly high incentives – had taken the lead. Incentive-based approaches might expect that pre-accession influence of such institutions is already very limited if they could not offer material inducements and if the EU did not tie their recommendations to improved prospects for EU accession. Whatever influence such an implicit link to EU accession yielded, it would be expected to erode quickly after accession.

Current candidate countries and the ENP

Candidate countries
Beyond the question of post-accession compliance in the EU's new member states, an incentive-based explanation of the influence of international institutions would also expect bigger obstacles to IO influence in two different geographical contexts: (i) the current candidate countries; and (ii) the remaining countries of postcommunist Europe that do not currently have a membership perspective and are included in the ENP.

As in the last enlargement rounds, the EU has offered the current candidate countries in the western Balkans and Turkey the incentive of membership. Still, in the current candidates, the conditions are much less conducive for this incentive to result in strong EU influence. First, for most of the candidates, the membership perspective is far more distant and less credible. The exception is Croatia, which started accession negotiations alongside Turkey in October 2005. For Turkey, even the start of accession negotiations did not ensure the credibility of the membership perspective. First, the member states simultaneously started a debate about whether the negotiations could only lead to membership. This debate marked a departure from the practice of earlier enlargement rounds when the start of negotiations indicated a commitment on both sides to conclude them successfully. Second, the 2005 amendment of the French constitution that subjects any enlargement (after Croatia) to a popular referendum takes the final decision out of the hands of the member state governments (although this constitutional amendment might be reversed again).

Furthermore, most of the remaining candidate countries face much higher domestic adjustment costs to meet the EU's political conditionality. In many areas, the EU's demands touch directly on questions of national identity and statehood, and the EU's demands threaten more directly the political support of governments.

European neighbourhood policy
In the postcommunist countries currently included in the ENP, the EU's ability to wield influence through conditionality is even more circumscribed. The most potent incentive that the EU has on offer – membership – is explicitly not on the agenda ('everything but institutions'). Moreover, the domestic conditions in the eastern ENP countries are much less conducive to meeting the EU's political conditionality than in the 2004/07 candidate countries. Their democratization is generally much less advanced, which implies high domestic adjustment costs with regard to the EU's accession criteria.

In sum, an incentive-based approach expects a significant deterioration of the influence of international institutions in postcommunist Europe after the EU's first two eastern enlargement rounds. The conditions are least favourable in the ENP, where the EU does not use membership as an incentive; in current candidates where the membership incentive is less credible and domestic political adjustment costs are high; and in the new member states with regard to rules that are not part of the *acquis*. Compliance with the *acquis* in new member states could be expected to deteriorate, but non-compliance should be temporary – albeit possibly drawn out – rather than durable. Compliance in areas in which the EU continues to apply issue-specific conditionality after accession is likely to vary according to issue- and country-specific cost/benefit calculations.

FINDINGS

In order to explore both the power and limits of international institutions in postcommunist Europe after enlargement, contributors to this book explicitly address one or more of the following dimensions in which the EU operates beyond conditionality as applied in the 2004/07 enlargements.

The first set of contributions analyses the temporal move 'beyond conditionality' and assesses the ongoing compliance record of the EU's newest members following the 2004 and 2007 enlargements. Sedelmeier (2008) examines compliance with the *acquis communautaire*. Johnson (2008) analyses the impact of the ongoing conditionality for EMU. Sasse (2008) and Vachudova (2008) examine areas affected by the EU's political conditionality in which EU institutions have no leverage after accession – minority rights and the orientation of political parties, respectively. Finally, Epstein (2008a) and Orenstein (2008) analyse two areas in which the EU has neither competences nor applied political conditionality prior to accession – the internationalization of the banking sector and partial privatization of pension systems.

Contributions in the second and third contexts go geographically beyond conditionality as applied in the 2004/07 enlargements. The second context concerns states currently in various stages of negotiation with the EU. Schimmelfennig (2008) examines the EU's political conditionality in Croatia, Serbia, and Turkey to whom the membership perspective is more distant and less firm and the compliance costs for governments are much higher than they had been in the early 2000s in the first ten postcommunist candidates. The third context refers to states outside the current accession orbit over which the EU has no membership leverage but that the EU still seeks to influence. Lavenex (2008) examines the EU's influence through the ENP, in particular in the sectoral policies of air transport regulation, transboundary waters management, and immigration control.

Finally, a fourth category is a conceptual extension of influence 'beyond conditionality'. That is, although international institutions' use of conditionality was an ongoing feature of postcommunist transition and enlargement, the question arises as to whether other mechanisms were nevertheless more powerful in securing domestic reform. The framework does not rule out the power of incentives, but it also broadens the analysis to include constructivist and constructivist-rationalist synthetic explanations that centre on persuasion, social context, socialization and social learning (see respectively Checkel 2001; Epstein 2008b; Gheciu 2005; Schimmelfennig and Sedelmeier 2005).

Assessing the influence of international institutions

Contrary to the expectation that compliance with IOs' prescriptions should falter among postcommunist states after enlargement, this book finds that, in a significant number of cases across a range of issues, compliance has actually endured. Compliance among the EU's newest members continues in areas that include the implementation of EU law (Sedelmeier 2008), the openness to foreign investment in central and east European banking sectors (Epstein 2008a), and convergence on some (though not all) key indicators of European monetary integration (Johnson 2008). In the area of pension reform, in which the EU's only prescription was that aspiring members heed the World Bank's advice, ECE states have adopted private pillars in large numbers and have stayed with that strategy following accession (Orenstein 2008). And in the area of minority protection, formal compliance has continued as Latvia met the demand to ratify the Council of Europe's Framework Convention for National Minorities (FCNM) in 2007 (Sasse 2008).

Yet in other areas in which the EU used to apply political conditionality there are signs that IO influence is limited. For example, Sasse (2008) finds that underneath formal legal compliance, problems with the application of minority rights in practice persist. Moreover, the involvement of IOs has had unintended consequences that deepened some structural problems and limit or undermine the effect of formal legal change. Vachudova (2008) finds that, while political parties moderated their agendas to bring them in line with the prescriptions of the EU's political conditionality, after EU accession the parameters for party competition broadened again. The lifting of accession-related constraints is especially apparent among parties that adopt more nationalist and culturally conservative positions.

The deterioration of the influence of IOs is also noticeable beyond the new members. Schimmelfennig (2008) argues that setbacks in the EU's attempts to obtain compliance in the various relations with Croatia, Serbia, and Turkey are due to the high political costs to the target governments, since parts of the EU's political conditionality are highly salient for national identity. Lavenex (2008) also notes the limits of using conditionality as a source of influence in the ENP. However, she suggests that, under specific conditions, a different mode of network governance can emerge in the ENP, which might provide an alternative to conditionality in creating new forms of horizontal flexible integration.

Beyond conditionality: mechanisms of influence after enlargement

In addition to the fact that external incentives have apparently done more than provide short-term motivation for compliance, this book highlights the myriad other ways in which IOs have exercised their power in postcommunist Europe. In some instances, IOs have attempted to encourage certain policy innovations in the absence of conditionality – with varying success (Orenstein 2008; Lavenex 2008). In other cases, this book finds that conditionality can have uneven effects for heretofore unexamined reasons – namely because of the social context between IOs and domestic actors (Epstein 2008a) or the existence of particularly strong domestic inhibitors (Schimmelfennig 2008). Finally, conditionality, as well as other kinds of policy guidance, can have unintended consequences that not only fail to elicit the intended response but that create new dilemmas (Sasse 2008). This research is therefore suggestive of the ways in which IOs will exercise their power in postcommunist Europe after enlargement, but also of the ways in which IOs globally will behave and with what consequences.

To varying degrees, the chapters in this book then confirm, undermine or complicate the explanatory power of the incentive-based approach to IO influence that predicts domestic compliance will follow the credible promise of rewards if the domestic costs of compliance are low. Vachudova (2008) and Schimmelfennig (2008) largely confirm the incentive-based approach. Sedelmeier's (2008) finding of good post-accession compliance with the *acquis* despite generally unfavourable compliance conditions fits much less easily. Sasse's (2008) observation of Latvia's ratification of the FCNM in 2007 also appears puzzling from a conditionality perspective. However, she finds that EU influence is only tied to legal change; it is not effective in bringing about behavioural and attitudinal change either pre- or post-accession. The lack of behavioural compliance could either fit a rationalist explanation (as it avoids the costs of correct application) or a constructivist explanation focusing on the lack of domestic resonance of new norms. Johnson (2008) presents similarly mixed results. However, the importance of the absence of a clear deadline for combined euro adoption and of variation in national economic structures for the uneven EU influence over new member states' monetary and fiscal policies fits well with an incentive-based explanation. The remaining contributions are not explicit tests of the conditionality hypothesis as it applies to EU membership, but they question in different ways its explanatory power. They emphasize the importance of alternative mechanisms of influence, such as network governance in the ENP, or a more general form of IO policy guidance, and the significance of the social context in (Bretton Woods) conditionality.

CONCLUSIONS

In recent years, the study of the influence of IOs in postcommunist Europe, and in particular of the EU on its candidate countries, has become a major growth area of research in the study of IOs and EU enlargement. The completion of the 2004 and 2007 rounds of EU enlargement does not mark the end of this research agenda – on the contrary. Post-accession and post-enlargement present a very promising context in which to refine and develop some of the central insights gained from research on pre-accession influences in the ECE.

First, the post-accession context allows researchers to probe the extent and durability of pre-accession influences, as well as the role of different mechanisms of influence. The countries that acceded to the EU in 2004/07 generally presented the EU with particularly conducive conditions for influence through incentives. Many scholars have concluded that incentives were strong enough to provide sufficient conditions to generate the broader patterns of adjustment. But the mixed record of the incentive-based approach after enlargement should encourage us to revisit those original findings to assess the explanatory power of competing approaches. The uneven legitimacy of IOs, the social context, persuasion and socialization could have been a bigger part of the story than is often recognized because of the methodological difficulty of separating incentives from social forces.

Furthermore, pre-accession conditionality was not a level playing field to test analytically distinct mechanisms of external influence. Given the overpowering incentives on the one hand, and the legitimacy problems of the conditionality process on the other, it presented arguably a most likely case for rationalist, and a least likely case for constructivist, approaches. Post-accession could be a more favourable context for observing alternative mechanisms, as they are no longer crowded out by overwhelming incentives.

Moreover, the post-accession phase might prove a fertile testing ground for whether the mechanisms of pre-accession rule transfer make a difference for post-accession compliance. Are rules that were transferred through social learning and persuasion more likely to be durably implemented than rules that were instrumentally adopted to achieve the objective of membership?

Finally, only the long-term perspective of the post-accession phase will allow researchers to identify and appreciate the full importance of socialization processes that accompanied the use of conditionality, including unexpected, unintended, or failed socialization. Of course, in over 15 years of 'transition', and often even before enlargement, many effects of socialization were on display (see, e.g., Checkel 2001; Epstein 2008b; Gheciu 2005). However, the accession period could still be considered rather short, and constructivist approaches will be particularly appropriate to capture the longer-term social processes. Some of these processes will only become apparent post-accession, and they include cases in which IOs failed to engender social learning. IOs might have been able to overcome a lack of domestic resonance of international rules in the short term through powerful incentives, but the lack of resonance could turn out to be a major long-term obstacle to behavioural compliance.

Second, in current candidate countries, and especially in those countries for whom membership is not currently on the EU's agenda, the incentives that the EU has to offer are less powerful because of a combination of higher domestic costs and fewer sizeable and/or credible rewards. In these cases the EU cannot expect simply to reproduce the policies that were deemed successful in eastern enlargement. The EU either needs to rethink how to use the incentives at its disposal more effectively and/or how to go 'beyond conditionality' – through different mechanisms of influence and different modes of external governance.

In both these broad areas, further research is necessary to provide more systematic evidence across issue areas and across new members and non-members, both with and without a membership perspective. The contributions in this book suggest that the influence of IOs and of the EU in particular does not necessarily end with the 2004 and 2007 enlargements. The new member states' compliance has been surprisingly durable, especially with the *acquis communautaire*, but also to some extent in areas of political conditionality. In the postcommunist non-member states, the EU's influence is generally much more limited than in the recent enlargement rounds. Yet even in the ENP, in certain sectoral policy areas, promising new forms of co-operation have emerged. The weakening of external incentives after accession creates obstacles for IO influence, but the contributions provide plenty of evidence of instances in which the EU and other IOs have successfully gone 'beyond conditionality' to exercise influence on postcommunist politics.

REFERENCES

Checkel, J.T. (2001) 'Why comply? Social learning and European identity change', *International Organization* 55(3): 553–88.

Epstein, R.A. (2008a) 'The social context in conditionality: internationalizing finance in postcommunist Europe', *Journal of European Public Policy* 15(6): 880–98.

Epstein, R.A. (2008b) *In Pursuit of Liberalism: International Institutions in Postcommunist Europe*, Baltimore, MD: Johns Hopkins University Press.

Gheciu, A. (2005) 'Security institutions as agents of socialization? NATO and the "New Europe"', *International Organization* 59(4): 973–1012.

Johnson, J. (2008) 'The remains of conditionality: the faltering enlargement of the euro zone', *Journal of European Public Policy* 15(6): 826–41.

Kelley, J.G. (2004) *Ethnic Politics in Europe. The Power of Norms and Incentives*, Princeton, NJ: Princeton University Press.

Lavenex, S. (2008) 'A governance perspective on the European neighbourhood policy: integration beyond conditionality?' *Journal of European Public Policy* 15(6): 938–55.

Orenstein, M. (2008) 'Out-liberalizing the EU: pension privatization in Central and Eastern Europe', *Journal of European Public Policy* 15(6): 899–917.

Sasse, G. (2008) 'The politics of EU conditionality: the norm of minority protection during and beyond EU accession', *Journal of European Public Policy* 15(6): 842–60.

Schimmelfennig, F. (2005) 'Strategic calculation and international socialization: membership incentives, party constellations, and sustained compliance in Central and Eastern Europe', *International Organization* 59(4): 827–60.

Schimmelfennig, F. (2008) 'EU political accession conditionality after enlargement: consistency and effectiveness', *Journal of European Public Policy* 15(6): 918–37.

Schimmelfennig, F. and Sedelmeier, U. (2005) 'Introduction: Conceptualizing the Europeanization of Central and Eastern Europe', in F. Schimmelfennig and U. Sedelmeier (eds), *The Europeanization of Central and Eastern Europe*, Ithaca, NY: Cornell University Press, pp. 1–28.

Sedelmeier, U. (2008) 'After conditionality: post-accession compliance with EU law in East Central Europe', *Journal of European Public Policy* 15(6): 806–25.

Vachudova, M.A. (2005) *Europe Undivided: Democracy, Leverage and Integration after Communism*, Oxford: Oxford University Press.

Vachudova, M.A. (2008) 'Tempered by the EU? Political parties and party systems before and after accession', *Journal of European Public Policy* 15(6): 861–79.

After conditionality: post-accession compliance with EU law in East Central Europe

Ulrich Sedelmeier

INTRODUCTION

Opponents and proponents of the European Union's (EU's) eastern enlargement shared one major concern: the ability of the central and eastern European countries (CEECs)[1] to apply and enforce the large and complex body of EU legislation – the *acquis communautaire* – after accession. Persistent compliance problems in the new members could undermine the functioning of the EU's internal market, which relies on all member states' credible commitments to play by the rules and their mutual trust in each other's ability to do so. These concerns led the EU to impose a strict pre-accession conditionality that demanded the alignment of the candidate countries' legislation and institutions with the entirety of the *acquis* prior to accession (see, e.g., Sedelmeier 2005: 141–53).

EU conditionality has attracted much criticism. Many conditions are ambiguous, inconsistently applied and more demanding of candidates than full members (see, e.g., Grabbe 2006; Hughes *et al.* 2004; Schimmelfennig and Sedelmeier 2005b: 12–5). Conditionality also had unintended consequences in domestic politics, including a strengthening of the executive over parliaments (Grabbe 2006: 207–8) and limiting party-political competition on socio-economic issues, which favoured populist and nationalist parties (Grzymala-Busse and Innes 2003). These criticisms notwithstanding, EU conditionality was generally very effective in prompting the CEECs' alignment with the *acquis* (Andonova 2003; Grabbe 2006; Jacoby 2004; Schimmelfennig and Sedelmeier 2005a; see also Kelley 2004; Vachudova 2005).

However, there are doubts whether this success of the EU's pre-accession conditionality is sustainable after accession. The EU's ability to elicit compliance 'beyond conditionality' might be more limited (see also Epstein and Sedelmeier 2008). The success of pre-accession conditionality depended primarily on the conditional incentive of membership, rather than on processes of persuasion and social learning (Kelley 2004; Schimmelfennig and Sedelmeier 2005a). The change in the incentive structure after accession should then lead to changes in the CEECs' compliance – unless there are mitigating factors. However, the main factors that influence compliance in member states – compliance costs, administrative capacities, societal mobilization – are less conducive in the CEECs than in the incumbents. Furthermore, while EU institutions can sanction non-compliance in member states after accession, the overwhelming threat of withholding membership is no longer available. The literature on EU compliance and on pre-accession conditionality therefore suggests that compliance patterns in the enlarged EU will be characterized by an 'eastern problem'.

Four years after accession, have these fears materialized? Are the post-communist new members (EU8) particularly prone to breaching EU law? How do their compliance records compare to the older member states (EU15)? Is conditionality as an instrument to induce compliance with the rules of an international institution only effective in the short term, but not sustainable in the longer term? This article presents a first step to answering these questions through descriptive statistics of – yet unexplored – data on transposition and infringements of EU law in the member states.

The data suggest that far from constituting an 'eastern problem', compliance in the new members has been surprisingly good. Not only is the enlargement sceptics' nightmare scenario of an avalanche of infringement cases against the new members after accession unfounded. Since joining the EU, virtually all of the EU8 outperform virtually all of the EU15. There are also striking differences in how the new and old members react to detected infringements: the EU8 settle such cases much faster and at an earlier stage of the EU's infringement procedure. A promising line of inquiry for explanations of the unexpectedly good post-accession compliance are two legacies of pre-accession conditionality. First, the new members might be more susceptible than the old members to the shaming strategy of the EU's compliance system and they might be more inclined to conceive of good compliance as appropriate behaviour. Second, a more material legacy of conditionality is the CEECs' pre-accession institutional investment in improving their legislative capacity – i.e. their ability to transpose EU legislation rapidly into national law and to respond to emerging compliance problems with legislative amendments. These inquiries should be complemented with longer-term studies of the evolution of post-accession compliance patterns and qualitative studies on the application and enforcement of the *acquis* in the new members.

WHY SHOULD THERE BE AN 'EASTERN PROBLEM'? PRE-ACCESSION ALIGNMENT AND COMPLIANCE CONDITIONS IN THE NEW MEMBERS

EU compliance research: high costs, low mobilization and capacity limitation

Research into member states' compliance with EU law has become a large and thriving subfield in EU studies, but it still remains somewhat inconclusive with regard to the factors that account for (non-)compliance (for recent overviews, see, e.g., Mastenbroek 2005; Treib 2006). The literature has resulted in a fairly long list of factors that plausibly affect compliance in the EU, without reaching a consensus on a master variable or on the relative importance of these factors. However, even in the absence of a generally accepted explanation of the causes of (non-)compliance, the two dominant rationalist institutionalist perspectives on compliance in the EU – enforcement and management (Tallberg 2002) – both expect that the new member states are particularly prone to compliance problems, owing to shared characteristics in their domestic structures.

Adjustment costs
The 'enforcement approach' emphasizes the costs of implementing EU legislation, which lead to deliberate 'cheating' at the implementation stage. It focuses on politico-economic variables such as issue-specific adjustment costs, levels of socio-economic development, or domestic institutional structures, including veto players. Alignment with the *acquis* generally creates high financial and administrative costs for the CEECs. The EU's regulatory templates reflect the specific socio-economic developments of Western Europe and particular bargains among EU members rather than the priorities of post-communist transition (McGowan and Wallace 1996). The domestic disruption associated with the transfer of EU policy regimes increases 'the likelihood of persistent compliance problems in key policy areas' (Goetz 2005: 274).

Despite the high costs of compliance, the dismantling of pre-accession reforms is not cost-free either. However, Goetz (2005) precisely identifies a strategic 'institutionalization for reversibility' in the EU8, which was kept deliberately 'shallow'; and Jacoby (1999) observes a 'Potemkin harmonization', designed exclusively for the purpose of EU pre-accession monitoring. Post-accession compliance might also suffer even if the CEECs did not strategically plan to exploit the weakening sanctioning capacity of EU institutions. During the pre-accession phase, the strong domestic consensus on the strategic goal of EU accession silenced opposition from potential veto players. After accession has been achieved, it is much more difficult for governments to use arguments about the overall benefits of membership to constrain actors unwilling to bear the costs of EU legislation in specific issue areas.

Weak post-communist societal mobilization
Another factor affecting enforcement is for structural reasons generally more problematic in the new member states. Some more recent studies have emphasized the importance of societal mobilization for compliance in the EU (Alter and Vargas 2000: 457–9; Börzel 2003: 38–9, 53–4; 2006; Cichowski 2007; Conant 2002; Falkner *et al.* 2005: 36–7). The EU's decentralized monitoring mechanism relies heavily on private actors at the domestic level to raise complaints with the Commission or to litigate in national courts against breaches of EU law. Yet in the CEECs, societal interest organizations are generally weak (Howard 2003).

Although transnational links with international institutions and nongovernmental organizations (NGOs) might partly compensate for the weakness of post-communist civil society (Petrova and Tarrow 2007; Stark *et al.* 2006), it is a key obstacle to the mobilization of societal groups benefiting from EU rules in support of the proper application and enforcement of such rules.

Administrative capacity limitations
The 'management' approach to compliance focuses on sources of involuntary non-compliance, especially on administrative capacity limitations. The legacies of communism make severe limitations of state capacity a distinctive challenge for the CEECs (see, e.g., Sissenich 2007). The administrative and institutional structures necessary to implement and enforce EU rules often had to be created from scratch. The magnitude of these challenges led the EU to include the creation of administrative capacities in the CEECs in its accession conditionality, but with mixed results (see, e.g., Dimitrova 2002). The scarcity of technical expertise in implementing EU law is exacerbated by continued problems with a politicized civil service (Meyer-Sahling 2004). The enforcement of EU rules through national court systems may also be problematic, as the European Court of Justice's (ECJ's) legal doctrine and the preliminary ruling system are not yet embedded and technical expertise in the legal profession is scarce (Kühn 2005). For Curtin and van Ooik, these capacity problems render it a

> rather obvious observation that there will be a serious enforcement problem in the accession aftermath [since] ... [eastern] enlargement will indeed be 'suboptimal' mainly in terms of the administrative capacity of the new

members to apply the *acquis* as a matter of daily practice as well as the capacity of the national judiciary to supervise the application of EU law by administrative authorities.

(Curtin and van Ooik 2000: 11)

In sum, the high costs of compliance in the generally much poorer EU8, as well as administrative capacity limitations and weak societal mobilization, create unfavourable conditions for a durable influence of rules adopted during the pre-accession period.

Mechanism of pre-accession rule transfer: changing incentive structure

Although EU conditionality was able to overcome the high adjustment costs during the pre-accession period, a central finding of the conditionality literature suggests that these unfavourable conditions will undermine sustained compliance after accession. Pre-accession alignment was largely underpinned by the conditional incentives of membership, rather than processes of persuasion and social learning (Schimmelfennig and Sedelmeier 2005a). The membership incentive was strong enough to overcome domestic opposition even in highly sensitive issue areas (see, e.g., Kelley 2004). However, the dominance of incentive-driven pre-accession rule transfer suggests that compliance should remain sensitive to changes in the incentive structure after accession.

Accession affects which instruments EU institutions can use to sanction non-compliance in the member states. The ECJ can ultimately impose financial sanctions on members that infringe EU law: a lump sum payment and/or daily penalty payments until compliance with the ECJ decision is achieved (according to the severity of the infringement and the capacity of the member state to pay). Furthermore, a novelty of the 2004 enlargement was a specific safeguard clause in the accession treaties that could be used to suspend certain membership rights during the first three years of membership. However, the most powerful sanction instrument of the pre-accession phase – withholding membership – is no longer available.

An incentive-based perspective would then expect the EU8 to capitalize on the sanctioning gap that EU institutions face after enlargement. This gap is both temporal – it can take a very long time until the ECJ imposes financial penalties for continued non-compliance – and with regard to the severity of the sanctions available. If the EU8 strategically exploit the weaker sanctioning capacity of EU institutions, we would expect that good formal compliance is not followed by proper application and enforcement and a marked difference in the formal transposition of rules before and after accession.

Incentive-driven rule transfer would also lead some constructivists to expect post-accession compliance problems. For constructivism, the mode of pre-accession rule transfer can be an important scope condition for post-accession compliance. EU rules that were transferred through processes of social learning and persuasion are internalized by élites, administrators and publics. If the appropriateness of these rules is taken for granted, achieving accession does not make a difference to compliance. By contrast, rules that are not adopted because they – or the international institution that promotes them – are considered legitimate, but transferred instrumentally, are more likely to remain contested after accession (see, e.g., Epstein 2005). Moreover, a top-down, hierarchical rule transfer suffers from a legitimacy problem as the candidates had no say in the creation of the rules, and thus lack 'ownership'. Once on the inside, resentment against such rules can therefore not only lead to strategic non-compliance, but to an open backlash against rules that are perceived as unfair external impositions (Schimmelfennig and Sedelmeier 2004: 676). Thus, the absence of persuasion-driven pre-accession rule transfer and the legitimacy problems of the conditionality process increase the likelihood of non-compliance (unless other processes establish compliance as socially appropriate).

In sum, the literature on pre-accession alignment and EU compliance would expect accession to result in much more serious compliance problems in the post-communist new members compared to the older member states. The dominance of the conditional membership incentive for pre-accession rule transfer, as well as the high costs of compliance and capacity limitations in the EU8, suggest that the good performance of the EU8 during the pre-accession period will quickly erode. The likelihood that formal rule adoption will result in behavioural rule adoption is low. Compliance will be only reluctant and incremental if the EU8 are threatened with sanctions from the EU's compliance system or the safeguard clause in the accession treaty. Conditionality might have been highly effective in prompting pre-accession rule adoption, but is much less so when it comes to sustained post-accession compliance.

POST-ACCESSION COMPLIANCE: TRANSPOSITION AND INFRINGEMENTS OF EU LAW

Quantitative data on the member states' compliance with EU legislation collected by the European Commission are very useful for a general overview of the magnitude of relative compliance problems. The two main types of quantitative data are transposition rates and infringements of EU law in the member states. This section presents the insights that can be gained from descriptive statistics, before discussing possible objections to the data.

Transposition of EU legislation

EU directives need to be transposed into national law by an agreed deadline, and the member states must notify the Commission that they have taken such national implementation measures. Since 2000, the Commission's Secretariat General publishes regularly – usually six times a year – tables about the member states' respective progress in notifying transposition, measured as the percentage of directives actually transposed on a given date compared to all directives that had to be transposed by then.

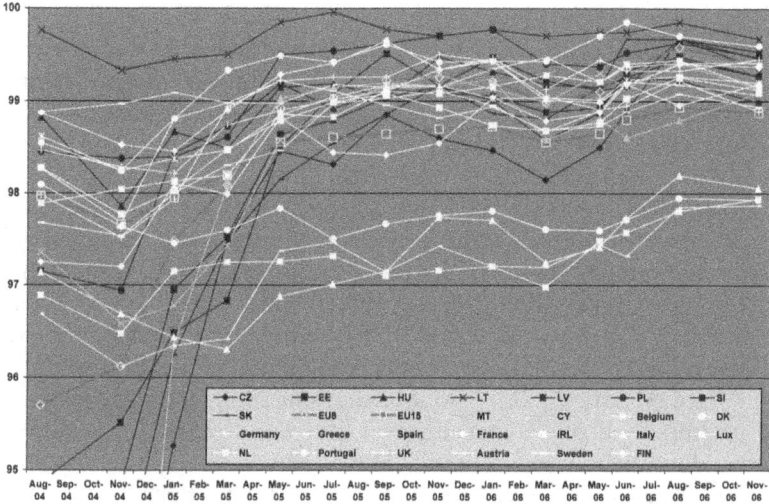

Figure 1 Transposition rates in the enlarged EU EU25 (% of directives notified)
Source: Compiled from the website of the Commission's Secretariat General (various dates).

According to transposition data, the EU8 have done extremely well since early 2005. Figure 1 shows transposition rates for all member states since the 2004 enlargement (EU15 in light colour and EU8 in dark), as well as the average rates for the EU15 and the EU8. Initially, transposition rates among the EU8 diverged significantly. Five of the EU8 started with rates well below the average for the EU15. However, since 2005, the EU8 have done consistently better than the EU15. Only the Czech Republic temporarily dropped again below the average of the EU15. Since accession, Lithuania has had almost continuously the highest transposition rate among all member states. At the end of 2006, four of the EU8 were in the top five, with a further three in the top 11. Thus, after initial problems for some of the EU8, they have rapidly improved and maintained transposition rates that are clearly better than the EU15 on average and for most of them individually.

Infringements of EU law

The second data source published by the Commission concerns infringements of EU legislation. They record actions taken by the Commission against member states that violate EU law (the other strand of the EU's compliance system is private litigation in national courts). The infringement procedure at the EU level includes a number of stages during which the Commission communicates with a member state in order to rectify the problem.

Most cases are solved informally before the Commission starts the infringement procedure according to Article 226 of the treaty. The next step is a 'letter of formal notice' by the Commission, which establishes its initial legal assessment of the case. The Commission does not consider the formal notice as part of the official procedure, but rather as a preliminary stage that provides an opportunity for consultations and an exchange of information (Börzel 2003: 9). For cases that remain unresolved, the Commission delivers a 'Reasoned Opinion', a detailed legal justification of its position. Of all the cases closed from 2000 to 2004, 86–89 per cent were solved at the latest after the infringement procedure reached this stage (own calculations from Commission, various years). If the problem persists, the Commission refers the case to the ECJ. Hardly any of these ECJ judgments go against the Commission (see, e.g., Falkner *et al.* 2005: 208). If a member state does not comply with an adverse ruling by the ECJ, the Commission can start a new infringement procedure (based on Article 228). It follows the same stages and includes the possibility to impose financial penalties on the non-compliant member state. However, less than 2 per cent of closed cases entered this post-litigation phase; and instances of a second referral to the ECJ are rare.

The Commission publishes an Annual Report on infringements (Commission, various years). Unfortunately, there is a long delay until these data become available, since the reports are often only published at the very end of the following year. The dataset used in this paper is therefore compiled from the infringement decision that the Commission's Secretariat General publishes periodically (some 12 to 17 times per year) on its website (Commission, various dates). Oddly, the dataset compiled from these individually published decisions does not exactly match the aggregate data for Reasoned Opinions and ECJ referrals in the Annual Report. However, since the dataset's numbers are slightly higher, especially for ECJ referrals, and do not appear to arise from a duplication of records, they appear more accurate.

Figure 2 presents the number of Reasoned Opinions and referrals to the ECJ for each member state from 2005 to 2007. The performance of the EU8 is not only better on average, but almost every individual EU8 also performed better than almost every old member state. Lithuania is the outstanding performer in the EU25, and the top nine include seven of the EU8, as well as Denmark (and Cyprus). The Czech Republic lags somewhat behind the other EU8, but mainly because of a poor performance in 2005, which improved significantly in 2006 and 2007. By contrast, Poland drops out of the leading group owing to its deteriorating performance, especially in 2007. This case apart, the data do not show a deterioration of the record of the EU8 over time, but rather an improvement. In sum, compared to the old member states, the infringement record of the EU8 – both on average and for most of them individually – is excellent.

The good record of the EU8 also holds if we only consider directives that had an implementation deadline after the accession of the EU8 in 1 May 2004. Table 1 considers only directives that had to be implemented between 1 May 2004 and the end of 2005. It shows the percentage of these directives that were infringed; for which a Reasoned Opinion was sent; and that were referred to the ECJ.[2] The compliance patterns are very similar to the data presented in

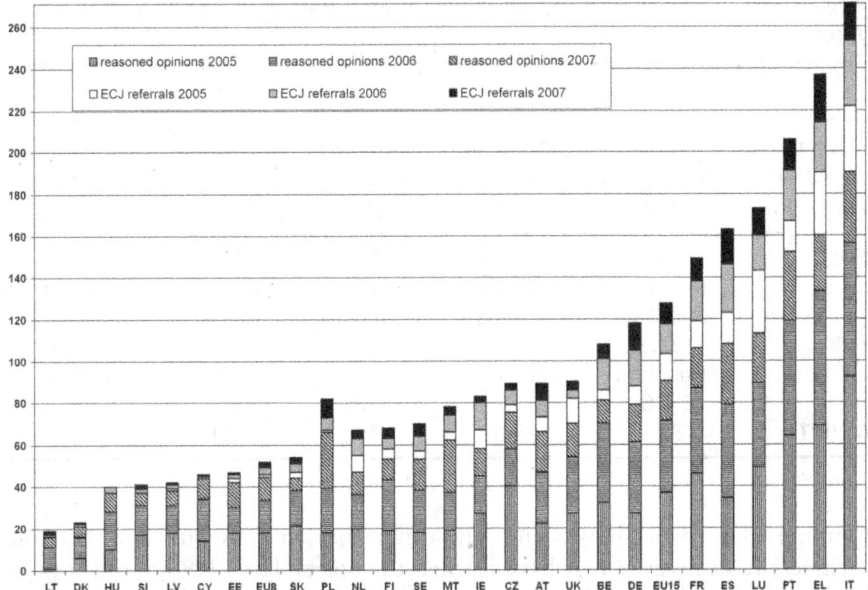

Figure 2 Commission infringement decisions, 2005–07

Figure 1. The EU8 have on average well under half as many Reasoned Opinions as the EU15 and less than one fifth of their ECJ referrals. The EU8 therefore do not seem to experience more serious infringement problems with regard to the legislation that they had to implement after accession than with legislation that had to be implemented before or upon accession.

Settlement of infringements

Table 1 also shows that the number of initial infringements is not much lower for the EU8 than for the EU15 (around 35 per cent of the directives for median members of both groups; the average is somewhat lower for the EU8). However, in the EU8 fewer cases reach subsequent – official – stages of the infringement procedure, particularly with regard to ECJ referrals. Thus, the EU8 not only tend to have a lower incidence of infringement cases; in fact the number of initial infringements might not even be much lower. However, they settle emerging cases at a much earlier stage than the EU15. The EU8 also tend to settle individual infringements – measured from the transposition deadline until the Commission's decision to close a case – faster than the EU15. On average, their infringement cases are closed around two and a half months earlier.

Figure 3 examines differences in the settlement behaviour of the member states further. It traces for 2005 and 2006 the subsequent developments for each infringement case in which a member state received a Reasoned

Table 1 Infringements of directives with an implementation deadline after 1 May 2004

n = 191 (2004: 95, 2005: 96)	Infringements (%)	Reasoned Opinions (%)	Referrals to the ECJ (%)	Average duration of infringement cases (months)	Open cases (by 1 May 2007)
EU15	39.2 (median: 35.1)	16.4 (median: 14.1)	7.1 (median: 5.8)	13.4 (median: 13.8)	7.9 (median: 5)
EU8	32.8 (median: 35.6)	6.7 (median: 6)	1.3 (median: 1.3)	11 (median: 11)	2.3 (median: 1)
CY/MT	38.7	7.9	2.4	11	3

Opinion. The data show significant differences in how the new and old members react in cases that have reached this stage. The EU8 are much more likely to close such cases in the next step rather than seeing it referred to the ECJ.

The contrast in settlement behaviour is particularly striking for Reasoned Opinions issued in 2005. The EU15 closed on average 49.8 per cent of these cases (by May 2007), but the EU8 closed 81.1 per cent. Only 14.7 per cent of Reasoned Opinions resulted in a referral to the ECJ for the EU8, while for the EU15 it was 40 per cent. In 2006, the contrast was no longer as striking, but still significant. Owing to their more recent nature, more cases in both groups had not yet seen any subsequent decisions by May 2007. Where further steps were taken, the EU8 were still far more likely to have closed them (32.8 per cent) than to have them referred to the ECJ (21.1 per cent). For the EU15, it was the opposite, with less than 20 per cent closed and

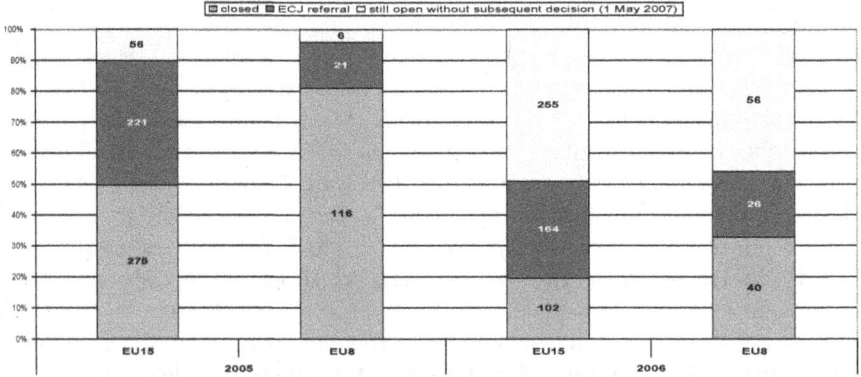

Figure 3 Subsequent actions after receiving a Reasoned Opinion

almost 32 per cent referred to the ECJ. Thus, the EU8 tend to settle emerging cases at an earlier stage than the EU15.

In sum, the available quantitative data show that far from constituting an 'eastern problem' in the enlarged EU, the compliance record of the EU8 is far better than that of the EU15. This record holds for the transposition deficit (after initial problems for some new members) and is particularly good for infringements of EU law. Furthermore, the new member states not only incur fewer serious infringements, they also exhibit a particular settlement behaviour characterized by a greater propensity to settle infringement cases before they reach more serious stages of the compliance process. This good post-accession compliance in the new member states contrasts with the expectations of research on pre-accession alignment and on EU compliance. The key question that emerges for post-accession compliance is, why are the new members so good?

RELIABILITY OF THE DATA AND FINDINGS

One possible objection to the findings concerns the data on which they are based. This section discusses these objections and argues that they are not sufficiently strong to question the broader compliance patterns that the data suggest.

More generally, the suitability of quantitative data as an indicator of *actual* compliance is limited. These problems are particularly serious for transposition data. They only cover one type of EU law – directives – which have to be transposed into national law (as opposed to regulations). Crucially, the data only measure *formal* implementation of EU law. They only attest that the Commission has been notified in time that national laws have been adopted to implement a directive, but not whether it has been transposed correctly, let alone applied and enforced on the ground. In any case, the importance of the transposition data should not be overstated since by the end of 2006 the differences across the member states' transposition deficit appear rather low. Most member states have a transposition deficit of less than 1 per cent and none much lower than 1.5 per cent. The important trend that the transposition data capture is that some of the EU8 struggled initially but continuously improved to achieve excellent performances, rather than initially peforming well but then deteriorating.

Infringement data have the advantage that they also focus on correct application of legislation, but nonetheless have shortcomings as an indicator of compliance (Börzel 2003: 11–8; Falkner *et al.* 2005: 19–20). They obviously cover only non-compliance that has been detected and taken up by the Commission. As the Commission largely has to rely on aggrieved parties – such as individuals, firms, or interest groups – to bring complaints against member states that do not properly apply and enforce EU law, the infringement data might well only represent the tip of the iceberg. Infringement data therefore should not be used to draw inferences about the *absolute* extent of compliance. However, to the extent that there are no reasons to suspect systematic bias in undetected non-compliance across member states, they are not only the best available, but also a highly suitable *comparative*, indicator for variation in relative compliance across countries and over time (Börzel 2003: 18). Thus, infringement data provide an obvious point of departure for studying post-accession compliance patterns and for follow-up qualitative case studies on the application of the *acquis* in the new member states.

Short observation period in the early post-accession phase

Another possible objection to the data is that the time factor might bias the results. There is a time lag between detecting an infringement and subsequent stages of the infringement procedure. It can take a couple of months until a Reasoned Opinion is issued. However, by focusing only on infringement decisions from 2005 onwards, the time lag should not introduce a bias. The only potentially problematic cases are some ECJ referrals for the EU15 in 2005 which resulted from Reasoned Opinions issued between July and December 2004, and which could have been initiated before May 2004. On the other hand, excluding 2004 could introduce a bias *against* the EU8, which had an almost spotless record in 2004, with a single Reasoned Opinion (against Poland) in December 2004.

Another objection might be the use of data at this early stage of membership. How indicative is the early performance of longer-term compliance patterns? We might be tempted to compare the record of the EU8 with earlier enlargement rounds. Figure 4 compares the average record of the EU8 to other newcomers from their second to fourth year of membership. Most new members

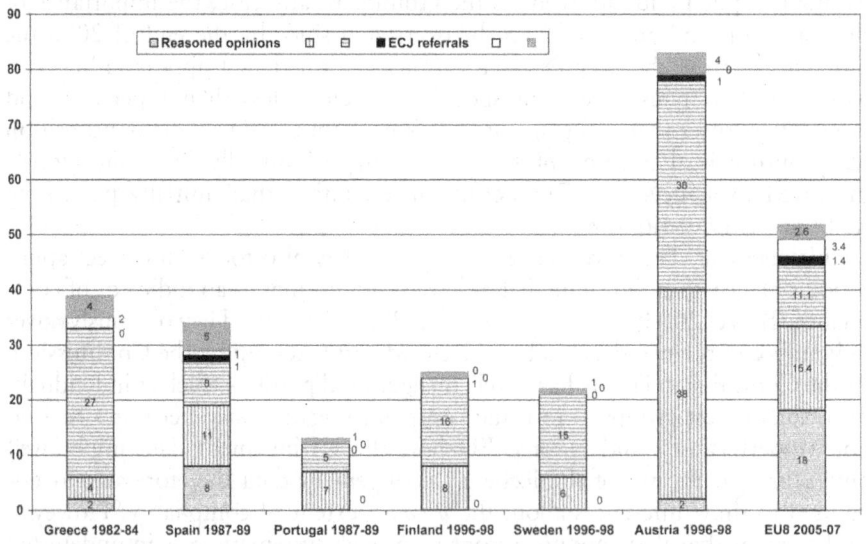

Figure 4 Infringements in the EU8 compared to earlier enlargements

in the Mediterranean and European Free Trade Association (EFTA) enlargements appear to do better than the EU8, but the comparison is misleading. First, new members in previous enlargement rounds enjoyed a 'period of grace' which the Commission explicitly ruled out for the EU8. Second, specific factors make earlier enlargements unsuitable for comparison. The Mediterranean enlargement took place before the completion of the single market. The body of the *acquis* and hence the number of 'violative opportunities' (Börzel 2003: 19) was much smaller. Comparisons with the early years after the EFTA enlargement are not representative either. First, the countries concerned had already applied most of the *acquis* under the European Economic Area agreement. Second, as the Nordic countries are now among the very best performers in the EU15, they present the toughest comparator.

The time factor may also play a role as the EU8 secured some post-accession transition periods during which they do not yet have to apply the *acquis*, especially for some areas of environmental policy, which is traditionally the policy area that attracts most infringements. However, these transition periods do not apply to some of the sectors in which non-compliance is most frequent, such as nature protection and environmental impact assessment. While it is therefore difficult to establish what impact the transition periods had, it is unlikely that they had a dramatic impact.

Weak domestic compliance mechanism in the EU8

Another key reservation about the infringement data is that they could indeed be biased in favour of the EU8. In other words, there might be a reason to believe that the extent of undetected non-compliance is systematically higher in the EU8 than in the EU15. The weakness of post-communist civil society could be a structural obstacle to the effectiveness of the EU's decentralized compliance system in the EU8, which relies on complaints from aggrieved parties. Data on the sources of detected infringements (Commission, various years) might provide some evidence for such an argument.

For the EU8, complaints are a much less significant source of detecting infringements than in the EU15. Figure 5 shows that in 2005 and 2006 complaints led to the detection of about half of the infringements in the EU15, but for the EU8 it was only around 22 and 24 per cent respectively. By contrast, 'non-communication' of transposition measures – which are the easiest for the Commission to monitor – account for only around one third of infringements detected in the EU15, but for around 56 and 46 per cent in the EU8. Of course, one interpretation could be that there is no reason to raise complaints as application and enforcement of EU law is diligent. Another interpretation is that citizens, firms and interest groups in the EU8 are not yet fully aware of their rights that might be infringed or are not yet accustomed to using the complaints procedure. In the latter case, the record of the EU8 with regard to detected infringements might not be indicative of equally good compliance with regard to proper application and enforcement of EU law.

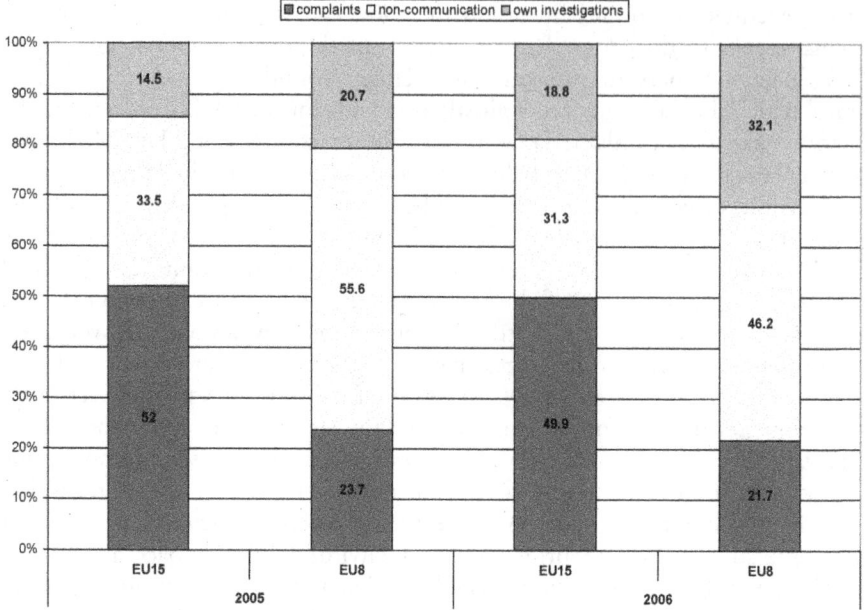

Figure 5 Source of detected infringements (%)
Source: Compiled from Commission (various years).

In fact, the lesser importance of complaints as a source for detecting infringements in the EU8 might again be related to the observation period, rather than to the specific characteristics of post-communist societies: the records of Cyprus and Malta are very similar to the EU8 across years and detection sources. Therefore, it might simply be a question of time until the complaints procedure is sufficiently developed at the domestic level. Yet even if a lesser development of complaints introduced a bias into the data, can it fully account for the differences in compliance patterns? Ultimately, only laborious qualitative research can establish whether there is a systematic bias towards undetected non-compliance in the EU8, and a longer observation period has to show whether the differences in the sources of detection remain. In any case, even if the lower incidence of complaints explained some of the difference in the infringement patterns, it does not affect the differences in settlement behaviour – the greater inclination of the EU8 to settle emerging infringement at an earlier stage of the infringement procedure.

In sum, while the short observation period should caution us against overstating the positive performance of the EU8, at an absolute minimum, we can safely conclude that the nightmare scenario of a flood of court cases against the new members after accession has not materialized. Much rather, the research question that emerges from descriptive statistics of infringement data is, why do the new members perform so well, despite plausible expectations to the contrary?

TOWARDS EXPLANATIONS FOR GOOD POST-ACCESSION COMPLIANCE

This article aimed primarily to establish how the compliance patterns of the EU8 compare to the old member states, as a starting point for generating research questions on post-accession compliance. It provides only a rather tentative answer to the question of how the good record can be explained. Enforcement approaches to compliance focus on the threat of sanctions that new members face post-accession. I contrast this explanation with two factors that relate to the legacy of pre-accession conditionality.

The threat of post-accession sanctions

Although EU institutions can no longer withhold the reward of membership, they still have sanctions at their disposal. In addition to financial penalties through the ECJ, the EU8 face a specific safeguard clause; a novelty in the history of enlargement. Article 38 of the accession treaty allows the Commission to take 'appropriate measures' if a new member causes within the first three years of membership 'a serious breach of the functioning of the internal market' or if there is an 'imminent risk of such breach'. This threat might indeed explain why the EU8 are particularly quick in resolving emerging compliance problems before they reach more serious stages of the infringement procedure.

However, the safeguard clause cannot explain the performance of the EU8, certainly not on its own. After the safeguard clause expired in May 2007, compliance in the EU8 did not deteriorate. Of course, a longer observation period is necessary for firmer conclusions about this trend, but so far the performance in 2007 even presents an improvement on 2006 (except for Poland). Moreover, if the threat of sanctions motivated the EU8's compliance, it is not clear that they would need to perform any better than the worst performers among the EU15. Finally, the threat of sanctions cannot explain the variation in the compliance records across the EU8.

The legacy of conditionality: legislative capacity and socialization

Legislative capacity-building
Other than the threat of post-accession sanctions, two further factors might explain the good post-accession compliance of the EU8; both are related to the experience of pre-accession conditionality. The first factor is in line with rationalist institutionalist 'management' approaches to compliance. Pre-accession conditionality impelled the EU8 to build up a very particular 'legislative capacity'.

The EU8 made an institutional investment to increase the effectiveness of national arrangements for the adoption of EU law, which allowed them to transpose a massive amount of *acquis* into national legislation within a very short period of time (see, e.g., Zubek 2005). As Sadurski (2006: 7) observes, 'given the notorious inefficiency and incompetence of parliamentary institutions in post-communist states', the EU8 often used fast-track procedures to enact EU-related laws, 'with little or no serious parliamentary discussions, and with the executive controlling the process throughout', allowing governments 'to by-pass parliament and to justify the centralization of decision-making by the emergency-like circumstances'. The EU repeatedly emphasized the institutional capacities to ensure proper application and enforcement. But maybe unwittingly it rewarded managerial efficiency of EU8 administrations in meeting formal indicators of compliance, like a speedy transposition of EU legislation.

Many of the EU8 may have maintained some of the pre-accession procedures, which increased their capacity for timely and formally correct transposition of EU directives into national law, and a quick resolution of compliance problems. Indeed, in Lithuania – the top performer in the EU25 – EU legislation is still treated differently from purely domestic legislation. Many observers consider the Lithuanian procedures for managing the implementation of EU legislation, from its adoption in the Council to the deadline for national implementation measures, as exemplary in the EU.

However, a focus on legislative capacity as an explanation for compliance may raise doubts among those sceptical about the good record of the EU8. An overemphasis on formal compliance indicators may well mask – or even generate – problems of (undetected) non-compliance with regard to practical application and enforcement. The transposition of a literal translation of the text of EU directives into national law can facilitate high rates of correctly and timely transposed legislation. However, the lack of substantive debate about legislation and the most appropriate ways to achieve their aims in the national context entails the risk of simply delaying the emergence of problems until the stage when the law has to be applied and enforced. At the same time, such a practice is not necessarily synonymous with behavioural compliance problems. In some instances, for example, where key legal definitions are highly specific, EU institutions even consider a literal translation of EU texts desirable. In any case, one task for further research is to establish whether such practices are particularly prevalent in the EU8.

Socialization

A complementary constructivist argument about the legacy of pre-accession conditionality is that the experience of conditionality has been a socialization process for the EU8. The jockeying for positions in the accession regatta could have been internalized by the élites in the EU8, who then remain sensitive to their countries' relative performance. Despite their resentment against the hierarchical and top-down nature of conditionality, the process of continuous monitoring and assessment may have triggered a form of 'hegemonic socialization' (Ikenberry and Kupchan 1990). Rather than creating a backlash against legitimacy problems of the process, the experience of conditionality may have socialized the EU8 into perceiving good compliance as appropriate behaviour for good community members. The EU8 have started to take for granted that problems identified by the Commission need to be rectified quickly. They therefore remain sensitive to criticism and are generally more susceptible to the shaming strategies that are built into the EU's compliance system. Thus, as compliance problems emerge and are detected at the EU level, these problems are settled fairly quickly.

The question of whether the EU8 are more susceptible to shaming strategies than the EU15 would need to be put on firmer theoretical foundations, not least to understand how the desire to be a respectable community member may vary across the EU8. Furthermore, its empirical implications also need clearer specification. At a first glance, variation in attitudes towards the EU in the EU8 may be an indicator of susceptibility to shaming by the Commission. The compliance laggards among the EU8 appear to be those with higher Euroscepticism within national parliaments. If a more systematic analysis confirmed this relationship, it would contrast with the situation in the old members, where Euroscepticism and compliance are (counterintuitively) positively correlated.

CONCLUSIONS

The literature on pre-accession conditionality and on compliance with EU law would lead us to expect a deterioration of compliance with EU law in the new members after they obtained accession. The incentive-induced pre-accession compliance remains sensitive to the changing incentive structure after accession, and compliance conditions are generally unfavourable in the new members. However, data on infringements of EU law indicate that concerns about an 'eastern problem' in the enlarged EU are unfounded. On the contrary, the EU8's compliance records during the first four calendar years of membership are generally far better than the old member states' and most of the EU8 are among the best performers in the enlarged EU. They not only incur fewer infringements than the EU15, but also show a characteristic settlement behaviour. Emerging infringement cases are solved faster and at earlier stages of the infringement procedure than in the EU15. Compliance after conditionality appears surprisingly durable.

Sceptics may consider the main question for further research to be whether compliance in the EU8 is really as good as the data suggest. Indeed, the complaints procedure may yet have to take root more fully at the domestic level. Furthermore, if the good record was only achieved through an emphasis on formal indicators, there might be a gap between good formal compliance and undetected non-compliance through deficient application and enforcement. Only systematic qualitative research and a longer observation period can validate or invalidate such concerns. Yet even if we had doubts about the record of the EU8, at a minimum the data disconfirm the sceptics' scenario of a flood of infringement cases against the new members after accession, or of a backlash against the EU's pre-accession conditionality. Moreover, even if the good compliance of the EU8 was found to be limited to the formal level, it would then still constitute an important finding about the characteristics of post-accession compliance after conditionality: why is *formal* compliance so good and why do the EU8 settle cases earlier?

This article has made tentative suggestions for further research into explanations of the good post-accession compliance patterns. It suggests that the threat of post-accession sanctions – including the special safeguard clause in the accession treaties – does not seem to be able to account for the good compliance records; certainly not exclusively. Instead, two lines of inquiry that relate to the experience of pre-accession conditionality appear promising. First, the then candidate countries were under pressure to invest heavily in an institutional infrastructure that increased their legislative capacity. Maintenance of such institutional arrangements could explain the ability to transpose EU law correctly and timely, and to settle infringement cases rapidly. Second, the decision to maintain and use such procedures could be attributed to socialization during the pre-accession process which makes the EU8 more susceptible to shaming and to consider good compliance as appropriate behaviour.

NOTES

1 This article focuses only on the eight post-communist countries included in the 2004 enlargement.
2 There is no big difference between directives with a deadline in 2004 and those in 2005. For both EU8 and EU15 there is an increase of around 2 per cent in all categories.

REFERENCES

Alter, K.J. and Vargas, J. (2000) 'Explaining variation in the use of European litigation strategies. European Community law and British gender equality policy', *Comparative Political Studies* 33(4): 452–82.

Andonova, L.B. (2003) *Transnational Politics of the Environment: The European Union and Environmental Policy in Central and Eastern Europe*, Cambridge, MA: MIT Press.
Börzel, T.A. (2003) *Environmental Leaders and Laggards in Europe: Why There Is (Not) a 'Southern Problem'*, Aldershot: Ashgate.
Börzel, T.A. (2006) 'Participation through law enforcement: the case of the European Union', *Comparative Political Studies* 39(1): 128–52.
Cichowski, R.A. (2007) *The European Court and Civil Society: Litigation, Mobilization and Governance*, Cambridge: Cambridge University Press.
Conant, L.J. (2002) *Justice Contained: Law and Politics in the European Union*, Ithaca, NY: Cornell University Press.
Curtin, D.M. and van Ooik, R.H. (2000) 'Revamping the European Union's enforcement system with a view to eastern enlargement', *WWR Working Documents*, No. W110.
Dimitrova, A. (2002) 'Enlargement, institution-building and the EU's administrative capacity requirement', *West European Politics* 25(4): 171–90.
Epstein, R.A. (2005) 'Diverging effects of social learning and external incentives in Polish central banking and agriculture', in F. Schimmelfennig and U. Sedelmeier (eds), *The Europeanization of Central and Eastern Europe*, Ithaca, NY: Cornell University Press, pp. 178–98.
Epstein, R.A. and Sedelmeier, U. (2008) 'Beyond conditionality: international institutions in postcommunist Europe after enlargement', *Journal of European Public Policy* 15(6): 795–805.
European Commission (various dates) Recent Commission decisions on breaches of EU law; http://ec.europa.eu/community_law/infringements/infringements_decisions_en.htm
European Commission (various years) *Annual Report on Monitoring the Application of Community Law*.
Falkner, G., Treib, O., Hartlapp, M. and Leiber, S. (2005) *Complying with Europe: EU Harmonisation and Soft Law in the Member States*, Cambridge: Cambridge University Press.
Goetz, K.H. (2005) 'The new member states and the EU', in S. Bulmer and C. Lequesne (eds), *The Member States of the European Union*, Oxford: Oxford University Press.
Grabbe, H. (2006) *The EU's Transformative Power: Europeanization through Conditionality in Central and Eastern Europe*, Basingstoke: Palgrave.
Grzymala-Busse, A. and Innes, A. (2003) 'Great expectations: the EU and domestic political competition in east central Europe', *East European Politics and Societies* 17(1): 64–73.
Howard, M.M. (2003) *The Weakness of Civil Society in Post-Communist Europe*, Cambridge: Cambridge University Press.
Hughes, J., Sasse, G. and Gordon, C. (2004) *Europeanization and Regionalization in the EU's Enlargement to Central and Eastern Europe: The Myth of Conditionality*, Basingstoke: Palgrave.
Ikenberry, G.J. and Kupchan, C.A. (1990) 'Socialization and hegemonic power', *International Organization* 44(3): 283–315.
Jacoby, W. (1999) 'Priest and penitent: the European Union as a force in the domestic politics of eastern Europe', *East European Constitutional Review* 8(1–2): 62–7.
Jacoby, W. (2004) *The Enlargement of the European Union and NATO. Ordering from the Menu in Central Europe*, Cambridge: Cambridge University Press.
Kelley, J.G. (2004) *Ethnic Politics in Europe. The Power of Norms and Incentives*, Princeton, NJ: Princeton University Press.
Kühn, Z. (2005) 'The application of European law in the new member states: several (early) predictions', *German Law Journal* 6(3): 563–82.

Mastenbroek, E. (2005) 'EU compliance: still a "black hole"?' *Journal of European Public Policy* 12(6): 1103–20.

McGowan, F. and Wallace, H. (1996) 'Towards a European regulatory state', *Journal of European Public Policy* 3(4): 560–76.

Meyer-Sahling, J.H. (2004) 'Civil service reform in post-communist Europe: the bumpy road to depoliticisation', *West European Politics* 27(1): 71–103.

Petrova, T. and Tarrow, S. (2007) 'Transactional and participatory activism in the emerging European polity: the puzzle of east-central Europe', *Comparative Political Studies* 40(1): 74–94.

Sadurski, W. (2006) 'Introduction: The law and institutions of new member states in year one', in W. Sadurski, J. Ziller and K. Zurek (eds), *Après Enlargement: Legal and Political Responses in Central and Eastern Europe*, Florence: European University Institute, pp. 3–18.

Schimmelfennig, F. and Sedelmeier, U. (2004) 'Governance by conditionality: EU rule transfer to the candidate countries of Central and Eastern Europe', *Journal of European Public Policy* 11(4): 661–79.

Schimmelfennig, F. and Sedelmeier, U. (eds) (2005a) *The Europeanization of Central and Eastern Europe*, Ithaca, NY: Cornell University Press.

Schimmelfennig, F. and Sedelmeier, U. (2005b) 'Introduction: Conceptualizing the Europeanization of Central and Eastern Europe', in F. Schimmelfennig and U. Sedelmeier (eds), *The Europeanization of Central and Eastern Europe*, Ithaca, NY: Cornell University Press, pp. 1–28.

Sedelmeier, U. (2005) *Constructing the Path to Eastern Enlargement: The Uneven Policy Impact of EU Identity*, Manchester: Manchester University Press.

Sissenich, B. (2007) *Building States without Society: European Union Enlargement and the Transfer of EU Social Policy to Poland and Hungary*, Lanham, MD: Lexington Books.

Stark, D., Vedres, B. and Bruszt, L. (2006) 'Rooted transnational publics: integrating foreign ties and civic activism', *Theory and Society* 35(3): 323–49.

Tallberg, J. (2002) 'Paths to compliance: enforcement, management, and the European Union', *International Organization* 56(3): 609–43.

Treib, O. (2006) 'Implementing and complying with EU governance', *Living Reviews in European Governance*; http://europeangovernance.livingreviews.org/.

Vachudova, M.A. (2005) *Europe Undivided: Democracy, Leverage and Integration after Communism*, Oxford: Oxford University Press.

Zubek, R. (2005) 'Complying with transposition commitments in Poland: collective dilemmas, core executive and legislative outcomes', *West European Politics* 28(3): 592–619.

The remains of conditionality: the faltering enlargement of the euro zone

Juliet Johnson

INTRODUCTION

On 1 May 2004, ten new states – eight of them in postcommunist Central and East Europe – joined the European Union (EU), followed by Bulgaria and Romania in January 2007. Policy-makers and scholars worried that having devoured the long-dangling carrot of EU membership, these states had moved 'beyond conditionality.' Without the potential threat of withholding membership, the EU arguably no longer had the same ability to co-opt and coerce these states into further adjusting their political, economic, legal, and social institutions to mesh with European norms and practices. Lost in this discussion has been one remaining set of unfulfilled conditions, with the carrot of membership still hanging in the air: the Maastricht criteria required for countries to join the euro zone.

'Conditionality,' or the political and economic influence of the conditions placed on countries aspiring to join the EU, has been a central theme in the literature on EU enlargement (Kelley 2004; Schimmelfennig 2007; Epstein 2005; Hughes et al. 2004; Jacoby 2004; Vachudova 2005; Grabbe 2006; Schimmelfennig and Sedelmeier 2004). Numerous scholars have persuasively argued that EU conditionality has both coerced and persuaded would-be member states to adopt policies that they otherwise might not have, ranging from political democratization to minority protection to economic restructuring. EU conditionality has also forced aspiring member states to extensively restructure their legal codes to comply with the EU's *acquis communitaire*. Vachudova (2005) refers to this conditionality as 'active leverage,' in contrast to the 'passive leverage' exerted by the more general attraction of EU membership. The Copenhagen criteria of 1993 provided the basis for this active leverage, laying out the specific conditions that states must fulfill before joining the EU. The Maastricht criteria (or convergence criteria), part of the Maastricht Treaty signed in 1992 and in force since 1993, similarly detailed the conditions that a state must meet before being eligible to join the euro zone.

The key Maastricht provisions included achieving a 'high degree of price stability,' maintaining sustainable government debt and deficit levels, ensuring convergent long-term interest rates, and successfully participating in the exchange-rate mechanism of the European monetary system (ERM II). In practice, this means inflation rates of no more than 1.5 percent and long-term interest rates of no more than 2 percent above the average of the three member states with the lowest rates, a public debt less than 60 percent of gross domestic product (GDP), a budget deficit below 3 percent of GDP, and participation in ERM II for at least two years. ERM II commits the aspiring euro-zone country to maintain an agreed-upon exchange rate with the euro within a fluctuation band of $+/-15$ percent.

When the postcommunist states became EU members, they formally committed to joining the euro zone as soon as they met the Maastricht criteria. However, after an initial burst of enthusiasm for the euro across the region, by 2005 the postcommunist new member states had split into two groups: 'pacesetters' and 'laggards' (Dyson 2006). While five states continued to profess a government commitment to rapid euro adoption (the Baltic states, Slovenia, and Slovakia), regional heavyweights Poland, the Czech Republic, and Hungary all began expressing euro-skepticism and pushed back or cancelled their prospective entry dates. As euro-zone membership conditions were identical for all, the mere existence of conditionality cannot explain this variation. The candidate states' divergent preferences also stood in stark contrast to the run-up to EU membership, when they all bent over backwards to meet EU conditions in a range of seemingly more sensitive areas such as minority rights. What explains this division between the pacesetters and the laggards? Why did the conditionality of Maastricht prove less potent than that of Copenhagen?

I argue, first, that a straightforward domestic cost–benefit analysis turned the smaller new member states into pacesetters. This is consistent with other evidence from this volume that domestic conditions mediate the power of conditionality (Epstein and Sedelmeier 2008; Schimmelfennig 2008). The pacesetters all had far lower GDPs than the laggards. In great part because of their size, and again in contrast to the laggards, most had fixed exchange-rate regimes and all had highly trade-dependent economies. As a result, the material benefits of meeting the Maastricht criteria and joining the euro zone seemed to outweigh the costs for these states. Moreover, for those that had already ceded their monetary autonomy in an environment of capital mobility, entering ERM II did not represent a significant, difficult, or especially controversial change. Once these small states had entered ERM II in the heady honeymoon period soon after EU membership, they found themselves effectively locked in to the euro adoption process.

Second, I argue that Maastricht conditionality not only allowed but encouraged the laggards to further delay their entry, a clear example of the unintended consequences of EU policy (see also Sasse 2008). Unlike in the smaller states, the governments of the larger ones had a difficult choice to make. For these states, the potential economic benefits of joining the euro zone were less clear-cut. It would also require their central banks, all inflation targeters, to cede control over monetary policy. Therefore, European influences could tip the political scales either way. By making it possible for new member states to delay entry, by increasing the difficulty of the entry conditions, and by displaying internal problems and disputes undermining the euro zone's legitimacy and attraction, EU actors discouraged the laggards from making euro-zone entry a domestic priority. While EU membership conditionality pushed applicant states to exert maximum efforts to meet the criteria, in these cases euro-zone conditionality had the opposite effect.

EURO-PHILES AND EURO-SKEPTICS

Although all postcommunist new member states expressed enthusiasm for the euro before they entered the EU, once in the EU their governments' commitments to rapid euro adoption diverged. ERM II entry represents the best measure of credible commitment to post-accession euro adoption, as postcommunist governments uniformly stated their intentions to remain in ERM II for only the minimum two-year period before adopting the euro. Moreover, once a state joins ERM II, international financial markets also expect it to move quickly towards euro adoption and will punish government backsliding on the Maastricht criteria. Joining ERM II represents a potentially risky and near-irrevocable commitment to the euro.

Of the May 2004 entrants, the five postcommunist 'pacesetters' confirmed their intent to join the euro zone by entering ERM II in 2004–05 (see Table 1). On the other hand, the three 'laggards' – Poland, Hungary, and the Czech Republic – still had not joined ERM II in March 2008, and had no immediate plans to do so. The 2007 EU entrants Bulgaria and Romania seemed poised to diverge as well, with the Bulgarian government anticipating an early entry into ERM II while the Romanian government planned to enter ERM II only in 2010–12.

Table 1 New EU members' convergence status

	GDP 2006 (EUR billions)	Exchange rate regime (immediately pre-ERM II)	ERM II member	Inflation (HICP) 2006 (01–05 avg.)	Deficit as % GDP 2006 (03–05 avg.)	Debt as % GDP 2006 (03–05 avg.)	Long-term interest rates 12/06 (12/05)
Reference values	–	–	2 years	3.0*	−3.0	60.0	6.4**
Poland	271.5	Float	No	**1.3 (2.7)**	−3.9 (−5.4)	**47.8 (46.6)**	5.14 **(5.16)**
Czech Republic	114	Managed float	No	**2.1 (2.0)**	−2.9 (−4.4)	**30.4 (30.2)**	3.68 **(3.61)**
Romania	97.1	Managed float	No	6.6 (18.3)	**−1.9 (−1.5)**	**12.4 (18.7)**	7.42 (N/A)
Hungary	89.9	Float	No	4.0 (5.8)	−9.2 (−7.2)	66.0 (59.7)	6.81 (6.89)
Slovakia	43.9	Managed float	11/2005	4.3 (5.8)	−3.4 (**−2.6**)	**30.7 (39.3)**	4.15 **(3.62)**
Slovenia (1/07)	29.7	Managed float	6/2004	**2.3 (5.5)**	**1.8 (−2.2)**	**29.1 (27.6)**	3.8 **(3.69)**
Bulgaria	25.1	Currency board	No	7.4 (5.5)	**3.3 (1.4)**	**22.8 (37.6)**	4.18 (N/A)
Lithuania	23.7	Currency board	6/2004	3.8 (0.9)	**−0.3 (−1.1)**	**18.2 (19.7)**	4.28 **(3.79)**
Latvia	16.2	Euro peg	5/2005	6.6 (4.1)	**0.4 (−1.0)**	**10.0 (13.8)**	4.9 **(3.59)**
Cyprus (1/08)	13.5	Euro peg	5/2005	**2.2 (2.5)**	−1.5 (−4.3)	65.3 (69.4)	4.44 **(4.09)**
Estonia	13.1	Currency board	6/2004	4.4 (3.5)	**3.8 (1.8)**	**4.1 (5.0)**	N/A
Malta (1/08)	5.1	Basket peg	5/2005	**2.6 (2.5)**	−2.6 (−5.9)	66.5 (70.9)	5.18 **(4.39)**

Notes: **Bolded** values meet euro-zone entry requirements; **bolded** countries have joined the euro zone. Primary statistics are 2006 averages, except for Slovenia, Cyprus, and Malta (these figures come from the relevant *Convergence Reports*). HICP, Harmonized index of Consumer Prices.
*Poland (1.5), Finland (1.3), Sweden (1.6) → Average 1.5, Reference +1.5%.
**Poland (5.3), Finland (3.9), Sweden (3.8) → Average 4.4, Reference +2%.
Sources: *ECB Monthly Bulletin and Statistics Pocket Books*; *May 2007 Convergence Report* (reference values, April 2006–March 2007); *May 2006 Convergence Report on Slovenia* (Slovenian Maastricht criteria statistics).

Government statements confirmed this division. Officials in the Baltic states, Slovenia, and Slovakia expressed their desire to reap the benefits of euro-zone membership. When Slovenia successfully joined the euro zone in January 2007, Baltic governments expressed regret and irritation that they had not been welcomed as well. Similarly, Slovakia's government began to worry that the EU would not allow it to join even if it met the Maastricht criteria. Prime Minister Robert Fico complained in September 2007 that 'new political criteria that were not here have started appearing,' and that he feared Slovakia's robust efforts to adopt the euro will have been wasted (SITA 2007). Meanwhile, Poland's government refused to set a date for ERM II entry and suggested that euro adoption should be put to a referendum; Hungary's government made no sustained effort to fulfill the fiscal Maastricht criteria and continually pushed back its planned euro entry date; and the Czech Republic under euro-skeptical President Vaclav Klaus and a bitterly divided parliament undermined the Czech National Bank's commitment to the euro and refused to set a proposed entry date (Epstein and Johnson, forthcoming; Johnson 2006).

On reflection, many proposed reasons for this divergence do not match the evidence especially well. For example, in the most comprehensive study Dyson (2007) argues that the Baltic states and Slovenia were more eager to adopt the euro because it would provide 'a vital underlying shared identity' and serve to separate them from Russia and the former Yugoslavia, respectively. If this were a key factor, then Poland, another strongly anti-Russian country, should be a pacesetter as well. Moreover, according to the regular Flash Eurobarometer polls, citizens of the Baltic states were consistently among the least likely to believe that adopting the euro would make them feel more European. For all these states, EU membership rather than the euro represented their acceptance into the community of 'Europe.'

Legacies of inherited debt and deficit, capacity for fiscal discipline, and attitudes towards the market economy likewise do not adequately differentiate the two sides. In the laggard camp, Poland's massive inherited debt burden was erased and Hungary's was not, while of the postcommunist states only the Czech Republic and Slovenia did not need to take advantage of International Monetary Fund (IMF) lending programmes. The ramifications of size determined in great part whether or not a postcommunist country had a sustainable capacity for fiscal discipline, as I discuss below. Just as importantly, the simple ability to meet the Maastricht criteria did not clearly separate the pacesetters from the laggards (see Table 1). While Hungary stood out in consistently not meeting any of the four monetary and fiscal criteria, the record was mixed among the other countries. Of the remaining candidate states the Czech Republic was the only country to meet all four criteria as of 2006, while Poland met three of the four. In contrast, all three of the Baltic states missed the inflation criterion, while Slovakia missed both the inflation and the deficit criteria. Objective readiness to join and government eagerness to join were separate phenomena.

Lingering skepticism towards the market economy was not widespread in any of these countries either. Unlike citizens in many post-Soviet states (such as in

Russia and Central Asia), postcommunist EU citizens generally did not express much nostalgia for the non-market economic past. Perhaps more importantly, public attitudes towards the euro itself did not distinguish the government europhiles from the euro-skeptics. According to the regular Flash Eurobarometer polls, citizens of the Baltic states were consistently among those who most wanted to postpone the introduction of the euro as long as possible and who felt that the introduction of the euro would cause prices to rise and jeopardize their national identities.[1] The Baltic states also were consistently more likely than others to expect negative consequences from euro adoption. In contrast, citizens of Romania, Slovakia, and Hungary were the most sanguine about the euro. Of the 2004 postcommunist EU entrants, only Poles, Hungarians, and Slovaks said that most people were happy that the euro would eventually replace their national currencies.

Instead, I argue that the key difference is the size of these countries' economies. It is no accident that the smallest new member countries as measured by GDP entered ERM II quickly while the largest countries did not (see Table 1). Size is important for two related reasons: it affects foreign trade dependence and exchange-rate regime choices. In small states with open economies, external market forces tend to discipline fiscal policy more effectively than in larger ones. All of the smaller postcommunist states, from Slovakia on down, had already met both of the fiscal criteria for Maastricht well before joining the EU. In Slovenia, for example, economic openness and extensive trade ties to the EU made the country a natural pacesetter. Unlike the other postcommunist new member states, Slovenia already had extensive trade ties with the EU when it became independent in 1991. In 2001, three years before EU membership, its trade openness and concentration of trade with EU member states were both above the EU average – that is, non-member Slovenia already traded more intensively with the EU than did over half of EU member states (Gaspari 2005). Tiny, prosperous Slovenia thus had achieved significant economic integration with the EU and a political consensus on the desirability of euro-zone membership when it joined the EU in 2004, making it relatively costless to enter ERM II right away.

Size affects exchange-rate regime choice as well. Most Central and East European transition states initially adopted fixed exchange-rate regimes because of the need to quickly establish monetary policy credibility. In moving from a non-market to a market economy with inexperienced central bankers and economic uncertainty, exchange-rate pegs or currency boards signaled to domestic and international actors that a government intended to pursue conservative monetary and fiscal policies. However, the larger states all eventually adopted floating, inflation-targeting regimes, while most of the smaller countries maintained or strengthened exchange-rate pegs or currency boards (see Table 1). Governments in the larger states decided that economic convergence with Europe required this move to floating regimes. The complexity of their internal markets meant that inflation stubbornly persisted under exchange-rate pegs, particularly as rapid economic development put upward pressure on their currencies. Large-state central bankers also felt that they needed the tool of flexible monetary policy to offset inflationary pressures from government spending.

But in smaller, more open economies, exchange-rate stability typically matters more to policy-makers than does the flexibility offered by independent monetary policy. In small states, the external, trade-based market is more important than the internal market in affecting prices, economic growth rates, and government revenue streams. Such states put a high value on maintaining stable, predictable exchange rates *vis-à-vis* their main trading partners. The easiest way to do this is by pegging the exchange rate, establishing a formal currency board, or simply adopting the currency of the major trading partner. In fact, some countries seriously debated adopting the euro unilaterally (most notably Estonia), and refrained only because of European Central Bank (ECB) threats forbidding them to do so.[2] The smallest states saw fixing their currencies to the euro as a way to achieve both economic stability and convergence with the EU market. In turn, because these states had already relinquished monetary policy-making flexibility by fixing their currencies, they would give nothing up when entering ERM II or adopting the euro. For the same reason, they found it easy to enter ERM II relatively quickly, as ERM II mirrored their existing exchange-rate regimes. Therefore, the governments of the small, fixed-rate states consistently pressed for more rapid euro adoption because the benefits of doing so appeared to far outweigh the costs. Not surprisingly, the Baltic states (and Cyprus and Malta) entered ERM II as soon as they could do so, without real political dissent.

Nevertheless, as the more complicated Slovak case demonstrates, size was not destiny. Having a smaller, more open economy may make it objectively easier and more desirable to meet the Maastricht criteria, enter ERM II, and join the euro zone, but the decision to do so is ultimately a political one. Slovakia spent much of the 1990s as a veritable pariah state under Prime Minister Vladimír Mečiar, fiscally profligate and rejected from consideration for the first round of EU membership. Only when the pro-EU public brought a centre-right coalition led by Prime Minister Mikuláš Dzurinda to power in 1998 did Slovakia pursue EU membership. Re-elected in 2002, the Dzurinda government used its mandate to carry out extensive fiscal reforms, shepherd the country into the EU, and meet the Maastricht criteria. As Dzurinda's economic policies increasingly began to bite, it became clear that he might lose power in the June 2006 elections. In order to preserve fiscal discipline and Slovakia's path to the euro, the Dzurinda government effectively tied the hands of future governments by moving Slovakia into ERM II in November 2005.

Entering ERM II locks a country into maintaining a commitment to fiscal rectitude because it immediately becomes the country's central symbol of economic credibility. This is the one effective part of Maastricht's conditionality, but ironically the EU is not the enforcer. Instead, once in ERM II a country will abandon it only under extreme circumstances because financial markets would read it as a strongly negative development (Frieden 1997; Woodruff 2005). Slovak Prime Minister Robert Fico's post-election predicament demonstrated the force of the ERM II commitment, one that kept Slovakia in the group of pacesetters. His centre-left coalition came to power in June 2006 because the Slovak public was fed up with the previous government's austere, Maastricht-oriented policies. However, Fico quickly found that he had to abandon pursuit of his more expensive campaign promises. The moment Fico implied that Slovakia might consider postponing its planned 2009 euro adoption for fiscal reasons, currency speculators began to attack the Slovak crown, forcing him to reiterate Slovakia's commitment to the 2009 target date. As Fico rightly suspected, the EU is holding Slovakia to a high standard before allowing it to join the euro zone under his government, as the EU expects fiscal backsliding once Slovakia has safely introduced the euro. Nevertheless, Slovakia remained poised to be the next postcommunist state to adopt the euro.

CONDITIONALITY AND THE LAGGARDS

Although the smaller states' pro-euro stance can be explained in instrumental terms, such a cost–benefit approach did not resolve the issue for the larger states. While they recognized the long-term benefits of euro adoption, in the short and medium term the economic benefits were less clear and the costs potentially high. Academics and policy-makers alike raised concerns over the possible negative economic effects for the larger states of entering the euro zone too quickly. These states had both significant investment needs and productivity and price levels well below the EU average, so racing to fulfill the Maastricht criteria could retard economic growth (Dumke and Sherman 2000; Krenzler and Senior Nello 1999; Égert et al. 2003). Other potential risks included misalignment from entering the euro zone with an overvalued exchange rate or the possible inflationary impact of euro-zone entry in the wake of high productivity growth in the traded-goods sector (the Balassa-Samuelson effect) (Watson 2004; Kenen and Meade 2004; Vintrová 2004; Dumke and Sherman 2000; Begg 2006). Many of the same observers also argued that allowing more time for financial market deepening, coordinating payments systems, working with EU statistical and accounting systems, and other elements of financial system development would improve the transmission mechanisms for monetary policy and allow the central banks to more effectively implement the ECB's monetary policies.

Just as importantly, these large, inflation-targeting states strongly objected to the ERM II requirement. Polish, Czech, and Hungarian central bankers, for example, repeatedly spoke out against ERM II. As Czech National Bank governor Zdeněk Tůma observed:

> Policymakers designed a set of rules 15 years ago ... back then these rules might have been perfectly legitimate, but today they are outdated and counter-productive ... what is the sense in asking countries that already use inflation targets and floating rates to enter the ERM-2? ... It implies switching

from a regime that is perfectly compatible with the European Central Bank framework to a semi-fixed exchange rate, which is incompatible.

(Tůma 2007)

The ECB responded to these concerns not only with stern warnings that it would not relax the Maastricht criteria, but with suggestions that aspiring euro-zone members might want to stay in ERM II longer than the minimally required two years. ECB officials often repeated that ERM II should not be seen as a 'waiting room' but as a 'testing room,' one in which prospective euro members could fine-tune their economies to mesh with the euro area before joining. Central bankers and governments in the larger states thus became wary of entering ERM II, as it would imply giving up useful monetary-policy flexibility with no guarantee of subsequent timely euro adoption. This concern has borne fruit, as five post communist new member states had entered ERM II by 2005, but only one, Slovenia, succeeded in adopting the euro two years later.

As a result, European actors would need to work hard to coerce or persuade the governments of these larger states to repress their economies long enough to meet the Maastricht criteria and risk the ERM II lock-in. But instead, issues surrounding the timing, difficulty, and legitimacy of Maastricht conditionality had the opposite effect, reinforcing these states' 'laggard' status. First, the lack of a formal deadline for euro adoption permitted the timing of euro-zone membership to become a political issue in new member states. The ECB itself opened the door to further politicization on timing by emphasizing that new member states should not necessarily rush to adopt the euro. Indeed, on occasion ECB president Jean-Claude Trichet (2006) resorted to analogy to make this argument:

> It needs to be borne in mind that enlargement, in particular euro area enlargement, could also bear some risks if a country were to rush too quickly to join the euro area. To illustrate this point let me return to sporting imagery. While it is fully understandable for a young, ambitious and talented sportsperson to want to join the champions league as soon as possible, this person might sometimes be better off taking a bit more time for training in order to further develop and strengthen his talents in a favourable environment ... My main message is, do not worry about whether [entry] will be quick or slow. The team is ready and happy to receive new members when they are ready and patient for them to become ready.

Other ECB officials also sent clear, public messages not to rush. With the ECB urging caution, domestic policy-makers who supported rapid euro adoption in the larger states lacked a vital source of external legitimation for their policy-preferences. While domestic politicians previously manufactured consensus on difficult reforms required for EU accession by saying that EU directives left no scope for policy choice, such ECB statements emphasized that euro entry timing was entirely a domestic policy choice.

The ECB issued these warnings because of concerns over governance issues, credibility, and past history with expansion. In terms of governance, as new members join the euro zone the Governing Council of the ECB must be restructured in order to absorb them (Eijffinger 2006; Howarth 2007). Gradual expansion would give the ECB's decision-making apparatus more time to adjust. More importantly, the ECB worried that aspirants might push to meet the criteria only in a nominal fashion, one that would prove unsustainable once eurozone membership was attained. As José Manuel González-Páramo (2006) noted, the 'overall credibility of the euro area ... could be negatively affected by a lack of sustainable convergence and flexibility in an individual country.' The ECB's fears were based not simply on theory, but on past experience with expansion. The EU previously bent the rules to allow Italy, Belgium, and Greece to join despite not meeting the required public-debt levels, and experienced some regret over this decision. The Greek example was perhaps foremost in their minds. Greece made massive political and economic efforts to reach nominal convergence in time to adopt the euro along with the other first-round entrants, but was subsequently dogged by economic problems, as well as persistent allegations that it 'cooked the books' to make it appear as though it had fulfilled the Maastricht criteria when it had not (Featherstone 2003). Given these experiences, the ECB was wary of bringing in new members who might not be completely prepared.

Second, and as a result, the EU governing bodies let the new member states know that they planned to interpret the Maastricht criteria in strict terms. In particular, ECB president Jean-Claude Trichet repeatedly warned that states would only be permitted to adopt the euro if they fulfilled the Maastricht criteria in a 'sustainable manner,' emphasizing that decisions would be made 'case-by-case' on the basis of 'equal treatment.' Dyson (2007) argues that it is this combination of strict formal and informal euro adoption requirements with temporal uncertainty that most undermined euro-zone conditionality. The EU demonstrated its credibility in this matter by denying Lithuania's bid to join the euro zone in January 2007 on the grounds that it did not meet the inflation criterion. Lithuanians found this decision galling. Not only did Lithuania come close to meeting the criterion (it had an inflation rate of 2.7 percent in the relevant time period, with a benchmark rate of 2.6), but the EU strictly interpreted the Maastricht criteria in taking its benchmark to be an inflation rate within 1.5 percent of the three lowest inflation rates in EU member states at the time – two of which were Sweden and the UK, which were outside the euro zone. Jonas Lionginas, chairman of the Lithuanian parliament's finance and budget committee, opined that 'it seems now that declarations of equality of all member states are not worth anything,' stating that the EU had shown 'disrespect' towards his country (White 2006).

ECB officials were thus forced to defend themselves in the face of allegations that the EU used the Maastricht criteria arbitrarily in order to keep the postcommunist states out of the euro zone.[3] Trichet (2007) fought back, saying that 'we have to protect the credibility of the euro area, so there is a joint interest in being as efficient and as professional as possible in organizing this enlargement. We are not a closed shop. We have proved that with the entry of Slovenia.' The protestation that the euro zone was 'not a closed shop' or was 'an open shop' appeared repeatedly in ECB officials' speeches and public statements after the Lithuanian decision.

Finally, the euro's weak legitimacy within the EU itself made joining the euro zone seem much less attractive. Most fundamentally, a country can be 'European' without adopting the euro, but not without joining the EU and adopting the *acquis*. The United Kingdom and Denmark both negotiated opt-outs from the Maastricht Treaty and are not required to adopt the euro. Many in the United Kingdom in particular were vocal about the potential negative effects, both economic and political, of joining the euro zone, and public opinion remained firmly against joining. In addition, although Sweden did not have an opt-out, it nevertheless remained outside the euro zone simply by failing to meet the Maastricht criteria – it has refused to join ERM II. This decision followed a failed referendum on euro adoption in September 2003, in which 56 percent voted against the euro. Therefore, the new accession states saw the open dissent among older members over the benefits and viability of the euro zone, and saw that, despite their lack of a formal opt-out clause, opting out was viable in practice. Moreover, they saw that these three non-euro states had relatively vibrant economies, active inter-European trade relationships, and stable prices. In fact, the inflation levels in these three countries on average have been consistently lower than those in the euro zone. Perhaps as a result, polls showed that Central and East European publics widely believed that their countries were not actually required to adopt the euro, in contradiction to the commitment these countries made upon accepting EU membership. Fully 67 percent of those surveyed in the new member states in 2006 thought that their country could choose whether or not to adopt the euro, with only 26 percent correctly answering that no such legal choice existed.[4] Although EU membership criteria effectively set limits on what policies were open to legitimate political debate in the postcommunist accession states, euro adoption criteria did not have the same effect.

The troubles that euro-zone members have experienced with policy coordination and public opinion since the euro's full introduction in January 2002 reinforced this skepticism among would-be members. Many euro-zone governments at first accused the independent ECB of conducting an overly conservative monetary policy, one that showed it was willing to squelch growth in Europe in order to build up its own credentials as an inflation hawk. Since then the debate has grown more broadly to critique the ECB's 'democratic deficit' (Verdun 1998; Henning 2007; Berman and McNamara 1999). Modeled in great part by and after the Bundesbank, the ECB was widely considered to be the world's most independent central bank. Critics argued that this independence led the ECB to adopt inappropriate monetary policies and prevented it from coordinating its actions effectively with the fiscal policies of the member states. More recently, concerns have arisen that the ECB's policies have exacerbated the euro's appreciation *vis-à-vis* the US dollar, hurting exports.

The problems that euro-zone states, especially France and Germany, have experienced with meeting the fiscal conditions of the Stability and Growth Pact resonated as well. New member states fairly wondered whether the combination of a unified ECB monetary policy and diverse, nationally controlled fiscal policies would be sustainable over the long run. They also feared that their countries' adjustment needs might take a permanent second place to those of the original member states. All of this was further compounded by the continuing public skepticism about the euro in the current euro-zone states, with only 48 percent of those surveyed in 2006 finding that euro adoption had been advantageous overall for their countries.[5] The biggest public complaint was about the perceived rise in prices caused by euro adoption. Although the ECB, supported by academic studies, denied that euro introduction led to inflation, the general European public widely disbelieved this claim (Deroose et al. 2007).

These governance problems and mixed public feelings about the euro in current euro-zone states, combined with the robust economic health and views of the non-euro three, made joining a relatively less attractive option. As a result, the appropriate timing of euro adoption became an issue of heated political debate in the Czech Republic, Poland, and Hungary. Central bankers wanted to adopt the euro in order to impose its fiscal discipline on their governments, but objected to the Maastricht criteria (Johnson 2006). Powerful centre-left and euro-skeptical parties did not want to relinquish fiscal and monetary flexibility in the short term for an uncertain future in ERM II and the euro zone, and persistently pressed for delay (Bönker 2006; Greskovits 2006; Zubek 2006). In this sense, for the larger new member countries Maastricht conditionality may have more in common with IMF or World Bank conditionality than with EU membership conditionality – while governments pay lip service to the requirements, this is accompanied by grumbling, backsliding, and a questioning of both the value of the goal and the legitimacy of the condition-setting institution (see, for example, Epstein 2008).

STAGGERING TOWARDS THE EURO

With all but Slovenia having missed the initial post-accession window of opportunity to speed into the euro zone, the other postcommunist new member states will likely trickle in over the course of the next decade or so, complaining about Maastricht all the way. Ironically, despite their original preferences, the Baltic state euro-philes may end up adopting the euro at the same time as some of the laggards. Their rapidly growing economies and fixed exchange rates have led to rising inflation in recent years, meaning that none of the three now expect to meet the Maastricht inflation criterion any time soon. Although their governments responded by criticizing the inflation criterion, the ECB suggested that such inflationary problems demonstrated that these governments still needed to undertake serious structural reforms. Nevertheless, stuck in ERM

II, the Baltic states (as well as the Slovaks) have committed themselves to the euro path.

Under what conditions will the large country governments do the same? Three sets of circumstances could temper their euro-skepticism. First, serious domestic financial crises could make the discipline of Maastricht and the stability of the euro look more attractive, especially if they bring conservative governments to power who wish to tie the government's free-spending hands.[6] Second, the EU could adjust its approach to conditionality. While it cannot change the flexible timing, it could make the Maastricht conditions easier to meet. Despite ECB protestations that the criteria are 'strict,' there is clearly room for interpretation even without changing the monetary and fiscal targets. The postcommunist new member states are all looking to the EU's decision on whether or not to admit Slovakia in 2009. If Slovakia nominally meets the criteria and is still turned away, this will have a chilling effect on the others. Governments will be much less likely to spend the political capital necessary to meet the Maastricht criteria if they believe that the euro reward may not follow. Finally, there will likely be a regional snowball effect. As more postcommunist states join the euro zone, others will be less comfortable on the outside looking in. This will especially be the case if new member entries into the euro zone appear to progress smoothly. Slovenia presents a mixed example in this regard so far. While the introduction of the euro itself went off without a hitch, Slovenians – like other Europeans before them – overwhelmingly believed that the euro's introduction led to increased prices.[7]

But even if and when these postcommunist new member states join the euro zone, will they be able to deal with the fiscal implications? As Cohen (2007) rightly points out, the euro zone not only maintains a more restrictive monetary policy than might be appropriate for these states, but EU membership has already placed new fiscal demands upon them that could raise their deficits by as much as 3 to 4 percent of GDP. Not only must they contribute to the EU's central budget, but meet the expenses of conforming to the *acquis*. Unless they follow the lead of France and Germany in breaching the Stability and Growth Pact, euro-zone membership will likely engender a constant struggle to contain government spending in many postcommunist states, even in circumstances where the economy may need it and the public expects it. Seen from this angle, the less attractive conditionality of Maastricht may be a blessing in disguise.

NOTES

1 See the successive Flash Eurobarometer surveys on new member states and the euro conducted from 2004 to 2007, available at http://ec.europa.eu/public_opinion/archives/flash_arch_en.htm
2 This did not stop tiny non-members Montenegro and Kosovo from unilaterally euroizing.
3 The issue arose again when Malta and Cyprus were given the green light to join in January 2008 despite not meeting the public debt criterion.
4 Fully 75 percent of Poles felt that their country had the right to make this decision. In no country was the percentage agreeing less than 50. Flash Eurobarometer 195 (2006), http://ec.europa.eu/public_opinion/flash/fl191_sum_en.pdf
5 Flash Eurobarometer 193 (2006), http://ec.europa.eu/public_opinion/flash/fl193_en.pdf. The most skeptical citizens were in Italy, Greece, Germany, and the Netherlands. This approval percentage has fallen steadily since 2002.
6 Walsh (2007) argues that such a crisis would be most likely to put Britain back on the euro track as well.
7 Inflation in Slovenia has risen significantly since the euro's introduction, but the European Commission and the ECB deny that this has occurred because of the euro (Vuković 2007).

REFERENCES

Begg, I. (2006) 'Real convergence and EMU enlargement: the time dimension of fit with the euro area', in K. Dyson (ed.), *Enlarging the Euro Area: External Empowerment and Domestic Transformation in East Central Europe*, Oxford: Oxford University Press, pp. 71–89.
Berman, S. and McNamara, K. (1999) 'Bank on democracy', *Foreign Affairs* 78: 2–8.
Bönker, F. (2006) 'From pacesetter to laggard: the political economy of negotiating fit in the Czech Republic', in K. Dyson (ed.), *Enlarging the Euro Area: External Empowerment and Domestic Transformation in East Central Europe*, Oxford: Oxford University Press, pp. 160–77.
Cohen, B.J. (2007) 'Enlargement and the international role of the euro', *Review of International Political Economy* 14(5): 746–73.
Deroose, S., Hodson, D. and Kuhlmann, J. (2007) 'The legitimation of EMU: lessons from the early years of the euro', *Review of International Political Economy* 14(5): 800–19.
Dumke, R. and Sherman, H. (2000) 'Exchange rate options for EU applicant countries in Central and Eastern Europe', in B. Granville (ed.), *Essays on the World Economy and Its Financial System*, London: The Royal Institute of International Affairs, pp. 153–95.
Dyson, K. (2006) 'Euro entry as defining and negotiating fit: conditionality, contagion, and domestic politics', in K. Dyson (ed.), *Enlarging the Euro Area: External Empowerment and Domestic Transformation in East Central Europe*, Oxford: Oxford University Press, pp. 7–44.
Dyson, K. (2007) 'Euro area entry in east-central Europe: paradoxical Europeanization and clustered convergence', *West European Politics* 30(3): 417–42.
Égert, B., Gruber, T. and Reininger, T. (2003) 'Challenges for EU acceding countries' exchange rate strategies after EU accession and asymmetric application of the exchange rate criteria', *Focus on Transition* 2: 152–72.
Eijffinger, S. (2006) 'Change at the ECB Executive Board', *Intereconomics* 2: 93–9.
Epstein, R.A. (2005) 'Diverging effects of social learning and external incentives in Polish central banking and agriculture', in F. Schimmelfennig and U. Sedelmeier

(eds), *The Europeanization of Central and Eastern Europe*, Ithaca, NY: Cornell University Press, pp. 178–98.

Epstein, R.A. (2008) 'The social context in conditionality: internationalizing finance in postcommunist Europe', *Journal of European Public Policy* 15(6): 795–805.

Epstein, R.A. and Johnson, J. (forthcoming) 'The limits of Europeanization: the Czech Republic, Poland and European monetary integration', in K. Dyson and M. Marcussen (eds), *The Changing Power and Politics of European Central Banking: Living with the Euro*, Oxford: Oxford University Press.

Epstein, R.A. and Sedelmeier, U. (2008) 'Beyond conditionality: international institutions in postcommunist Europe after enlargement', *Journal of European Public Policy* 15(6): 806–25.

Featherstone, K. (2003) 'Greece and EMU: between external empowerment and domestic vulnerability', *Journal of Common Market Studies* 41(5): 923–40.

Frieden, J. (1997) 'The politics of exchange rates', in S. Edwards and M. Naím (eds), *Mexico 1994: Anatomy of an Emerging-Market Crash*, Washington, DC: Carnegie Endowment for World Peace, pp. 81–94.

Gaspari, M. (2005) 'Comments on "Two roads to the euro: the monetary experiences of Austria and Greece"', in S. Schadler (ed.), *Euro Adoption in Central and Eastern Europe: Opportunities and Challenges*, Washington, DC: International Monetary Fund, pp. 202–7.

Grabbe, H. (2006) *The EU's Transformative Power: Europeanization through Conditionality in Central and Eastern Europe*, London: Palgrave Macmillan.

Greskovits, B. (2006) 'The first shall be the last? Hungary's road to EMU', in K. Dyson (ed.), *Enlarging the Euro Area: External Empowerment and Domestic Transformation in East Central Europe*, Oxford: Oxford University Press, pp. 178–96.

Henning, C.R. (2007) 'Democratic accountability and the exchange-rate policy of the euro area', *Review of International Political Economy* 14(5): 774–99.

Howarth, D. (2007) 'Running an enlarged euro-zone – reforming the European Central Bank: efficiency, legitimacy and national economic interest', *Review of International Political Economy* 14(5): 820–41.

Hughes, J., Sasse, G. and Gordon, C. (2004) 'Conditionality and compliance in the EU's eastward enlargement: regional policy and the reform of sub-national government', *Journal of Common Market Studies* 42(3): 523–51.

Jacoby, W. (2004) *The Enlargement of the European Union and NATO: Ordering from the Menu in Central Europe*, Cambridge: Cambridge University Press.

Johnson, J. (2006) 'Two-track diffusion and central bank embeddedness: the politics of euro adoption in Hungary and the Czech Republic', *Review of International Political Economy* 13(3): 361–86.

Kelley, J. (2004) 'International actors on the domestic scene: membership conditionality and socialization by international institutions', *International Organization* 58(3): 425–57.

Kenen, P.B. and Meade, E.E. (2004) 'EU accession and the euro: close together or far apart?' in R. Pringle and N. Carver (eds), *EU Enlargement and the Future of the Euro*, London: Central Banking Publications, pp. 79–98.

Krenzler, H. and Senior Nello, S. (1999) 'Implications of the euro for enlargement: report of the working group on the eastern enlargement of the European Union', *RSC Policy Paper* 99.

Manuel González-Páramo, J. (2006) 'The enlargement of the euro area'. Speech at the conference on 'EMU Governance and Euro Changeover – Cyprus on the Path to the Adoption of the Euro', Cyprus, 30 November. Accessed at http://www.ecb.eu/press/key/date/2006/html/sp061130.en.html

Sasse, G. (2008) 'The politics of EU conditionality: the norm of minority protection during and beyond EU accession', *Journal of European Public Policy* 15(6): 842–60.

Schimmelfennig, F. (2007) 'European regional organizations, political conditionality, and democratic transformation in eastern Europe', *East European Politics and Societies* 21(1): 126–41.

Schimmelfennig, F. (2008) 'EU political accession conditionality after the 2004 enlargement: consistency and effectiveness', *Journal of European Public Policy* 15(6): 918–37.

Schimmelfennig, F. and Sedelmeier, U. (2004) 'Governance by conditionality: EU rule transfer to the candidate countries of Central and Eastern Europe', *Journal of European Public Policy* 11(4): 661–79.

SITA Slovenska Tlacova Agentura (2007) 'Double standard complicates euro introduction, says PM Robert Fico', *SITA Slovenska Tlacova Agentura*, 29 September.

Trichet, J.-C. (2006) 'Looking at EU and euro area enlargement from a central banker's angle: the views of the ECB'. Speech at the Diplomatic Institute, Sofia, 27 February. Accessed at http://www.ecb.eu/press/key/date/2006/html/sp060227.en.html

Trichet, J.-C. (2007) Interview with Jean-Claude Trichet conducted on 14 May by Lionel Barber, *Financial Times* editor, Ralph Atkins, *Financial Times Frankfurt* bureau chief, and Mark Schieritz, *Financial Times Deutschland*. Accessed at http://www.ecb.eu/press/key/date/2007/html/sp070518.en.html

Tůma, Z. (2007) 'Europe's club of nations needs a rule change', *Financial Times*, 4 January.

Vachudova, M. (2005) *Europe Undivided: Democracy, Leverage and Integration after Communism*, Oxford: Oxford University Press.

Verdun, A. (1998) 'The institutional design of EMU: a democratic deficit?', *Journal of Public Policy* 18(2): 107–32.

Vintrová, R. (2004) 'The CEE countries on the way into the EU – adjustment problems: institutional adjustment, real and nominal convergence', *Europe-Asia Studies* 56(4): 521–41.

Walsh, J.I. (2007) 'How and why Britain might join the single currency: the role of policy failure', *Review of International Political Economy* 14(5): 868–92.

Watson, M. (2004) 'Challenges for central banks in the new member states', in R. Pringle and N. Carver (eds), *EU Enlargement and the Future of the Euro*, London: Central Banking Publications, pp. 53–63.

White, A. (2006) 'Slovenia on track to adopt euro currency', *Washington Post*, 16 May.

Woodruff, D.M. (2005) 'Boom, gloom, doom: balance sheets, monetary fragmentation, and the politics of financial crisis in Argentina and Russia', *Politics and Society* 33(1): 3–45.

Vuković, M. (2007) 'Happy anniversary or the winter of our discontent?', *Slovenia Times*, 7 December.

Zubek, R. (2006) 'Poland: unbalanced domestic leadership in negotiating fit', in K. Dyson (ed.), *Enlarging the Euro Area: External Empowerment and Domestic Transformation in East Central Europe*, Oxford: Oxford University Press, pp. 197–214.

The politics of EU conditionality: the norm of minority protection during and beyond EU accession

Gwendolyn Sasse

INTRODUCTION

While 'the respect for and protection of national minorities' was enshrined in the first Copenhagen criterion and is often singled out as a prime example of the European Union's (EU's) positive impact on democracy in Central and Eastern Europe, the EU has in fact promoted norms which lack a foundation in EU law and remain controversial, even in the 'old' member states. This paradox points to the fact that the EU's 'minority condition' is a political and social construct. Constructs can have very 'real' effects, both intended and unintended, and direct and indirect. It is important to understand the context and rationale underlying the construction of the EU's minority condition in 1993, the dilemmas involved in translating the construct into EU policy, and the resonance of the construct in international and domestic politics in the pre- and post-accession periods. The EU's minority condition has proven to be 'sticky': it is a powerful cognitive framing device for both international institutions and domestic actors in the accession countries. At first glance, EU conditionality may appear as something fixed and constant but its chameleon-like characteristics can turn it into a dynamic process itself. Through an empirical case study of the medium-term effects of the minority condition in Latvia (and Estonia), this article challenges some of the conceptual and empirical findings of previous research on conditionality.

The post-enlargement context provides a new testing ground for the study of the effectiveness of EU conditionality in anchoring political, economic and legal reforms in Central and Eastern Europe (see Epstein and Sedelmeier 2008). In the post-accession period, the continued compliance with the *acquis* might be primarily a question of administrative capacity and the political will to be a 'good EU citizen' (see also Sedelmeier 2008), while the components of 'democratic conditionality', as defined by the first Copenhagen criterion, regain in significance as a litmus test of the medium- to long-term consolidation of the polities in question. So far the study of 'democratic conditionality' has been tied most convincingly to the early phase of regime change prior to the onset of the EU accession negotiations (Vachudova 2005). The scope for EU leverage in the post-accession period is clearly limited, in particular in the political sphere. The question is whether the EU created a certain momentum in the pre-accession period through sustained rhetoric and involvement with domestic actors, which carries over into the post-accession period. This momentum might be reinforced either by the EU itself or by other international actors specializing in a particular issue area (e.g. the Council of Europe and the Organization for Security and Co-operation in Europe (OSCE) with their expertise in minority issues). Domestic actors might seek to enhance or limit the EU-induced pre-accession momentum in the post-accession phase depending on their own interests, thereby providing us with an insight into the domestic consensus and commitment behind the EU's prescribed democratic values.

The study of the effects of democratic conditionality generally suffers from the broad nature of the first Copenhagen criterion which combines exceptionally large concepts, such as the 'stability of institutions' or the 'rule of law'. These criteria lack clear measures and benchmarks and, therefore, turned the EU's own monitoring and assessment into a political judgement (Grabbe 2006). How can we measure 'compliance' if conditionality itself is in flux? What does compliance mean in the case of a constructed norm like minority protection that lacks an internal EU consensus, a firm legal base and clear benchmarks, and is used flexibly over time? Thus, in the areas where conditionality was weakly defined or its interpretation changed over time, the seemingly precise term 'compliance' can be as fuzzy as the term 'conditionality' itself. At best, we can formally measure post-accession 'compliance' against the domestic follow-up on the actual complaints and recommendations, including legal changes, made by the EU during the accession process, or against international norms of minority protection, as propagated and monitored by the Council of Europe and the OSCE. What did the EU actually do during the accession process, and to what extent have legal, policy or behavioural changes been implemented in the issue areas raised during the accession process? In the field of minority protection the EU borrowed legal tools and policy recommendations from the Council of Europe and the OSCE in particular. This incorporates the interplay between different international actors into the study of conditionality pre- and post-accession. An in-depth assessment of the effects of the EU's minority condition that takes a more long-term perspective and connects the pre- and post-accession periods has to go beyond measuring 'compliance' and probe the domestic context in the accession countries for the political resonance (or lack thereof) of the EU's condition. Has the EU's 'minority condition', constructed in a particular historical and political context, shaped the domestic politics in the accession countries, and if so, how?

Taking the well-documented ambiguity and contested nature of the minority condition as a starting-point (de Witte 2000; Schwellnus 2001, 2006a, 2006b; Hughes and Sasse 2003; Vermeersch 2003, 2004; Sasse 2005a, 2005b; Toggenburg 2004, 2006; Wiener and Schwellnus 2004), this article traces the medium-term effects of the EU condition by focusing on the case with the most significant international emphasis on minority issues – Latvia (and Estonia as a variation on the same case). Though being a single case, it is the strongest test case for the EU's ability to assert direct influence and encourage the adoption of an EU-promoted norm associated with democratic conditionality. We would expect the intensity and visibility of the EU's involvement in specific minority issues to underpin a momentum for legal and behavioural change in the new member states before and after accession. This question is ultimately about the politics of conditionality, and it allows us to revisit the balance between international and domestic actors shaping legal and behavioural change.

CONCEPTUAL CHALLENGES IN THE STUDY OF EU CONDITIONALITY

Research on the impact of EU conditionality struggles with the difficulty of isolating the effect of international factors from the domestic incentives for legal, institutional or behavioural change. The gradually growing body of work that empirically tests the scope of conditionality has demonstrated that the record of conditionality is mixed across countries and policy areas. This evidence has led to the EU's role being conceptualized as a 'reinforcement mechanism' or a 'lock-in effect' (Schimmelfennig *et al.* 2003; Sasse 2005a). As part of this ongoing conceptual refinement, 'effective' conditionality has been tied primarily to consistency and credibility as well as low domestic adoption costs (Schimmelfennig and Sedelmeier 2005). The minority condition is neither consistent (in its application in any one country or across candidates) nor credible (the opening of the accession negotiations began when the first Copenhagen criterion was deemed 'fulfilled', though monitoring and criticism continued, and non-compliance with elements of the minority condition, such as the ratification of the Framework Convention for the Protection of National Minorities (FCNM), did not hold up accession).

While the adoption of minority-sensitive legislation may not derail a government, the domestic costs (mostly political, but also financial) of adopting and implementing progressive norms on minority protection and participation cannot be considered to be 'low'. Thus, the minority condition violates some of the requisites of effective conditionality and points to a necessary distinction between rule adoption and implementation.

Some scholars have tried to empirically unpack the concept of conditionality itself by pointing to its constructed, flexible, continuously evolving and highly politicized content (Hughes *et al.* 2004; Brusis 2005; Epstein 2006). Conditionality is being shaped by various actors at the EU level, in member states or in candidate countries. The preferences and norms of these political actors change over time, and they regularly instrumentalize references to EU conditionality in order to shape an agenda or silence opposition. Hughes *et al.* (2004: 3–4) conceptualized conditionality as a process shaped by the interaction of multi-level actors, perceptions and interests, differentiated rewards and sanctions, temporal factors and different degrees of institutional or policy compliance. This definition highlights the pitfalls inherent in treating conditionality as a variable, but it remains rather broad and calls for further conceptual and empirical precision. The minority condition fits the broad definition of conditionality as a process and thereby points us to the importance of the politics surrounding conditionality.

When extended into the post-accession period, the methodological difficulty of isolating the EU impact amidst the dynamics of domestic politics is amplified, in particular with regard to the components of 'democratic conditionality'. It is unclear to what extent any post-accession policy implementation and behavioural change can be accredited to the EU rather than to domestic political contestation. The lack of an EU effect would be most apparent where a legislative, policy or behavioural change occurs that goes openly against an EU priority stressed during the accession process. Conversely, an EU effect can manifest itself in at least two ways in the post-accession period: either through new domestic initiatives in an issue area initially put on the domestic agenda by the EU (and potentially followed up by other international institutions), or through a steady continuity of deepening structural or behavioural trends from the pre-accession period.

Analysing conditionality as a construct, as suggested here, is closely related to the conceptualization of conditionality as a process. Process-tracing starts from the actual construction of conditionality itself, and it traces the utilization, redefinition and politicization of a condition over time. This approach is particularly, though not exclusively, relevant to the study of the expansive first Copenhagen criterion ('democratic conditionality'), including the norm of minority protection. Process-tracing is not a new method, though the term has recently regained in prominence. Process-tracing can fit both a rationalist and a constructivist line of argument. So far it has been presented as primarily rooted in the research of linear causal mechanisms, although its creation of a series of 'mini-checks' has been credited with raising awareness of the limits of causal stories (Checkel 2005). If we accept that an outcome at one stage in the process can shape or determine a different outcome at a later stage in the process, process-tracing goes beyond a basic causality model. If we factor in the fluidity of a construct shaping a process of legislative or behavioural change, the linearity of causality is further disrupted. In the area of conditionality research, the use of the word 'process' starts with unpacking the construction and malleability of a specific condition. A condition might be weakly defined, as in the case of regional policy (Hughes *et al.* 2004; Jacoby 2004), or it may lack a solid foundation in the *acquis* or international law, as in the case of the minority condition.

Most empirical studies of the EU's impact on minority protection trace the successive legal and constitutional changes in Estonia and Latvia as proof of the EU's impact. Kelley's conceptually more nuanced study of the norm of minority protection in Central and Eastern Europe also emphasizes that EU membership conditionality was the key impetus for a change towards minority-friendly legislation (Kelley 2004). She concludes that only membership conditionality had the capacity to overcome domestic opposition, but she points to the importance of socialization supporting the process of legal change. According to Kelley, socialization without the leverage of membership conditionality fails to overcome domestic opposition. Similarly, Schimmelfennig and Sedelmeier (2005) and Jacoby (2004) point to mechanisms of social learning, lesson-drawing and emulation respectively. Ultimately, these studies find it hard to empirically pinpoint socialization or variants thereof in the accession context where they are difficult to separate from rationalist calculations.

So far the study of conditionality has not fully taken account of the political context of the minority condition during the accession process. It is here that the notion of socialization plays out empirically. Moreover, the temporal extension into the post-accession period has been absent from the study of EU conditionality so far. In principle, value and behavioural change that has taken effect during accession should be more consolidated and thus more apparent post-accession.

THE CONSTRUCTION OF THE EU'S MINORITY CONDITION

There are three stages to the construction of the EU's minority condition: the process of formulating the first Copenhagen criterion, its translation into a process of monitoring and assessment, and the anchoring of the minority condition in the political context of the Central and Eastern European (CEE) countries. The first two stages have been analysed at length in the literature, so a brief summary of the main findings will suffice in order to frame the analysis of the third stage.

The formulation of the conditions for membership, as set out by the Copenhagen Council of 1993, marked a significant disjuncture for the EU through the explicit mention of minority protection in addition to familiar human rights clauses among the political norms associated with democracy (de Witte 2000;

Toggenburg 2004). A number of security concerns arising from the post-communist transition process, especially the violent disintegration of the former Yugoslavia, formed the rationale for a greater internationalization of minority rights in the early 1990s. Sizeable minority groups in many CEE countries were associated with conflict potential in the context of a volatile transition process. The formulation of the EU's political conditions for accession took shape against the background of a changing pan-European framework of norms, driven by the OSCE and the Council of Europe in the early 1990s.

Once the EU had formulated the loose first Copenhagen criterion, it faced the challenge of translating it into policy and enforcing it in the absence of an EU-wide or international legal or political consensus on the norm of minority protection or, in fact, clear benchmarks or enforcement mechanisms (Vermeersch 2004; Sasse 2005a; Schwellnus 2006b). These dilemmas were further compounded by a procedural challenge, namely the fact that in the case of the first- and second-wave accession countries the first Copenhagen criterion had to be 'fulfilled' by the time the accession negotiations got under way, thereby limiting the EU's subsequent leverage in the political sphere.

The Commission's annual Regular Reports, following on from the Opinions of 1997 and the Accession Partnerships, have been the EU's key instrument to monitor and evaluate the candidates' progress towards accession. In the case of the minority criterion the EU based its monitoring exercise on a set of values and non-EU documents, namely the European Convention on Human Rights, the major OSCE documents of the early 1990s and the UN Declarations. Over time the Council of Europe's FCNM of 1995 became the Commission's primary instrument for translating the minority criterion into practice.[1] The Regular Reports frequently reminded the candidate states to sign and ratify the FCNM – despite the fact that several EU member states had not done so. This discrepancy and the fact that the first Copenhagen criterion lists the EU values embodied in Art. 6(1) Treaty on European Union (TEU) – with the notable exception of the minority criterion – gave rise to the discussion about 'double standards' (de Witte 2000; Hughes and Sasse 2003; Hoffmeister 2004; Sasse 2005a; Schwellnus 2006b).

The Regular Reports are a compendium of results compiled from a variety of sources. In the area of minority issues the Council of Europe and the OSCE were privileged sources of information. The coverage of the minority condition in the Regular Reports is characterized by a hierarchy of minority issues, ad hocery and inconsistencies resulting from the lack of clear benchmarks, and a lack of mechanisms to enforce implementation (Hughes and Sasse 2003; Sasse 2005a). The Reports primarily focus on the Russophones in Estonia and Latvia and the Roma across Central and Eastern Europe, reflecting the EU's soft security concerns. In the absence of clear benchmarks, the Reports track the adoption and amendment of laws on citizenship, naturalization, language and elections, the establishment of institutions or programmes targeting minority issues. The borrowing of different external 'standards' has at times confounded the ambiguity inherent in the minority condition and given rise to inconsistencies. The 2002 Reports on Estonia and Latvia, for example, report on the one hand that the OSCE mission in these states closed in late 2001, including the official OSCE reasons for this decision (that the improved situation no longer warranted their presence), but on the other hand also highlighting the EU's continued concerns (Hughes 2005). As a Commission official put it: 'Although the closure of the OSCE missions was not a formal condition, the Commission had a clear interest in it'.[2]

A closer analysis of the EU's monitoring exercise and the successive adoption of legislation in the candidate countries suggests that international actors and a vaguely defined European norm have framed the debates and perceptions and affected the timing and nature of specific pieces of legislation, especially the gradual modification of restrictive citizenship laws in Estonia and Latvia (Kelley 2004). In Commission circles the EU's actual impact has been described rather realistically: 'we help them do what they are already doing anyway.'[3] The post-accession period now allows us to go beyond the initial legislative changes in order to assess the more long-term effects of the EU on the norm of minority protection in Central and Eastern Europe.

The contingent construction of the EU minority condition, premised on a dual concern for security and democratization, highlights the importance of tracing the social and political process behind the component parts of the Copenhagen criteria. The logical conclusion of presenting the minority condition as a construct is the recognition that any notion of compliance is a construct as well. Thus, both conditionality and compliance become flexible constructs in need of a nuanced understanding through their politicization.

THE POLITICS OF THE EU'S MINORITY CONDITION

The intensity and visibility of international involvement in the area of minority protection singles out Latvia and Estonia as the strongest test case of the EU's transformative impact on legislative and behavioural change. The sizeable but loose category of 'Russophones', accounting for 35–42 per cent of Estonia's and Latvia's respective populations in 1989, represents a diverse group, including Russians, Ukrainians, Belarusians, and some smaller minority groups. With perceptions shaped by the Soviet era occupation and in the absence of organized minority interests, the domestic push for a minority-sensitive policy in Estonia and Latvia was small. Restrictive citizenship and language laws and naturalization procedures have been amended gradually in the context of EU accession (Norgaard 1996; Kolsto 2002; Kelley 2004), but the persistently high numbers of stateless Russophone residents suggest that the effect of international pressure on forging deeper societal cohesion has been limited (Hughes 2005).[4] As of April 2007 there were 392,816 non-citizens (17 per cent of the population) and 41,439 Aliens registered in Latvia (Latvian Naturalization Board 2007) and as of May 2006 there were 120,000 (9 per cent of the population) in Estonia (Estonian Ministry of Foreign Affairs 2006).[5]

The dimensions of this phenomenon of statelessness are unprecedented inside the EU. A discussion of this political reality neither calls into question the legitimacy of Estonian or Latvian sovereignty nor does it detract from the fact that the presence of such large Russophone minorities is primarily a legacy of Soviet imperial policies. The intensity and visibility of international involvement during the EU accession process, the closure of the OSCE missions at the end of 2001, and EU membership in 2004 have underpinned the impression that all the outstanding issues concerning the Russophones have been 'resolved'. Successive Estonian and Latvian governments, policy-makers and analysts have been eager to safeguard this image.

The discussion here will focus primarily on Latvia where the urgency of restrictive measures was fuelled by particularly extreme demographic statistics: in 1989 only 52 per cent of its residents were Latvian, compared to 42 per cent Russophones (by now the Latvian share of the population stands at 59 per cent). The details of the citizenship and language laws and their gradual changes over time have been documented elsewhere (e.g. Gelazis 2004; Kelley 2004; Hughes 2005; Sasse 2006). Suffice it to say that delayed membership in the Council of Europe and exclusion from the first wave of candidate countries opening accession negotiations with the EU provided important catalysts for a partial rethinking of the legal side of minority issues. The densely packed period was characterized by the interaction of different international actors (the EU, the OSCE High Commissioner on National Minorities, the OSCE missions, the Council of Europe, the North Atlantic Treaty Organization (NATO) and prominent government interventions from the USA, the Scandinavian countries and Russia). The OSCE High Commissioner, in particular, provided detailed legal input into the reformulation of the laws (Dorodovna 2003). Despite their limited constitutional remit, the Estonian and Latvian presidents have repeatedly played a moderating role, encouraging legal change. By June 1998 the Latvian parliament had passed amendments to the citizenship law, paving the way for the 'window' system, which imposed a restrictive timetable on citizenship applications, to be overturned. In line with the recommendations by the OSCE High Commissioner, echoed by the EU, a referendum in October 1998 abolished the 'window' system and confirmed the right of children of non-citizens to obtain citizenship. The timing of this decision was closely related to the annual Regular Reports of the EU, and the exclusion of Latvia from the first-wave accession countries in December 1997.

Measuring the EU effect against the EU's own 'benchmarks'

The Commission's Opinion and the Regular Reports concentrated on three particular areas: the amendments of the citizenship legislation and the rate of naturalization; the development of the language law and policy; and Latvia's ratification of the FCNM. While the legal provisions for citizenship were gradually amended and are now in line with those of many European countries, throughout

Latvia's accession process the take-up rate has remained low to moderate under the changed naturalization procedure, suggesting that the real or perceived 'costs' of naturalization, including administrative fees, learning Latvian or preparing for the citizenship test, were still too high, and people felt too alienated at this late stage in the transition process to be attracted by a new procedure or legal provision. Between 1 February 1995 and 30 November 2007, 124,797 naturalization applications were received, requesting 137,833 persons to be naturalized (of these 127,505 persons have been granted citizenship; see Latvian Naturalization Board 2007). The most significant increase in the number of successful applications trailed the legal changes: from 4,439 (1998) it jumped to 12,427 (1999) and 14,900 (2000). A second increase occurred in the immediate run-up to EU accession from 10,049 (2003) to 16,064 (2004). The number peaked in the immediate post-accession period with 19,169 people being granted citizenship in 2005, followed by a decrease to 16,439 in 2006 and a further decrease to 6,545 in 2007 (data for December 2007 not included) (Latvian Naturalization Board 2007). In Estonia, the figures follow a similar trend: 3,706 (2003), 6,523 (2004), 7,072 (2005) (Estonian Citizenship and Migration Board 2006).

These figures suggest that the potential carrot of (eventual) labour mobility across the EU added an incentive but the figures quickly stabilized at a level that falls short of a speedy reduction of the number of stateless residents.[6] Given that the legal framework is now in place, the real issue is whether there is a lack of will to naturalize among the Russophones, and if so, what explains it. Estonia and Latvia are demonstrations of the detrimental consequences for socialization and integration that flow from exclusionary ethnified rhetoric and discriminatory policies in the early phase of post-communist state- and nation-building. The damage done to the Russophones' willingness to identify with the state cannot easily be undone by later modifications to citizenship and language laws and procedures.[7] The latest report on Estonia by the Council of Europe's Commissioner for Human Rights (Council of Europe 2007a) notes that

> the number of non-citizens is still high and the risk of alienation is present. There is obviously a connection between citizenship and social inclusion, both perceived and real ... increased importance should be given to awareness-raising measures targeting non-citizens about the possibilities of learning the Estonian language and the benefits associated with it.[8]

Latvia's 1999 Language Law, which toned down its 1989 and 1992 precursors, and which still aims to regulate Latvian language use down to private institutions and companies and self-employed persons, has remained an international concern beyond EU accession (Poleshchuk 2002). The law's definition of when these activities relate to public interests is vague, and only 'unofficial' and 'internal communication' of residents and national minorities are excluded, and reference is made to assessment procedures to check the required level of state language proficiency (Latvian Language Law 1999). The 2007 amendments to Estonia's Language Law have given the equivalent language inspectorates extended powers, including the right to recommend the dismissal of employees with insufficient language proficiency, to make people holding language certificates resit an exam. The Council of Europe's High Commissioner for Human Rights singled out this latest provision among his concerns (Council of Europe 2007a), following up on similar criticism by the Advisory Committee of the FCNM (Council of Europe 2006b).

During the EU accession process, the EU's calls for Latvia's ratification of the Framework Convention proved unsuccessful. On 26 May 2005 the Latvian parliament ratified the Framework Convention, which entered into force in October 2005. Latvia's post-accession ratification demonstrates the importance of domestic political considerations shaping the adoption of internationally binding documents. The adoption of the FCNM in the post-EU accession period rids international institutions of a concrete reminder of Latvia's lack of commitment to minority protection – not having ratified the FCNM can have a greater reputational effect over time than ratifying it with crucial reservations. Latvia's timing of the ratification ensures that the country-specific declarations added to the FCNM have come under less international scrutiny. Latvia added three declarations to its ratification of the FCNM (Council of Europe 2007b). The first one in particular goes beyond those attached by other signatories: in it the Republic of Latvia recognizes the diversity of cultures, religions and languages in Europe as a constituent of a common European identity and a particular value; refers to the experience of the Council of Europe member states and the wish to foster the preservation and development of national minority cultures and languages, while respecting the sovereignty and national cultural identity of every state; affirms the positive role of an integrated society, including the command of the state language, in the life of a democratic state; and refers to the specific historical experience and traditions of Latvia.

The term 'national minority', which remains undefined in the actual FCNM, applies to 'citizens of Latvia who differ from Latvians in terms of their culture, religion or language, who have traditionally lived in Latvia for generations and consider themselves to belong to the State and society of Latvia, who wish to preserve and develop their culture, religion or language'. A fuzzy formulation was adopted according to which 'persons who are not citizens of Latvia or another state but who permanently and legally reside in the Republic of Latvia, who do not belong to a national minority within the meaning of the FCNM as defined in this declaration, but who identify themselves with a national minority that meets the definition contained in this declaration, shall enjoy the rights prescribed in the Framework Convention, unless specific exceptions are prescribed by law.'[9] Latvia's further two declarations state that Latvia will apply Article 10, paragraph 2 (the recognition of the right to use minority languages in relations between individuals and administrative authorities), and Article 11, paragraph 2 of the Convention (an individual's right to display minority language signs, inscriptions and other information of a private nature visible to the public), in line with the Latvian constitution and other legislative acts defining the use of the state language, thereby effectively limiting their scope.[10]

The Council of Europe, less visible during the EU accession process, provides the main post-enlargement institutional follow-up to the EU's monitoring and the detailed OSCE recommendations during the accession process. The monitoring tied to the legally binding FCNM is very detailed – often pointing to the politicized definition of national minorities – and one monitoring cycle includes several reports by the governments and the Council of Europe, both based on consultation with a wide range of domestic actors. Latvia's first monitoring cycle attached to the FCNM has only just begun. In the Initial Report on the Implementation of the FCNM by the Republic of Latvia of October 2006, the Latvian government emphasized that it effectively opened the application of the FCNM to legally resident non-citizens who identify with a national minority (Council of Europe 2006a). Furthermore, it cross-references the OSCE High Commissioner's verdict that Latvia had fulfilled the OSCE recommendations on citizenship. With regard to Article 15 of the FCNM, 'effective participation' of national minorities is discussed as a matter of civil society participation rather than as a characteristic of the political system as a whole.

Other parts of the Council of Europe, namely the Commissioner for Human Rights and the Parliamentary Assembly, provide additional monitoring. There is considerable overlap and mutual reinforcement through these different mechanisms. The monitoring under the FCNM appears to be most immune to the politicization inherent in international organizations. A critical report by the Council of Europe's Parliamentary Assembly rapporteur György Frunda, asking Latvia to drop its FCNM declarations, waive the naturalization of Soviet era immigrants, and allow non-citizens to vote, was overruled by the Assembly's Monitoring Committee in November 2005. This decision, taken by an unusual majority vote, is noteworthy, as the Assembly tends to accept a rapporteur's recommendations.[11] The fact that Frunda is also an active member of the Hungarian minority party in Romania documents another trend: the proactive minority policies by Hungarian politicians, advisers and officials at home and abroad which gained legitimacy through the EU's minority condition.

While the EU accession process, with its emphasis on the ratification of the FCNM, paved the way for the Council of Europe's increased role in the post-EU accession period, the OSCE saw its scope for action weakened. The successor of OSCE High Commissioner on National Minorities Max van der Stoel, Rolf Ekeus, welcomed Latvia's ratification of the Framework Convention including its 'liberal' definition of 'national minorities' during a visit in June 2005 (Ministry of Foreign Affairs for the Republic of Latvia 2005). On a further visit in April 2006 he addressed education and naturalization issues, highlighting progress as well as the need for further 'attention'. The Latvian authorities have been keen to publicize the OSCE High Commissioner's general endorsement of their policies, but his domestic and international clout is small compared to the 1990s, in particular in the new EU member states (Ekus 2006). The ongoing election monitoring by the Office of Democratic Institutions and Human Rights (ODIHR), invited by the authorities, maintains a low level of visibility of international involvement and provides an update on the naturalization process in the context of voting. The politically motivated closure of the OSCE missions in Estonia and Latvia in late 2001, aimed at avoiding an anomaly inside the EU, limited the OSCE's scope for action in the Baltics and contributed to an internal crisis of the OSCE as a whole, not least as Russia has been less cooperative in response to the mission closure. The immediate post-Cold War period and the process of EU accession temporarily empowered the OSCE, particularly in the presence of a proactive High Commissioner like van der Stoel and in a context where detailed legal advice was asked for and encouraged by the EU as the international actor offering the biggest incentive structure.

When measuring the EU's medium-term effect against the EU's own benchmarks applied during the accession process, the evidence points to a limited impact. The language laws and their implementation have remained ambivalent beyond EU membership. The significant legal and constitutional changes during the accession period did not foster a trend of legislative activity in the post-accession period. Moreover, Estonia's 2007 Language Law points to follow-up through tougher monitoring of the use of the state language. The naturalization rate, a much referred to benchmark during the accession period, has dropped significantly after a temporary peak around the accession date. Naturalization benefited from the incentives of mobility tied to EU citizenship, but there is little evidence of a general acceptance of citizenship among the Russophones. The FCNM was the international document used as a shorthand reference to a commitment to minority protection during the EU accession process. The fact that Latvia did not heed the EU's rhetorical pressure on this issue at the time demonstrates the lack of commitment to enforcement on both sides – Latvia delayed the process of ratification, and the EU did not make this a stumbling block on the way to membership. The content of the declarations which Latvia has added to the FCNM illustrates that the post-accession ratification of the document is at best a lukewarm endorsement of the principle of minority protection and primarily a carefully timed matter of political convenience.

During the accession process the EU's leverage over minority issues was reinforced by the expertise and involvement of the OSCE and the Council of Europe. While the EU's own leverage on the various components of democratic conditionality ends with accession, the leverage of the other two international institutions is significantly shaped by the politics of conditionality during accession. The OSCE limited its own scope for action, and the institution's image remains tainted by the politically motivated decision on the mission closure in Estonia and Latvia. The Council of Europe's reputation is intact, and it is widely recognized as the only institution with a scope for action on minority issues beyond the EU's enlargement. However, owing to its political weakness, it can at best hope to gradually shape the engrained structural, attitudinal and behavioural trends.

Measuring the EU's effect against domestic politics

Proportional representation alone has not been conducive to effective minority representation. Since independence in 1991 Latvia's and Estonia's party landscape has been characterized by a missing political left.[12] The continuous centre-right or right-wing political consensus has had implications for the integration and political mobilization of minorities. The mobilization of a linguistic – rather than an ethnic or a clear-cut historical – minority has proven difficult in both countries. Divided interests among voters and party leaders, a higher living standard compared to other parts of the former Soviet Union, and early disillusionment with the post-Soviet regimes turning into political apathy, are among the key explanations for the lack of a coherent and sustained minority mobilization in either state. The ethnic divide has become more polarized over time, though this has not led to sustained societal mobilization on the part of the Russophones. The absence of an overarching ethnic identity among the Russophones and a tangible avenue for political mobilization have hindered the formation of coherent minority parties or organizations. In Estonia the minority vote is split between self-declared minority parties, such as Estonia's Constitution Party or the Russian Party of Estonia, which only secured 1.1 and 0.2 per cent respectively in 2007 and failed to enter parliament (the Constitution Party was represented with six seats 1999–2003), and mainstream parties that include minority concerns in their programmes, namely the Estonian Centre Party (26.1 per cent in 2007).

Latvia's political scene illustrates that even sizeable political representation at the national level does not necessarily guarantee influence over policy-making, especially if the other factions in parliament stand united on minority-relevant legislation. After Latvia's 2002 election 25 out of 100 deputies represented a loose bloc 'For Human Rights in a United Latvia' which combined a minority platform with a leftist outlook. The number of minority-friendly deputies decreased to 23 in the 2006 elections, and two former constituents of the bloc ran a separate campaign after internal disagreements. Despite their potential numerical strength, Lavia's minority-oriented deputies are easily outvoted by the overwhelming de facto majority Latvian 'ethnic' bloc whenever minority-relevant issues are being decided in parliament.[13] Parliamentary representation of minority interests even seems to feed directly into a more extremist rhetoric among the main parties of the right in the run-up to elections. Thus, in a political climate where the issue of minority integration is highly sensitive, continuous international emphasis on minority protection and political minority representation can deepen rather than bridge the gap in majority–minority relations. The continuing problems with integration after accession and occasional protests, including provocations by Russian organizations,[14] demonstrate that the legal changes promoted by EU pressure were not sufficient to bring about behavioural change – on the part of the majority of the Russophones as much as on the part of the political élites representing the majority. Rather than inducing a traceable change in the attitudes of representatives of the political establishment and society at large, the continuous emphasis of international institutions on minority issues in Estonia and Latvia has helped to successfully build a political majority consensus around the image that the minority issues have been resolved. Deeper structural issues have remained unaddressed or have, in fact, been further engrained through the politics of conditionality.

The domestic political context provides significant pointers as to the medium-term effects of EU conditionality. International pressure on minority issues did not per se increase the domestic political will for the effective implementation of integration policies, such as proactive measures on naturalization. Legal changes notwithstanding, the EU's minority condition – in particular the intensity and visibility of international actors emphasizing the minority issue – has not widened the domestic scope for a systematic engagement with the deeper structural problems. The empirical evidence suggests that this type of international involvement has triggered a strong negative reaction among the political élites which narrows rather than widens the domestic scope for a rethinking of minority policies. Moreover, the generally positive assessment by international institutions of the situation prior to accession has further eroded the space for political claim-making on the part of the minorities. The analysis of Latvia and Estonia illustrates the significance of the political system as an element in the more long-term assessment of the socialization of new values and behaviour through conditionality. By contrast, the empirical evidence from accession countries with sizeable, politically mobilized ethnic minorities but an absence of a comparable sustained and high-profile visibility of international involvement in minority issues, such as in Slovakia, Romania and Bulgaria, points to an indirect EU effect on the de facto ethnic power-sharing through party representation (Brusis 2003; Sasse 2006). Thus, the domestic political context in accession countries determines the EU's scope in promoting ethnically inclusive governments.

CONCLUSION

This paper has argued that any component of the EU's democratic conditionality, such as the condition on minority protection, is best understood as a social and political construct. As a framing device, this construct can have 'real' effects on domestic actors, but these effects are insufficiently captured by the focus on legislative change employed in most studies of EU conditionality. Methodologically, if we want to go beyond a formal or technical understanding of conditionality and compliance, we need to begin with the construction and malleability of the condition itself, taking seriously the political process by which it was devised and re-appropriated by different actors over time.

EU effects can be unintended and indirect. An intense and highly visible international involvement in a politicized issue area can produce an overlay of contradictory outcomes: a legal change can hide deeper political or societal trends which might, in fact, become more engrained in the context of the EU's involvement. An important conceptual clarification emerges from the case study presented in this article: in the realm of political conditionality, the concentration on formal measures, such as legal change, offers at best a very thin notion of conditionality effects. Rather, there is a different dimension to the lock-in effect of EU conditionality that has not been highlighted previously: deeper structural issues, underpinning polarization and segregation, can also be 'locked in' through the process of EU involvement as, in particular, the case of Latvia has shown. This is one of the ways in which the EU's political leverage carries over into the post-accession period. In this period the scope for EU involvement in minority issues is gone, the OSCE is politically weakened, and the Council of Europe remains the only international institution with a mandate to monitor minority issues in Europe.

In the short run, the socialization effects of conditionality are almost impossible to trace. They certainly play a role when a candidate country engages in proactive policy-making in an issue area outside the EU's official *acquis*-based remit or when a change occurs in the domestic political dynamics (e.g. through the representation of ethnopolitical parties). In the medium term, a wider range of socialization effects becomes apparent. Without at least a degree of socialization the implementation of rationally adopted laws and policies from the accession period is bound to remain patchy. Process-tracing over time can reveal where the patchiness exists and what its scale is. The study of conditionality, which has stressed either the alternative rationalist and constructivist explanations of policy change, or their compatibility, must open itself for a better understanding of the contradictory effects of the EU's involvement. Rational cost–benefit calculations about accession may inform legal changes in candidate countries, but this does not necessarily mean that legal changes are underpinned by successful socialization into European norms or indeed will promote such a normative and behavioural change. As the case study has demonstrated, socialization can in fact 'lock in' a majority consensus on the inappropriateness of a political norm as well as a minority's lack of engagement and thereby limit or undermine the effect of formal legal change. Thus, the socialization effects, revealed through a change in attitudes or behaviour, can point in the opposite direction from the rational motivation that informs legal change.

NOTES

1 Author's interviews with officials from the Country Desks in DG Enlargement, the Horizontal Co-Ordination Unit and the Legal Service, Brussels, 12–13 January 2004.
2 Author's interview with a Commission official, DG Enlargement, Brussels, 12 January 2004.
3 Author's interview with a Commission official in the Horizontal Co-ordination Unit, 13 January 2004.
4 Statistical data allowing for an assessment of ethnic employment and discrimination are rare and inconclusive. What is most striking is the lack of minority representation in certain sectors and institutions (local government and administration, most state institutions with the exception of the Ministry of the Interior, prison administration and the police) resulting from the Soviet era ethnic division of labour, the consequences of the citizenship and language policies, and a degree of self-segregation on the part of both the majority and the minorities (especially in educational institutions and small private companies) (see Pabriks 2002).
5 Compared to 22.4 per cent and 12.5 per cent of Latvia's and Estonia's resident population respectively before accession; see European Commission (2002a, 2002b).
6 The Council Directive 2003/109/EC has been interpreted to include all non-EU citizens irrespective of their citizenship or statelessness.
7 Amendments to Estonia's Law on Citizenship entered into force in March 2004, providing for the state to reimburse the fee for Estonian language training for persons who have passed the naturalization examination. The overall naturalization process has been shortened, and persons born before 1930 are now exempt from the written examination component, though the obligation to pass the oral language examination remains; see https://wcd.coe.int/ViewDoc.jsp?id=1163131#P106_4925).
8 In his last report (2003) on Latvia, the Council of Europe's High Commissioner also urged that 'the state should do even more to bring those populations into its fold, as a forthright demonstration to them of their place in Latvian society' (https://wcd.coe.int/ViewDoc.jsp?id=112881&Site=COE&BackColorInternet=9999CC&BackColorIntranet=&BackColorLogged=FDC864). He recorded 'that the communities concerned often perceive the positive changes as very slow and that there is a consequent danger that they may fail to achieve their purpose and thereby aggravate certain tensions between the minorities generally (non-citizens in particular) and those of Latvian stock, who frequently feel misunderstood despite all the efforts that have been made', and concluded that it was clear that 'the naturalizations have not achieved their objective in that the numbers naturalized are still on the low side and the tendency in the last two years (2001 and 2002) has been downwards.'
9 See http://conventions.coe.int/Treaty/Commun/ListeDeclarations.asp?NT=157&CM=8&DF=4/19/2006&CL=ENG&VL=1
10 http://www.mfa.gov.lv/en/news/press-releases/2005/May/27-3/?print=on
11 Vladimir Socor, 'Council of Europe's biased rapporteur overruled on Lativa', see http://www.jamestown.org/edm/article.php?article_id=2370534
12 In Estonia's 2007 elections the Social Democratic Party obtained 10.6 per cent of the vote and was easily accommodated as part of a centre-right governing coalition with the liberal Estonian Reform Party and the conservative Union of Pro Patria and Res Publica (http://www.valitsus.ee/?lang=en).
13 Author's interviews with members of the Latvian parliament, Riga, September 2005.
14 The removal of the 'Bronze Soldier' monument from the centre of Tallinn in early May 2007 triggered violent clashes, partly orchestrated by the Kremlin-sponsored Russian youth movement 'Nashi', and a political crisis in Estonian–Russian relations.

REFERENCES

Brusis, M. (2003) 'The European Union and interethnic power-sharing arrangements in accession countries', *Journal on Ethnopolitics and Minority Issues in Europe* 1: 1–21.
Brusis, M. (2005) 'The instrumental use of European Union conditionality: regionalization in the Czech Republic and Slovakia', *East European Politics and Societies* 19(20): 291–316.
Checkel, J. (2005) 'It's the process, stupid! Process-tracing in the study of European and international politics', *ARENA Working Paper*, No. 26. http://www.arena.uio.no/publications/working-papers2005/papers/wp05_26.pdf
Council of Europe (2006a) Initial Report on the Implementation of the FCNM by the Republic of Latvia, ACFC/SR(2006)001, 11 October; http://www.coe.int/t/e/human_rights/minorities/2._framework_convention_(monitoring)/2._monitoring_mechanism/3._state_reports_and_unmik_kosovo_report/1._first_cycle/PDF_1st_SR_Latvia_eng.pdf
Council of Europe (2006b) Advisory Committee on the Framework Convention for the Protection of National Minorities, Second Opinion on Estonia, ACFC/INF/OP/II(2005)001, adopted 24 February; http://www.coe.int/t/e/human_rights/minorities/2._framework_convention_%28monitoring%29/2._monitoring_mechanism/4._opinions_of_the_advisory_committee/1._country_specific_opinions/2._second_cycle/PDF_2nd_OP_Estonia_eng.pdf
Council of Europe (2007a) Commissioner for Human Rights, Report on Estonia; https://wcd.coe.int/ViewDoc.jsp?id=1163131#P106_4925
Council of Europe (2007b) Latvia's Declarations to the Framework Convention for the Protection of Minorities; http://conventions.coe.int/Treaty/Commun/ListeDeclarations.asp?NT=157&CM=8&DF=08/02/05&CL=ENG&VL=1
De Witte, B. (2000) 'politics versus law in the EU's approach to ethnic minorities', *EUI Working Paper* RSC No. 2000/4.
Dorodovna, J. (2003) 'Challenging ethnic democracy: implementation of the recommendations of the OSCE High Commissioner on National Minorities to Latvia 1993–2001', *CORE Working Paper* 9.
Ekus, R. (2006) OSCE High Commissioner on National Minorities, Statement to the 616th Plenary Meeting of the OSCE Permanent Council, Vienna, 29 June; available at http://www.osce.org/documents/hcnm/2006/06/19959_en.pdf, accessed 20-10-08.
Epstein, R.A. (2006) 'Cultivating consensus and creating conflict: international institutions and the (de)politicization of economic policy in postcommunist Europe', *Comparative Political Studies* 40(8): 1019–42.
Epstein, R.A. and Sedelmeier, U. (2008) 'Beyond conditionality: international institutions in postcommunist Europe after enlargement, *Journal of European Public Policy* 15(6): 795–805.
Estonian Citizenship and Migration Board (2006) http://www.mig.ee/index.php/mg/eng/citizenship_and_migration_board
Estonian Ministry of Foreign Affairs (2006) http://www.vm.ee/estonia/kat_399/pea_172/4305.html; http://web-static.vm.ee/static/failid/460/Nationalities.pdf
European Commission (2002a) *Regular Report Estonia*; http://ec.europa.eu/enlargement/archives/key_documents/reports_2002_en.htm
European Commission (2002b) *Regular Report Latvia*; http://ec.europa.eu/enlargement/archives/key_documents/reports_2002_en.htm
Gelazis, N.M. (2004) 'The European Union and the statelessness problem in the Baltic states', *European Journal of Migration and Law* 6(3): 225–42.
Grabbe, H. (2006) *The EU's Transformative Power. Europeanization through Conditionality in Central and Eastern Europe*, Basingstoke: Palgrave.

Hoffmeister, F. (2004) 'Monitoring minority rights in the enlarged European Union', in G. Toggenburg (ed.), *Minority Protection and the Enlarged European Union: The Way Forward*, Budapest: LGI Books, pp. 85–106.

Hughes, J. (2005) 'Exit in deeply divided societies: regimes of discrimination in Estonia and Latvia and the potential for Russophone migration', *Journal of Common Market Studies* 43(3): 739–62.

Hughes, J. and Sasse, G. (2003) 'Monitoring the monitors: EU Enlargement conditionality and minority protection in the CEECs', *Journal on Ethnopolitics and Minority Issues in Europe* 1: 1–36.

Hughes, J., Sasse, G. and Gordon, C. (2004) *Europeanization and Regionalization in the EU's Enlargement to Central and Eastern Europe. The Myth of Conditionality*, Basingstoke: Palgrave.

Jacoby, W. (2004) *The Enlargement of the European Union and NATO. Ordering from the Menu in Central Europe*, Cambridge: Cambridge University Press.

Kelley, J. (2004) *Ethnic Politics in Europe. The Power of Norms and Incentives*, Princeton, NJ: Princeton University Press.

Kolsto, P. (2002) *National Integration and Violent Conflict in Post-Soviet Societies: The Cases of Estonia and Moldova*, Oxford: Rowman & Littlefield.

Latvian Language Law (1999) http://unpan1.un.org/intradoc/groups/public/documents/UNTC/UNPAN018409.pdf

Latvian Naturalization Board (2007) http://www.np.gov.lv/index.php?en=fakti_en&saite=residents.htm; http://www.np.gov.lv/en/faili_en/stat_angl.xls

Ministry of Foreign Affairs for the Republic of Latvia (2005) 'Societal integration in Latvia: Towards mutual understanding and cooperation', 2 June; available at http://www.mfa.gov.lv/en/news/Newsletters/Integration/45/, accessed on 20-06-08.

Norgaard, O. (ed.) (1996) *The Baltic States after Independence*, Cheltenham: Edward Elgar.

Pabriks, A. (2002) *Occupational Representation and Ethnic Discrimination in Lativa*, Soros Foundation Latvia: Nordik Publishing House.

Poleshchuk, V. (2002) *Estonia, Latvia and the European Commission: Changes in Language Regulation in 1999–2001*; http://www.eumap.org/journal/features/2002/jan02/languagereg

Sasse, G. (2005a) 'EU conditionality and minority rights: translating the Copenhagen criterion into policy', *EUI Working Paper* RSCAS No. 2005/16.

Sasse, G. (2005b) 'Securitization or securing rights? Exploring the conceptual foundations of policies towards minorities and migrants in Europe', *Journal of Common Market Studies* 43(4): 673–93.

Sasse, G. (2006) 'The political rights of national minorities: lessons from Central and Eastern Europe', in W. Sadurski (ed.) *Political Rights under Stress in 21st Century Europe*, Oxford: Oxford University Press, pp. 239–82.

Schimmelfennig, F. and Sedelmeier, U. (eds) (2005) *The Europeanization of Central and Eastern Europe*, Ithaca, NY: Cornell University Press.

Schimmelfennig, F., Engert, S. and Knobel, H. (2003) 'Cost, commitment and compliance: the impact of EU democratic conditionality on Latvia, Slovakia and Turkey', *Journal of Common Market Studies* 41(4): 495–518.

Schwellnus, G. (2001) '"Much ado about nothing"? Minority protection and the EU Charter of Fundamental Rights', *Constitutionalism Web-Papers (ConWEB) 5*, available at http://www.bath.ac.uk/esml/conWEB/current.htm

Schwellnus, G. (2006a) 'Looking back at ten years of EU minority conditionality vis-à-vis Central and Eastern European candidate states', *European Yearbook of Minority Issues* Vol. 4, 2004/05: 321–40.

Schwellnus, G. (2006b) 'Double standards? Minority protection as a condition for membership', in H. Sjursen (ed.), *Questioning Enlargement: The EU in Search of Identity*, London: Routledge, pp.186–200.

Sedelmeier, U. (2008) 'After conditionality: post-accession compliance with EU law in East Central Europe', *Journal of European Public Policy* 15(6): 806–25.
Toggenburg, G. (ed.) (2004) *Minority Protection and the Enlarged European Union: The Way Forward*, Budapest: Local Government and Public Reform Initiative.
Toggenburg, G. (ed.) (2006) 'A remaining share or a new part? The Union's role vis-à-vis minorities after the enlargement decade', *EUI LAW Working Papers* No. 15.
Vachudova, M.A. (2005) *Europe Undivided. Democracy, Leverage and Integration after Communism*, Oxford: Oxford University Press.
Vermeersch, P. (2003) 'EU enlargement and minority rights policies in Central Europe: explaining policy shifts in the Czech Republic, Hungary and Poland', *Journal on Ethnopolitics and Minority Issues in Europe* 1: 1–32.
Vermeersch, P. (2004) 'Minority policy in Central Europe: exploring the impact of the EU's enlargement strategy', *The Global Review of Ethnopolitics* 3(2): 3–19.
Wiener, A. and Schwellnus, G. (2004) 'Contested norms in the process of EU enlargement: non-discrimination and minority rights', *Constitutionalism Web-Papers*, No. 2.

Tempered by the EU? Political parties and party systems before and after accession

Milada A. Vachudova

INTRODUCTION

The study of European Union (EU) conditionality has focused on how the governments of candidate states have changed domestic policies, laws and institutions in order to qualify for EU membership. However, political parties are arguably the most important and most proximate source of domestic policy change – and thus of compliance or non-compliance with EU requirements. Scholars have shown that ruling political parties rarely comply with the EU's external requirements if the costs of compliance are too high and threaten to undermine the domestic sources of their political power. Consequently, it is important to understand how parties construct and change their agendas, especially when they are in opposition and able more easily to recalibrate their appeals.

The purpose of this article is threefold. The first is to explore how parties and party systems in EU candidate states evolve over time. Can we identify a common sequence of change? The second is to explore whether and how EU leverage influences the positions of political parties. Has the EU helped to bring about a convergence in favor of liberal democracy and comprehensive economic reform in the party systems of candidate states? The third is to begin exploring how well mechanisms of EU influence on parties are working in conditions that are less auspicious because countries that have already acceded are no longer subject to the EU's membership conditionality (see Epstein and Sedelmeier 2008).

I argue in this article that the party systems of EU candidate states do follow a predictable evolution over time – and this is caused by participation in the EU's pre-accession process. In almost all cases, major political parties respond to EU leverage by adopting agendas that are consistent with EU requirements in the run-up to negotiations for membership. Consequently, the party systems – at least for a while – reflect a consensus on the general course of domestic policy-making. Candidate states where regime change in 1989 was followed by illiberal democracy or authoritarianism are the most interesting. For key parties in these states, pushing for EU accession is a marker of profound moderation in their agendas, including support for democratic standards and economic reform. Yet after EU accession, the parameters for party competition broaden again. The lifting of accession-related constraints is especially apparent among parties that adopt more nationalist and culturally conservative positions.

What does it mean to adopt an EU-compatible agenda? I use the Chapel Hill dataset on the positions of national political parties in 2002 that depicts the structure of political competition in the EU's post-communist member states (I use 'the post-communist candidates,' 'East Central Europe' (ECE) or simply 'the East' as shorthand for these states), and sheds some light on how political parties bundle different issues.[1] The dataset is built on expert surveys and provides the position of each party on European integration, as well as its position on two dimensions of political competition: the left/right economic dimension, and the gal/tan cultural dimension, where 'gal' stands for green/alternative/libertarian and 'tan' for traditional/authoritarian/nationalist.

Based on the content of the requirements for EU membership, we know that the EU expects parties in the East to take positions that tend toward the *right* and toward *gal*. Governments are instructed, for example, to decrease the role of the state in the economy and provide protection for the rights of ethnic minorities. We can see in Figure 1 that support for European integration in the post-communist candidates is highly correlated with party positions that are *right* and *gal*. Indeed, opposition to the EU is concentrated in the *left* and *tan* quadrant – and hard *left* and hard *tan* positions are *never* combined with support for European integration. This is consistent with earlier research that finds that pro-Europeanism in the East is concentrated among parties with *right* and *gal* positions, and anti-Europeanism among *left* and *tan* parties (Beichelt 2004; Kopecký and Mudde 2002; Rohrschneider and Whitefield 2005; Taggart and Szczerbiak 2004). This is distinct from the West, where pro-European attitudes are associated with *left* and *gal* party positions and anti-European attitudes with

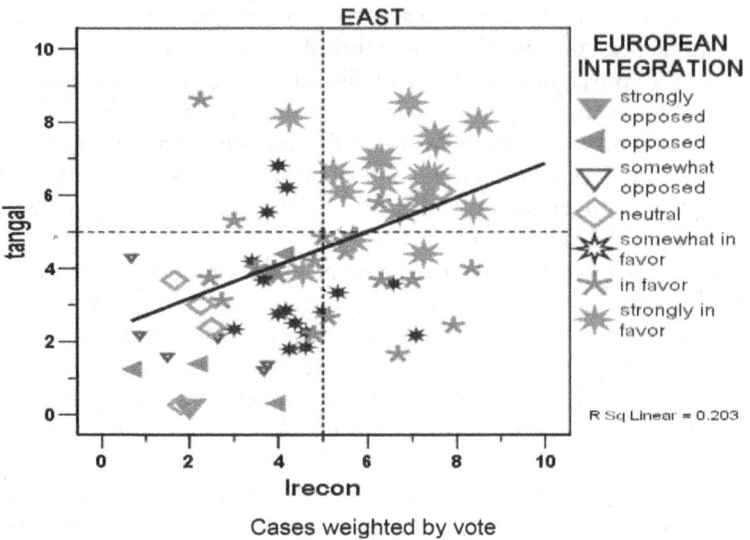

Figure 1 Structure of party competition and support for European integration: nine post-communist EU candidate states, 2002

right and *tan* positions (Marks *et al.* 2006). The main axis of domestic party competition in the East is at a 90 degree angle to that in the West (Evans and Whitefield 1993).

This article is divided into three parts. First, I describe the mechanisms that allow the EU to influence the positions of political parties in candidate states. Second, I trace the changes in party positions in two distinct groups of states – those that embark on a liberal and those that embark on an illiberal political trajectory after 1989. Third, I examine the timing and the sequence of changes in the two groups of states after EU accession, and explore what they mean for party positions in states that have now joined the EU.

MECHANISMS THAT SHAPE PARTY POSITIONS

One of the central challenges for comparative politics and international relations studies is to identify the specific mechanisms that translate international influence into changes in the positions of political parties and the behavior of domestic élites (for an overview, see Sedelmeier 2006). For all EU candidates, three mechanisms that guide and constrain the actions of governments are important. First, straightforward *conditionality* is at play: moving forward in the EU's pre-accession process is tied to adopting laws and implementing reform in different policy areas and also restructuring the state administration (Andonova 2003; Epstein 2008; Grabbe 2006; Hughes *et al.* 2004; Jacoby 2004; Kelley 2004; Pridham 2005; Sissenich 2007; Vachudova 2005). Often, this process creates external legitimation for domestic preferences, allowing politicians to sell policies that they have long supported (Grabbe 2006). Second, the process itself serves as a *credible commitment* mechanism to ongoing reform, because reversing direction becomes prohibitively costly for any future government. As candidates move forward in the process, governments are thus locked into a predictable course of economic policy-making that serves as an important signal to internal and external economic actors.[2] Meanwhile, moving toward EU membership changes the character and the strength of different *groups in society*, increasing the pressure on the governing political parties to deliver the necessary reforms (Epstein 2008; Vachudova 2005).

The conditionality and the credible commitment mechanisms work mainly on political parties that are in power and therefore have to deliver progress within the framework of the EU's pre-accession process. What positions on European integration did these parties bring with them to office? There is evidence that being in power during the pre-accession process does push parties to take positions that are somewhat more supportive of European integration than would otherwise be predicted by their ideological profile or party family (Vachudova and Hooghe, forthcoming). However, ruling parties with domestic sources of political power that are antithetical to the requirements of EU membership never make a radical shift to bring their domestic policies into compliance with the EU (Schimmelfennig and Sedelmeier 2005; Schimmelfennig 2007; Vachudova 2005). It follows that parties that govern while the country is making across-the-board progress in satisfying EU requirements must have adopted an EU-compatible agenda prior to taking power.

As I have argued elsewhere, the initial configuration of powerful domestic élites and institutions at the moment of regime change produced strong political competition in some states, and weak political competition in others (Vachudova 2005). In illiberal democracies[3] EU requirements were at loggerheads with the domestic agendas of political parties in power, and progress toward the EU was slow. Conditionality had little success in changing the policies of governing political parties in Slovakia, Bulgaria or Romania (or indeed in Croatia or Serbia) even after the EU's pre-accession process was in place in 1995. By influencing the information and the institutional environment, however, EU leverage helped to create what the illiberal democracies were missing at the moment of transition: a coherent and moderate opposition, and an open and pluralistic political arena.

For the purpose of understanding party systems, the key mechanism is *adapting*: when and why did political parties change their positions on European integration and concurrently on economic and cultural issues? In general, greater support for European integration goes hand in hand with party positions that are culturally more *gal* (green/alternative/libertarian), and economically more *right*. What distinguishes the party systems of the liberal and illiberal pattern states in the early 1990s is whether or not the majority of parties in parliament distanced themselves from hard *left* and hard *tan* positions almost immediately after regime change.

Even in the liberal pattern states, however, where this took place rapidly, we can trace the importance of *adapting* to a pro-Western agenda for opposition and communist successor parties alike. This process began decades before regime change for some opposition groups, and even for some communist parties that were already becoming more technocratic and open to capitalist economic innovations in the 1980s (Bozóki and Ishiyama 2002; Grzymala-Busse 2002). The impetus for oppositions and reforming communists alike was a general turn toward the West, and not a specific reaction to the leverage of the EU, which would not come online until about 1994.

In the illiberal pattern states, political parties with strong *left* and *tan* positions took power after 1989. These were either repackaged communist parties or new, opportunistic nationalist parties. They faced weak, fragmented oppositions that they further undermined by restricting access to the political arena. In this domestic context, EU leverage, in concert with other international actors (Epstein 2005; Gheciu 2005; Grabbe 2006), contributed to changing the nature of political competition by influencing the opposition (Vachudova 2005: 161–80). They offered information to opposition political élites and other domestic actors that were adapting to a political and economic agenda compatible with liberal democracy and comprehensive market reform. Parties designated as mainstream right or left had been neither strong nor unified in these countries after 1989, nor had they necessarily moderate and *gal* positions. Over time, many opposition politicians shifted substantially their position on ethnic minority rights and on economic reform to oppose the illiberal regime, and to make their parties fit the increasingly attractive 'pro-EU space' on the political spectrum. This space was particularly attractive, given the growing and increasingly visible costs of illiberal rule. What motivated individual political élites was in each case a different mixture of political calculation, on the one hand, and a desire to promote the 'European' vocation of their countries, on the other. But in most cases information given in interviews as well as the steady defection of politicians from the illiberal parties suggested that these individuals considered the political prospects of the opposition parties more attractive than the short-term gains of being part of the ruling clique.[4]

The mechanisms of conditionality and credible commitment explain why governments in the candidate states, despite their very different political backgrounds and profiles, do not halt or reverse reform. Indeed, these mechanisms ideally trigger a second wave of adapting as formerly illiberal (or even authoritarian) political parties transform themselves and adopt positions that are consistent with Western liberal democracy and economic reform. For EU leverage to transform the nature of the party system, this second wave of adapting is critical.

Around the time that formal negotiations begin between the EU and a candidate state, the party system tends to have the weakest hard *left* and/or *tan* parties, and the least Euroskepticism. In post-communist countries that are in the membership queue, there are generally no parties that oppose qualifying for EU membership that stand a chance of winning elections or taking part in a governing coalition. Even today, when the post-communist membership queue is composed of six or seven Western Balkan states, Serbia's party system is the only exception. As we see below, formerly illiberal or authoritarian political parties learn that they can improve their chances of re-election by adapting to the expectations of the EU and other international actors.

CHANGES IN PARTY POSITIONS AND THE CONSENSUS ON EU MEMBERSHIP

Communist rule in the East bundled together *left* and *tan* positions, especially as communist parties increasingly resorted to nationalism to shore up illegitimate regimes (Kitschelt 1992). As the unravelling of the communist system put the transition process in motion, proponents of marketization and liberal democracy converged to the opposite pole. And from the mid-1990s, the prospect of EU membership reinforced this axis as accession required delivering market-oriented economic reforms and upholding liberal democratic standards. Consequently, in the East, hard *left* positions and, more importantly, strong *tan* positions have been bundled with strong Euroskepticism. All Euroskeptic parties (a score between 1 and 3.5) or neutral parties (a score between 3.6 and 4.5) are located in the *left-tan* quadrant. The one exception is the Czech Civic Democratic Party (ODS), which I discuss below.

My purpose in this section is to show how important political parties in ECE changed their positions over time. The process of joining the EU is central to understanding changes in individual party positions as well as broad changes in the structure of political competition. The positioning of political parties on European integration in 2002 is depicted for each country in Figures 2 and 3. If we had data to draw these country tableaux for the early 1990s, we would have found a crowded radical *left-tan* quadrant in countries such as Bulgaria and Romania, as well as more widespread and more radical Euroskepticism. In others, such as Poland or Hungary, we would have observed a less populated *left-tan* quadrant, as well as less Euroskepticism. EU candidate states fit into one of two groups depending on whether they embarked on a liberal or illiberal trajectory of political change immediately after the collapse of communism. (On the impact of communist legacies, see Bunce 1999; Ekiert and Hanson 2003; Ekiert *et al.* 2007 and Orenstein 2001.) An important observable implication of these two trajectories is the timing of a consensus in the party system about the benefits of joining the EU: this consensus occurs earlier in liberal pattern states – and also dissipates earlier, just before accession takes place.

Party systems on a liberal trajectory

In states following a liberal trajectory immediately after the collapse of the communist regime in 1989, a consensus developed very early among mainstream political parties in parliament in favour of liberal democracy and comprehensive

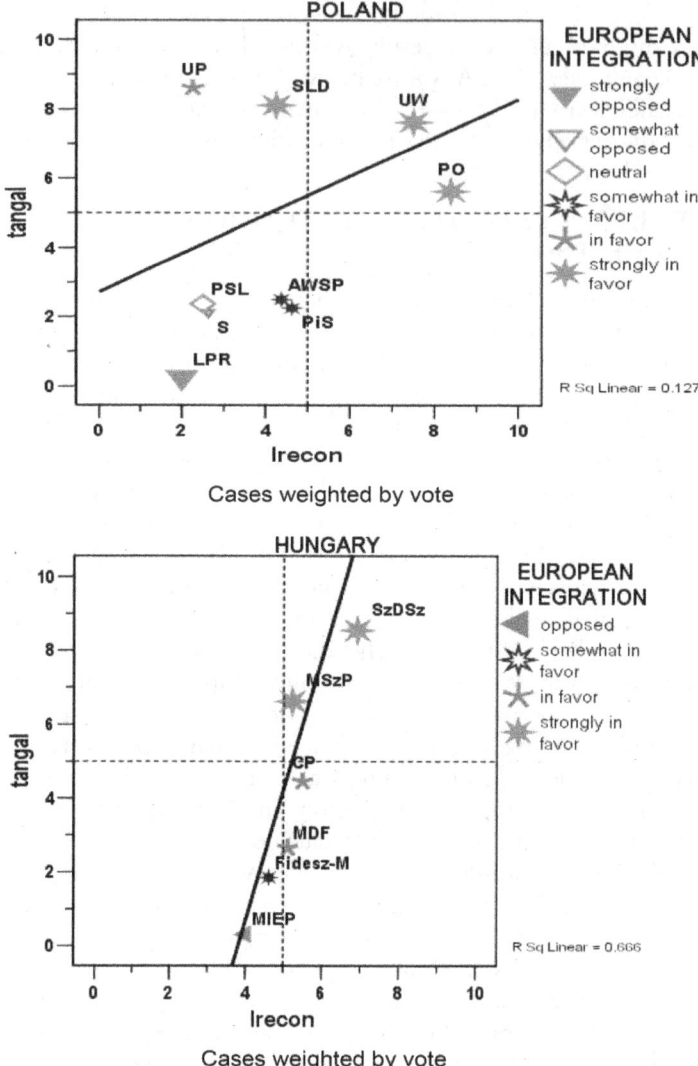

Figure 2 Structure of party competition and support for European integration, 2002. Early trajectory = liberal

economic reform. Joining the EU was rapidly embraced as an integral part of the country's transformation. In this group, including Poland, Hungary, Czechoslovakia, Latvia, Lithuania and Slovenia, a strong opposition to communism created movements and political parties that were able to win power at the moment of regime change, and immediately took positions that were *right* and *gal* (or only mildly *left* or *tan*). I only have space in this article to discuss the party systems in Poland, Hungary and the Czech Republic at any length.

And even among these three there were, of course, some exceptions. The Hungarian Democratic Forum (HDF) won the first democratic elections in Hungary, but its tenure in office from 1990 to 1994 was marked by what the international community considered to be overly *tan* foreign policy positions that were characterized as destabilizing and nationalist. In 1994 EU leverage arguably made its debut when it joined other Western actors to pressure the HDF to moderate its positions related to ethnic Hungarians living in neighbouring states (Vachudova 2005).

The communist party in states on the liberal trajectory exited from power and, in some cases, reformed itself rapidly into a modern European social democratic party, embracing comprehensive market-oriented reforms and EU membership.[5] This was critical because it enabled an early consensus on the direction of political and economic reform. The Polish and Hungarian communist parties best fit the ideal type: they were already reforming themselves in the 1980s in dialogue with a strong opposition and in advance of a negotiated end to communism. Far from being located in the *left-tan* quadrant in the early 1990s, the Polish and Hungarian socialist parties were much closer to the *right-gal* quadrant, and won the second free elections in 1993 and 1994 respectively on a *centrist-gal* platform. On national and cultural issues, both parties were hailed as moderate alternatives to the right-wing post-opposition parties that had ruled before them. On economic issues, the Polish Socialists (SLD) continued Poland's radical economic reforms, while the Hungarian Socialists (MSZP) initiated and implemented Hungary's most radical economic reforms. As Figure 2 shows, by 2002, Hungary's Socialists had become equally centrist on economic policy as Hungary's right-wing parties (see Bozóki and Ishiyama 2002; Grzymala-Busse 2002).

Early reform deprived Euroskepticism of a natural ideological and organizational base in the *left-tan* quadrant. Instead, ex-communist parties made preparing for EU membership a priority. Hence, a *centrist-gal* ex-communist party solidified the consensus in the party system. The Euroskeptic *left-tan* quadrant remained organizationally thinly populated throughout much of the 1990s. In Poland, one mildly *left-tan* party sat in parliament before 1997, the Polish Peasants (PSL). In 1997, two new *tan* parties, the Polish Peasants Self-Defence Party (Samoobrona) and the extremist Catholic-nationalist League of Polish Families (LPR), emerged as strongly Euroskeptic parties. But they were considered 'unusable' as government parties by Poland's mainstream. In Hungary, the extreme-right Justice and Life Party (MIEP) did not jump the 5 percent threshold to enter parliament in 1994 or 2002; it did in 1998, but it was also deemed 'unusable' by Hungary's mainstream parties.

The impact of EU leverage on the positions of political parties during this period thus took three main forms. First, it assisted in the transformation and adapting of the former communist parties: they could sell their technocratic expertise and *gal* positions as an asset in preparing the country for EU membership (Grzymala-Busse and Innes 2003). Second, it limited the choice of coalition partners. A major reason for excluding extremist parties from government was their hostility towards EU accession – and the EU's hostility toward their hard *tan* and hard *left* positions. Finally, once in government, all parties would be subject to the discipline of the conditionality embedded in the EU's pre-accession process.

The unique case of the Czech Republic

The Czech Republic is a strange case. Although it followed a liberal trajectory of political change – voting out the communist party and voting in an opposition-led government in 1990 – its party system is unique because of the positions of two major parties. The ODS was in 2002 the only party on the right to be openly hostile to the EU, and also the largest Euroskeptic party in the Eastern dataset. It has a score of 3.8 on a 7-point scale, which reflects the party leadership's position.[6] For over 15 years now Klaus has portrayed the EU as a dangerous socialist experiment, and a threat to national identity and sovereignty along the lines of *right-tan* Euroskeptic parties in Western Europe. Meanwhile, the radical *left* and *tan* Communist Party of Bohemia and Moravia (KSČM) is the only major communist successor party in ECE that remains unreformed and unrepentant. It has continuously garnered between 10 and 20 percent of the vote in parliamentary elections after 1989.

Thanks to the ODS and the KSČM, the Czech Republic has the highest percentage of voters casting their ballots for Euroskeptic or Euroneutral parties: 43 percent in the national elections in 2002, and 48.2 percent in 2006, and this in a party system without a radical *tan* party. The KSČM and the ODS have together put the Czech Republic's extreme right-wing *tan* party out of business. The KSČM has taken over its xenophobic, chauvinistic and anti-semitic agenda, while the ODS has appealed to more moderate voters who feel threatened by immigrants and ethnic minorities, distrust the EU, and identify with Czech parochialism (Williams 1997; Hanley 2007). In power from 1992 to 1997, and now again since 2006, the ODS's hallmark remains strong right-wing economic rhetoric and *tan* appeals.

Does it make sense to talk about the impact of the EU on party positions in this domestic context? What is striking is that the ODS lost power in 1997 – on the eve of the start of negotiations with the EU – and did not regain power until well after the Czech Republic had entered the EU. Since a majority of Czech voters did support EU membership, the ODS's anti-EU stance likely strengthened the hand of the relatively moderate Social Democratic Party (ČSSD) which governed in various forms from 1998 until 2006. ODS leaders, for their part, did limit their anti-EU activities, stopping short of attempting to scuttle the Czech Republic's accession even when they could have toppled a minority ČSSD government in power from 1998 until 2002. Ultimately the ODS's ideological and instrumental opposition to European integration had to give way to EU conditionality, which draws its power from the tremendous benefits of joining the EU (and the costs of being left outside).

Party systems that shift from an illiberal to a liberal trajectory

Romania, Bulgaria and Slovakia experienced an illiberal trajectory of political change in the early 1990s because ruling political parties did not embrace liberal democracy and comprehensive economic reform for many years. Hard-line communist parties in Romania and Bulgaria that had faced little opposition before 1989 found that the surest way to transform themselves into credible players on the new democratic scene was to exploit left-wing economic populism and ethnic nationalism while rewarding supporters with opportunities to extract resources from a partially reformed economy (Hellman 1998; Gould 2004). The Romanian Party of Social Democracy (PSDR) (now called the Democratic Party (PSD)), and the Bulgarian Socialist Party (KzB or BSP) were not only hard *left* but also hard *tan* well before the end of communism, brutally suppressing ethnic minorities during the 1980s to shore up the legitimacy of the regime. Even as they adopted the formal institutions of democracy and began some economic reforms after 1989, these parties did not adopt EU-compatible domestic policies. In Slovakia the dominant force was not a former communist party but a new nationalist-populist party. Vladimír Mečiar's Movement for a Democratic Slovakia (HZDS) ran election campaigns that were a textbook mixture of left-wing economic populism and xenophobic nationalism (Fisher 2006).

The PSDR, the BSP and the HZDS all kept to the economic left, promising to protect workers from radical 'Polish-style' economic reform. They also embraced xenophobic nationalism, out-competing but also befriending the radical *tan* parties that emerged after 1989. These parties, which supported the PSDR and the HZDS in governing coalitions in Romania (1994–1996) and Slovakia (1994–1998), respectively, blended nostalgia for fascism's national triumphalism with nostalgia for communism's economic security and closed polity.

Illiberal rule had major implications for party positioning on European integration. In the early reforming countries *left-tan* parties were marginalized, but here parties used radical *left-tan* appeals – defence of the nation from its enemies and defence of the citizen from unfettered capitalism – to win elections and concentrate political power. This delayed the effect of EU leverage. In their quest to hold power and divide up its spoils, these parties and their *left-tan* allies implemented policies that were inimical to progress towards EU membership.

As a consequence, EU leverage was confined to working slowly and indirectly by censuring governments and buttressing domestic opposition. By the second half of the 1990s, EU leverage gained enough momentum to impact domestic political change. As a variety of opposition parties campaigned against the *left-tan* policies of the governing parties, qualifying to join the EU became a common plank of their electoral platforms. Meanwhile, the EU became bolder in its assessments and criticisms of the candidates, and also in its threats to postpone negotiations indefinitely. Slovakia received the most explicit threat, when the EU made it known during the 1998 election campaign that a government under HZDS control would not be invited to the negotiation table.

Once countries became enmeshed in the EU's pre-accession process, the costs of backsliding became prohibitive. Formerly anti-EU parties learned, however, that they could adapt their agenda to the expectations of the EU and other international actors – and, in some cases, get back very quickly in the political game. The most dramatic turnarounds so far have been by the PSD in Romania and the Croatian Democratic Union (HDZ). Though Croatia was not part of our survey, it is an additional EU candidate that has, more recently, shifted from an illiberal to a liberal trajectory. While in opposition, both the PSD and the HDZ shed their extreme nationalist rhetoric and adopted a modernizing program based on economic reform and a more efficient state.

International party links have also played a role. For the PSD and the BSP acceptance by the Socialist International and the Party of Socialists (in the European Parliament) was an important additional external incentive from programmatic change (Petrova 2006). Upon winning re-election in 2000 and 2004, respectively, the PSD and the HDZ continued to satisfy EU requirements – and on some measures did a better job than their 'reformist' predecessors. In 2005 the BSP in Bulgaria was also re-elected after years of gradually shifting toward the agenda of a mainstream European socialist party. All three parties were returned to power while their country was still qualifying for EU membership, and made progress toward membership a priority of their government. Ironically, as part of the EU's process, the PSD, the HDZ and now the BSP governments have had to tackle endemic corruption in the economy and in state institutions that their party comrades helped to create.

Shut out of power from 1998 to 2006 while Slovakia implemented reforms that allowed it to join the EU in 2004, the HZDS has taken a different course. The EU made the tradeoff faced by the Slovak voter at the 2002 elections abundantly clear: re-elect Mečiar, and Slovakia will not be invited to become an EU member at the Copenhagen European Council summit in December 2002. The HZDS was increasingly frantic to gain some international respectability. The party program declared 'its irreversible decision to support Slovakia's integration into the EU with all of its might;' but the party's transformation appeared limited to these kinds of declarations (Bilčík 2002: 25). The HZDS entered government again in 2006 with other *left-tan* parties. Since Slovakia had already joined the EU, the constraints on its behaviour in government would be much looser, and its transformation quite different, from that of the PSD, the HZD or the BSP.

AS ACCESSION DRAWS NEAR

Before accession, a strong consensus developed in the party systems of the two groups of states about the course of domestic reform and EU membership, but at different times. In 1995, there were no parties embracing radical *left*, radical *tan*, or Euroskeptic platforms in government or even in parliament in Poland or

Hungary, while *all* parties in the coalition governments of Romania, Bulgaria and Slovakia fit these labels in deeds and rhetoric.

Yet when we look at Figure 3 depicting the party landscape in Romania, Bulgaria and Slovakia in 2002, we see that things had changed dramatically. EU leverage has pulled all parties away from radical *left* and *tan* positions, including Romania and Bulgaria's big late reforming ex-communist parties and Slovakia's HZDS. Romania's former communist party, now the PSD, has shed much of its *tan* political agenda. It is following the Polish and Hungarian socialist parties in hailing its technocratic skills and joining the Socialist International. After winning the 2000 elections, it pragmatically pursued the reforms necessary for EU membership. Similarly, the Bulgarian Socialist Party shed much of its radical *left* and *tan* agenda in preparation for the 2005 elections, which it won. Finally, the HZDS, after being defeated in 1998, gradually became more moderate and begged to be trusted as a party that could bring Slovakia into the EU, though the Slovak voters (and the EU) were in no mood to give it a chance in 2002. Instead, Slovak voters elected a *right-gal* government that continued with sweeping *right-gal* social and economic reforms.

In contrast, important shifts in the party landscape in Hungary and in Poland by 2002 had recalibrated the mainstream right as parties took advantage of new opportunities to oppose European integration, to take stronger *left* and especially *tan* positions, and to consider coalition partners that had previously been unacceptable. The strengthening of *tan* parties such as Samoobrona, LPR, and MIEP also signaled that these party systems were about to turn more critical toward the EU.

In Hungary, Fidesz vacated the *right-gal* quadrant, which had become crowded since the Socialists (MSZP) had moved into the centre, and adopted *tan* appeals. Under the leadership of Viktor Orban, it had by 2002 become the hegemon on the mainstream right. In the process, it appropriated the nationalist rhetoric of the radical-*tan* MIEP and took positions that appeared to the left of the MSZP on matters of economic reform.[7] As it adjusted its ideological profile, Fidesz also updated its European partners. In 2000, Fidesz left the pro-European, predominantly *gal* Liberal International and joined the more conservative European People's Party, where it is closest to Forza Italia and the German Conservative CSU (Enyedi 2005). While Fidesz is not Euroskeptic, it protests EU encroachments on national sovereignty and culture in strident terms unlike its socialist competitor.

In Poland, a new party, the Polish Law and Justice Party (PiS), successfully organized disparate *tan* fractions and won the national elections in 2005. Its coalition government included two *left-tan* parties, Samoobrona and the extremist LPR. This government was strongly *tan*, taking nationalist, traditionalist, and populist positions while strongly criticizing European integration. It was also strongly *left*, advocating state aid for disadvantaged groups and trumpeting its mistrust of economic liberalism.

Over time, we can detect a similar sequence in how these party systems have evolved. By adopting a market-oriented, non-nationalist and pro-European

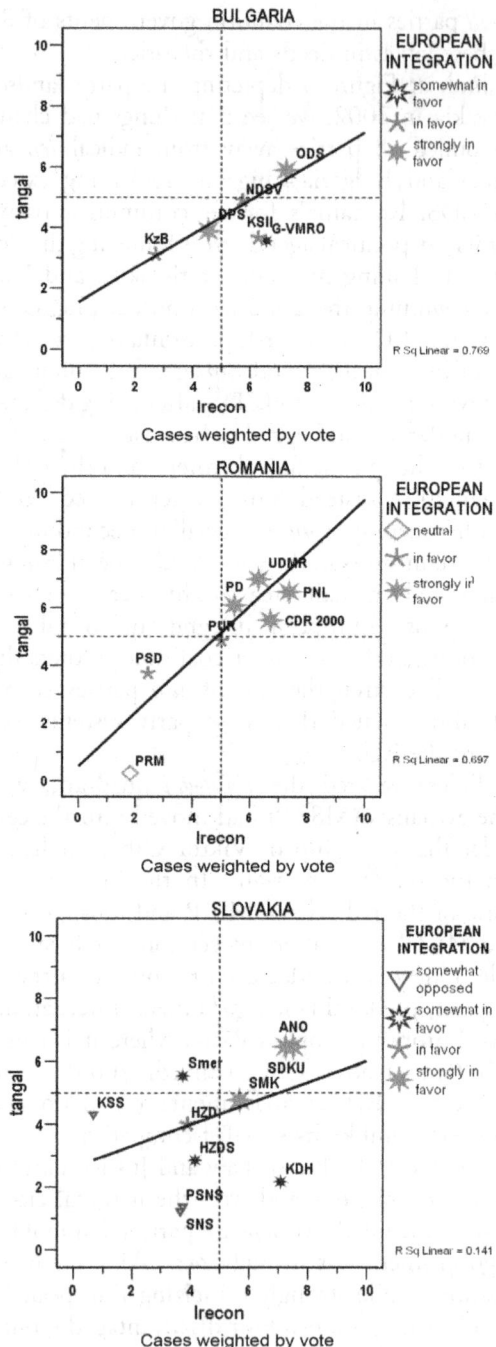

Figure 3 Structure of party competition and support for European integration, 2002. Early trajectory = illiberal

political agenda immediately after 1989, the opposition parties and the reforming communist party created a consensus on the direction of domestic policy-making. A communist party that reformed rapidly brought along a large portion of the traditionalist electorate that might otherwise have voted for radical *left-tan* parties.

As accession approached, however, other parties had emerged in the *left-tan* quadrant vacated by the reforming communist party. These parties took up, among other issues, Euroskepticism. The most dynamic new parties in this quadrant tended to be more *tan* than *left*, making few if any connections to the country's communist past. At the same time, conservative mainstream parties took more critical positions on Europe while also adopting more strongly *tan* positions. They were prone to appropriating some of the nationalist discourse of radical *tan* parties in the *left-tan* quadrant, or inviting them to support their government (Hanley 2004; Pop-Eleches 2004). Hungary's Fidesz, the Polish PiS, and the Czech ODS all used the nationalist discourse of radical *tan* parties. And the Polish PiS came into power in 2005 with the support of two *left-tan* parties, Samoobrona and the radical LPR. There is also speculation that Hungary's Fidesz would consider a coalition with the radical *tan* MIEP in the future.

The transformation was so great that, by 2002, more citizens were actually voting for Euroskeptic and Euroneutral parties in Poland and Hungary than in Romania and Bulgaria. Polish parties that fit these categories received 27.1 percent of the vote, and Hungarian parties 4.4 percent (this does not include 35 percent for Fidesz, which, with a score of 4.6 on the scale, fell just outside the range of Euroskeptic-Euroneutral parties in 2002). In contrast, Romanian parties received 19.5 percent and Bulgarian parties zero. In the *left-tan* quadrant, Romania's premier radical *tan* party, the Greater Romania Party (PRM) of Vadim Tudor, persevered with a hard *tan* agenda, although it had tempered its position on the EU considerably. In Bulgaria, the *left-tan* quadrant was emptied of parliamentary parties as the Bulgarian Socialist Party gradually shifted its agenda after 1997.

Using the earlier reformers as a guide, one would expect EU leverage to weaken on Bulgaria and Romania as accession nears. Indeed, during the elections of 2005, a new nationalist, anti-European party emerged in Bulgaria's hard *left-tan* political space. Named 'Attack,' this new Bulgarian party received 8.2 percent of the vote. Meanwhile, in Slovakia the election results of 2006 were very different from those in 2002: the populist *left-tan* SMER party of Robert Fico formed a government that includes the radical *tan* SNP, which had received 12 percent of the vote, as well as the *left-tan* HZDS. SMER, a social democratic party, has been suspended from the Socialist International for forming a coalition with the xenophobic and chauvinistic Slovak National Party (SNS).

Once more time has passed, however, scholars may be able to detect new trends and study new causal mechanisms that link EU membership with party positions. Even after EU membership is attained, European integration may temper the attraction of voters to *left-tan* parties through a different set of mechanisms, such as changing the preferences of important groups in society. Poland's early elections in 2007 provide some potential evidence because of the domestic backlash against the *left-tan* PiS government. This backlash may have been partly triggered by the PiS government's terrible relations with EU institutions and member governments, and their perceived costs for Poland. As the strongest party in parliament Polish voters replaced the PiS with the more *right* and also more *gal* centrist party, the Civic Platform. Moreover, the *left-tan* parties with the most radical positions and with the strongest Euroskepticism were resoundingly defeated: Samoobrana received 1.5 percent and the LPR 1.3 percent of the vote, well below the 5 percent threshold to enter parliament. Meanwhile, the 2006 elections in Hungary brought a surprising defeat to the *tan* Fidesz – and a surprising victory to the *gal* Hungarian Socialist Party, which became the first party to win two consecutive elections in Hungary since the regime change of 1989.

The preliminary data from the 2006 Chapel Hill dataset on party positions on European integration support a tentative conclusion that party systems have not turned more markedly *tan* or even Euroskeptic after accession. In 2002 there were nine parties that were opposed, somewhat opposed or strongly opposed to European integration – and in 2006 there were also nine such parties. We see a decrease in the number of parties in the *left-tan* quadrant from 25 in 2002 to 19 in 2006. This suggests that neither opposition to European integration nor strong *tan* appeals are considered resoundingly better political strategies after accession. However, we do see a decrease in the number of parties that *strongly* favor European integration from 19 to 15. And the number of parties in the *right-gal* quadrant has decreased from 17 to 13 as more parties move into the *left-gal* quadrant. The end of conditionality may have given parties more freedom in choosing their positions on economic and social issues. This kind of analysis, however, cannot tell us about the relative importance of parties with different positions in domestic politics.

CONCLUSION

The prospect of opening negotiations with the EU for membership creates incentives for political parties to make their agenda EU-compatible – and this means compatible with satisfying the EU's extensive domestic requirements. Major political parties shift toward more *right* and more *gal* positions, such as decreasing the state's role in the economy and protecting ethnic minority rights. As a result, I have argued that most party systems reflect a consensus on the benefits of European integration and, of necessity, on the priorities for domestic policy-making. For some states the EU's impact on party positions has arguably been decisive in pulling them from an illiberal to a liberal democratic trajectory.

After EU accession has become a certainty for the ECE candidates, EU conditionality has diminished and the importance of hard *left* and especially hard *tan* parties has increased. Governments in Poland and Slovakia have taken strong *tan* positions – and invited extreme *tan* parties to join their governing coalitions. However, in Poland this contributed to a domestic backlash that brought down the government in early elections. Moreover, preliminary data on party positions in 2006 show no increase in the number of parties opposed to European integration, and a decrease in the number of parties situated in the *left-tan* quadrant. Further research is needed to explore how EU membership may have activated different mechanisms – 'beyond conditionality' – that are contributing to this relative moderation in politics after accession.

APPENDIX

Position on European integration	Mean expert score along 7-point scale ranging from strongly opposed to European integration (1) to strongly in favor of European integration (7). Question: 'How would you describe the **general position on European integration** that the party's leadership has taken over the **course of 2002?**' *Source*: Chapel Hill dataset
Left/right position	Mean expert score on 11-point scale ranging from extreme left (0) to extreme right (10). Question: 'Political scientists often classify parties in terms of their ideological stance on **economic issues**. Parties to the **right** emphasize a reduced economic role for government. They want privatization, lower taxes, less regulation, reduced government spending, and a leaner welfare state. Parties to the **left** want government to play an active role in the economy. Using these criteria, indicate where parties are located in terms of their **economic ideology**.' *Source*: Chapel Hill dataset.

(Table continued)

Appendix Continued

Gal/tan position	Mean expert score on 11-point scale ranging from libertarian/postmaterialist (0) to traditional/authoritarian (10). This score is reversed in our analysis. Question: 'Parties may also be classified in terms of their views on **democratic freedoms and rights.** **"Libertarian"** or **"post-materialist"** parties favor expanded personal freedoms; for example, access to abortion, doctor-assisted suicide, same-sex marriages, and greater democratic participation. **"Traditional"** or **"authoritarian"** parties often reject these ideas; they value order and stability, and believe that the government should be a firm moral authority. Where are parties located in terms of their **ideological views on freedoms and rights?**" *Source*: Chapel Hill dataset.

NOTES

1 Dataset and codebook are available at http://www.unc.edu/~hooghe.
2 Interviews with officials from post-communist candidate countries, 1997, 1999, 2000, 2004 and 2005.
3 By liberal democracy I mean a political system in which state institutions and democratically elected rulers respect juridical limits on their powers and political liberties. They uphold the rule of law, a separation of powers, and boundaries between the state and the economy.
4 Interviews with former opposition members in Bratislava, Zagreb, Belgrade and Sarajevo, 2004 and 2005. On the evolution of the Slovak and Croatian opposition, see Fisher (2006).
5 In Lithuania and Latvia, the communist party was outlawed at independence in 1991.
6 There is a divide between the party leadership, which denigrates the EU regularly and champions pairing it down to a free trade zone, and the rank and file, who are in favor of EU membership but have reservations about a federal EU. The ODS has one of the highest scores on internal dissent in the dataset. On why the Czech party system has developed this way, see Hanley (2007).
7 On the challenges of categorizing parties on the economic left–right spectrum, see Vachudova, forthcoming.

REFERENCES

Andonova, L. (2003) *Transnational Politics of the Environment. The EU and Environmental Policy in Central and Eastern Europe*, Cambridge, MA: MIT Press.

Beichelt, T. (2004) 'Euro-skepticism in the EU accession countries', *Comparative European Politics* 2(1): 29–50.

Bilčík, V. (2002) 'Integrácie Slovenskej republiky do Európskej únie', in *Parlamentné voľby 2002: Zahraničná politika SR vo volebných programoch politických strán*, Bratislava: Slovak Foreign Policy Association, pp. 24–34.

Bozóki, A. and Ishiyama, J. (eds) (2002) *The Communist Successor Parties of Central and Eastern Europe*, Armonk, NY: M.E. Sharpe.

Bunce, V. (1999) 'The political economy of postsocialism', *Slavic Review* 58(4): 756–93.

Ekiert, G. and Hanson, S. (eds) (2003) *Capitalism and Democracy in Central and Eastern Europe: Assessing the Legacy of Communist Rule*, Cambridge: Cambridge University Press.

Ekiert, G., Kubik, J. and Vachudova, M.A. (2007) 'Democracy in the post-communist world: an unending quest?', *East European Politics and Societies* 21(1): 7–30.

Enyedi, Z. (2005) 'The role of agency in cleavage formation', *European Journal of Political Research* 44: 697–720.

Epstein, R. (2005) 'The paradoxes of enlargement', *European Political Science* 4: 384–94.

Epstein, R. (2008) *In Pursuit of Liberalism: The Power and Limits of International Institutions in Postcommunist Europe*, Baltimore, MD: Johns Hopkins Press.

Epstein, R. and Sedelmeier, U. (2008) 'Beyond conditionality: international institutions in postcommunist Europe after enlargement', *Journal of European Public Policy* 15(6): 795–805.

Evans, G. and Whitefield, S. (1993) 'Identifying the bases of party competition in Eastern Europe', *British Journal of Political Science* 23: 521–48.

Fisher, S. (2006) *Political Change in Post-Communist Slovakia and Croatia: From Nationalist to Europeanist*, New York: Palgrave Macmillan.

Gheciu, A. (2005) *NATO in the 'New Europe': The Politics of International Socialization After the Cold War*, Stanford: Stanford University Press.

Gould, J. (2004) 'Out of the blue? Democracy and privatization in post-communist Europe', *Comparative European Politics* 1(3): 277–311.

Grabbe, H. (2006) *The EU's Transformative Power: Europeanization through Conditionality in Central and Eastern Europe*, New York: Palgrave Macmillan.

Grzymala-Busse, A. (2002) *Redeeming the Communist Past*, Cambridge: Cambridge University Press.

Grzymala-Busse, A. and Innes, A. (2003) 'Great expectations: the EU and domestic political competition in East Central Europe', *East European Politics and Societies* 17(1): 64–73.

Hanley, S. (2004) 'Getting the right right: redefining the centre-right in postcommunist Europe', *Journal of Communist Studies and Transition Politics* 20(3): 9–27.

Hanley, S. (2007) *The New Right in the New Europe: Czech Transformation and Right-Wing Politics, 1989–2006*, New York: Routledge.

Hellman, J.S. (1988) 'The politics of partial reform in postcommunist transitions', *World Politics* 50(2): 203–34.

Hooghe, L. et al. (n.l.d.) 'Party positioning on European integration – east and west: crossvalidating the 2002 and 2006 Chapel Hill Expert Surveys', unpublished manuscript.

Hughes, J., Sasse, G. and Gordon, C. (2004) *Europeanization and Regionalization in the EU's Enlargement to Central and Eastern Europe: The Myth of Conditionality*, New York: Palgrave Macmillan.

Jacoby, W. (2004) *The Enlargement of the European Union and NATO: Ordering from the Menu in Central Europe*, Cambridge: Cambridge University Press.

Kelley, J. (2004) *Ethnic Politics in Europe: The Power of Norms and Incentives*, Princeton, NJ: Princeton University Press.

Kitschelt, H. (1992) 'The formation of party systems in East Central Europe', *Politics and Society* 20: 7–50.

Kopecký, P. and Mudde, C. (2002) 'The two sides of Euroscepticism: party positions on European integration in East Central Europe', *European Union Politics* 3(3): 297–326.

Marks, G., Hooghe, L., Nelson, M. and Edwards, E. (2006) 'Party competition and European integration in East and West: different structure, same causality', *Comparative Political Studies* 39(2): 155–75.

Orenstein, M. (2001) *Out of the Red: Building Capitalism and Democracy in Postcommunist Europe*, Ann Arbor: Michigan University Press.

Petrova, T. (2006) 'Differential impact of EU enlargement on first and second wave applicants: Europeanizing political parties in Poland and Bulgaria', *CDDRL Working Paper* No. 65, Stanford: Center for Democracy, Development, and the Rule of Law.

Pop-Eleches, G. (2004) 'Transition fatigue: the changing nature of post-communist anti-establishment parties'. Presented at the annual meeting of the American Association for the Advancement of Slavic Studies, Boston, 4–7 December.

Pridham, G. (2005) *Designing Democracy EU Enlargement and Regime Change in Post communist Europe*, London: Palgrave Macmillan.

Rohrschneider, R. and Whitefield, S. (2005) 'Responsible party government? Party stances on European integration in postcommunist Eastern Europe'. Presented at the annual meeting of the APSA in Washington, DC, 31 August–4 September.

Schimmelfennig, F. (2007) 'European regional organizations, political conditionality, and democratic transformation in Eastern Europe', *East European Politics & Societies* 21(1): 126–41.

Schimmelfennig, F. and Sedelmeier, U. (2005) 'Introduction: Conceptualizing the Europeanization of Central and Eastern Europe' in F. Schimmelfennig and U. Sedelmeier (eds), *The Europeanization of Central and Eastern Europe*, Ithaca, NY: Cornell University Press, pp. 1–28.

Sedelmeier, U. (2006) 'Europeanisation in new member and candidate states', *Living Reviews in European Governance (LREG)*: www.livingreviews.org/lreg-2006-3

Sissenich, B. (2007) *Building States Without Society: The Transfer of EU Social Policy to Poland and Hungary*, Lanham, MD: Lexington Books.

Taggart, P. and Szczerbiak, A. (2004) 'Contemporary Euroscepticism in the systems of the European Union candidate states of Central and Eastern Europe', *European Journal of Political Research* 43: 1–27.

Vachudova, M.A. (2005) *Europe Undivided: Democracy, Leverage and Integration After Communism*, Oxford: Oxford University Press.

Vachudova, M.A. (forthcoming) 'Center-right parties and political outcomes in East Central Europe', *Party Politics* 14(4).

Vachudova, M.A. and Hooghe, L. (forthcoming) 'Postcommunist politics in a magnetic field: how transition and EU accession structure party competition on European integration', *Comparative European Politics*.

Williams, K. (1997) 'National myths in the new Czech liberalism', in G. Schöpflin and Hosking, G. (eds), *Myths and Nationhood*, London: Hurst, pp. 79–89.

The social context in conditionality: internationalizing finance in postcommunist Europe

Rachel A. Epstein

INTRODUCTION

When it comes to embracing the European Union's (EU's) vision of building a fully integrated financial market, central and east Europeans have far out-performed their west European counterparts. After all, the EU and its previous incarnations have long aspired to a fully integrated financial market for the Continent that would bring down costs, increase efficiencies and facilitate cross-border transactions of all kinds.[1] Nowhere is the divergence between East and West more striking than in the strategic sector of banking. Across Central and Eastern Europe (CEE) it is now usual to find foreign investment levels in banking at 70 percent and upward. Among the 'old' 15 EU members, however, foreign control over banking assets more commonly hovers below 20 percent, and in many cases well below 10 percent. The outcome in CEE is even more surprising in light of the fact that in virtually no postcommunist country was there an élite consensus at the outset of transition in favour of high levels of foreign ownership. On the contrary, leaders initially sought to protect their banking sectors from foreign control.

In addition to examining the puzzle of why so many CEE states have diverged from their west European counterparts by allowing high levels of foreign investment in banking, this article addresses a second question: Why is there variation within CEE in the timing and extent of openness to foreign investment? Table 1 highlights both kinds of outcomes. I argue that, to a certain extent, the same evidence answers both questions.

Across CEE, transition states in the 1990s and early 2000s faced pressure from an array of international institutions that favoured internationally competitive bidding for state-owned assets. Often that pressure was in the form of

Table 1 Foreign and state ownership in selected industrialized and postcommunist banking sectors, 2002*

Ind. country	Assets foreign owned	Assets govt owned	Postcomm. country	Assets foreign owned	Assets govt owned
New Zealand	99.11	0.04	Estonia†	98.9	0
Luxembourg	94.64	5.05	Czech Rep.†	90	3.8
UK	46	0	Croatia	89.3	5
S. Korea	29.54	39.97	**Hungary†**	88.8	9
Norway	19.2	0	Slovakia†	85.5	4.4
US	19	0	Lithuania†	78.19	12.16
Portugal	17.7	22.8	Bulgaria††	74.56	17.6
Australia	17	0	Bos. & Herz.	73	10
Cyprus	12.7	4.2	**Poland†**	68.7	23.5
Greece	10.8	22.8	Latvia†	65.2	3.2
Switzerland	10.71	14.2	**Romania††**	47.3	41.8
Spain	8.5	0	Albania	46	54
Japan	6.7	0	Moldova	36.7	13.6
Finland	6.2	0	Belarus	26	74
Italy	5.7	10	Kyrgyzstan	24.7	16
Canada	4.8	0	**Slovenia†**	20.6	12.2
Germany	4.30	42.2	Kazakhstan	17.9	0.5
Turkey	3.47	31.82	Serbia & Mont.	13.2	3.8
Netherlands	2.2	3.9	**Ukraine**	10.5	12
China	1.9	98.1	Russia	8.8	35.5
Israel	1.2	46.1	Azerbaijan	4.6	58.3
Denmark	0	0			
Belgium	◆	0			
France	◆	0			

Source: Barth et al. (2006: 149–50, 152–3).
Notes: *Remaining assets are listed as privately owned (Barth et al. 2006: 154).
◆No data available.
†Countries admitted to the EU in 2004.
††Countries admitted to the EU in 2007.
Countries in bold face are those featured in this article.

conditionality. Owing to low levels of domestic capital accumulation in most CEE states, internationally competitive bidding often meant *de facto* sale of banks to foreigners. West European states never faced such an array of internationalizing pressure.[2] But in answering the second question more precisely about why, despite international pressure from multiple quarters, there was nevertheless variation in the timing and extent of openness to foreign ownership of banks in CEE, I argue that some CEE states were more resistant to international institutions' prescriptions than others.

Possible explanations for variation in CEE investment openness revolve around domestic preferences, financial crises, economic best practice, external demand or international institutions' conditionality as such. Instead, however, I argue that CEE susceptibility to international institutions' pressure, including conditionality, hinged on a particular social context (Epstein 2008). Where domestic actors viewed international institutions as authoritative sources of information and potential imprimaturs of their political platforms, postcommunist countries were likely to heed their advice and fulfill the terms of their conditionality. Domestic susceptibility in turn resulted in high levels of foreign ownership in banks. By contrast, where international institutions were unable to displace domestic sources of authority, namely nationalist striving and the desire for autonomy, international institutions' recommendations and conditionality wielded much less power, resulting in lower levels of foreign ownership in CEE banks.

After operationalizing the features of this social context, I test the argument in three core cases: Poland, Romania and Ukraine. These countries vary in terms of the values on the independent variables that constitute a facilitating social context. I also use evidence from both Hungary and Slovenia to provide additional observations on both the explanatory variables and outcomes. Additional variation over time provides still more explanatory leverage, particularly in the case of Romania. Ukraine's inclusion helps me to address possible alternative explanations concerning the effects of conditionality in the absence of a facilitating social context.

Explaining the internationalization of finance in CEE advances the central theme of this volume, 'Beyond Conditionality,' in three ways (see Epstein and Sedelmeier 2008). Most importantly, this article assesses international institutions' power in terms of a new mechanism – the social context – and demonstrates why conditionality is powerful in some instances but fails to elicit its intended effect in others. Second, the evidence draws in part from a case, Ukraine, which is beyond EU membership conditionality, even if that country has faced an abundance of other conditionality agreements with the World Bank and the International Monetary Fund (IMF). And finally, the article goes beyond conditionality in a temporal sense. I conclude that not only is it unlikely that CEE banks will ever recapture national ownership, but that in the decades to come, owing to changing EU law, European banks are even more likely to be transnational in character and ownership. Enduring compliance with international institutions' prescriptions even after enlargement mirrors other outcomes highlighted in this volume (Sedelmeier 2008).

THE SOCIAL CONTEXT IN CONDITIONALITY: ELABORATION OF THE ARGUMENT

The central argument of this article is that if external advice or conditionality is to produce its intended effect, it must be offered in a particular social context. That social context is most concisely described as one in which target states perceive themselves to be embedded in a hierarchy *vis-à-vis* international institutions. Three specific features of social context contribute to perceptions of authority: the discontinuity of sectors and regimes, domestic actors' perceived subordinated status *vis-à-vis* international institutions and the normative consistency underpinning the policies in question.

'Discontinuity' is operationalized here in terms of macro-economic liberalization, the endurance of business networks and party turnover in the transition. Discontinuity contributes to international institutions' power because domestic actors are likely to be uncertain about how to conduct reform and therefore prone to seek their assistance. Second, I measure the perceived subordinated status of domestic actors by assessing repeated political party turnover. Regular party turnover affords international institutions influence over domestic debates because they can take sides, confer legitimacy, mobilize the opposition and influence electoral outcomes. Lastly, normative consistency is assessed in terms of general practice – that is, the extent to which member states of organizations themselves pursue policies that the same organizations try to impose on target states. Where measures on all three variables are high, I would expect greater openness to external advice and stronger compliance with conditionality than where sectors and regimes are continuous, political competition muted, and the credibility of policies undermined by uneven practice.

What a social context informed by discontinuity, status and credibility captures is the power of international institutions to assign particular meanings to policies. From the perspective of CEE reformers in the early 1990s, planning to retain domestic ownership in banking was viewed as rational and desirable (Abarbanell and Bonin 1997; Tsantis 1997; Hjartarson 2004; Piroska 2005). As the evidence will show, however, where international institutions had the most influence over domestic debates by virtue of discontinuity, status and credibility, striving to retain domestic control came to be construed as embarrassing – in some cases as early as 1996. The shift in perception was not due to the availability of new information or incentives but to the exploitation of a permissive social context by international institutions to cast doubt on the wisdom of economic nationalism. They did this by emphasizing the extent to which they believed maintaining domestic ownership reflected communist, central planning instincts, anti-capitalist sentiment and a disregard for constructive relations with the liberal economic order of the West. The evidence also shows that the power of international institutions to orchestrate a shift in perceptions was at times limited by opposite measures on the same variables – i.e., continuity of regimes and sectors, domestic actors' lack of perceived subordinated status and the low credibility of the policies in question.

Another way of stating the argument is that in order for external advice or conditionality to 'work,' target actors must perceive the rewards on offer as worth the costs of compliance. This would seem to replicate other studies that assign objective values to both conditionality and compliance (Kelley 2004; Schimmelfenning 2005; Vachudova 2005). There is an important distinction, however. Although I also use the language of costs and trade-offs, I do so while arguing that incentives, whether they are in the form of money, membership or reputational rewards, have a subjective quality as well as material implications. In practice, the very same actors who reject conditionality in one period may comply with it in the next, not because their political position has changed, but because the social context has. Moreover, apparently similarly situated states may respond quite differently to a uniform set of incentives because perceptions of hierarchy differ, and the power of conditionality accordingly varies.

ALTERNATIVE APPROACHES

At least four rival explanations might also account for variation in the timing and degree of foreign participation in postcommunist bank privatization. The first is domestic preferences. Poland and Hungary in particular, which both saw democratic opposition movements assume power in the transition, might have been predisposed to pursue a liberalizing strategy in any case (Bockman and Eyal 2002; Shields 2003; Vachudova 2005). With respect to Bockman and Eyal's research specifically, liberal economists in Poland, Hungary, Czechoslovakia and Russia might have pushed for a major role for international capital. Although in those four countries such an approach would predict the correct outcome in all but Russia where domestic ownership of banks remained high, three kinds of evidence cast doubt on the power of domestic conditions alone to shape outcomes.

First, in none of the countries under consideration was achieving a high level of foreign ownership in finance an objective in and of itself – even among liberal economists. In fact, politicians across the spectrum explicitly sought to avoid foreign domination in the sector (Abarbanell and Bonin 1997; Tsantis 1997; Hjartarson 2004; Piroska 2005). Second, Romania, and to a certain extent Ukraine, show that even states without a liberal élite at the outset of transition can nevertheless be set on a liberalizing path. Third, political groupings that favoured a national approach to bank restructuring adopted an internationalizing strategy, not primarily in response to domestic pressure but because of international intervention. This was observable in the communist successor parties of Poland, Romania and to a lesser extent Hungary.

Economic best practice or financial crises may also have pushed states to seek out foreign investors as a way to shield the state from the burden of bank bailouts. But the best practice argument is undermined by the fact that states clearly disagree on what constitutes an optimal outcome. While Hungary, Romania and to a lesser extent Poland have accepted high levels of foreign ownership,

Slovenia and Ukraine have not. The financial crisis explanation would seem to get at least some of the predictions correct. Hungary and Romania had financial crises and subsequently invited foreign strategic investors to buy their banks; Slovenia was never under the same level of stress and was successful for more than a decade in keeping foreign investment in banking to a minimum. But the financial crisis hypothesis is notably off the mark when it comes to Poland and Ukraine. Moreover, if one is concerned about timing, then Romania, according to the severity of its ongoing financial crises (Cernat 2006), should have been the first to solicit foreign investors. And according to the financial crisis argument, it was *only* through foreign investment that postcommunist states could escape the burden of repeated bail-outs. But in fact a number of state-owned and operated CEE banks have performed well, including in Poland, Slovenia and even Romania.

A third kind of explanation posits that variation in external demand accounts for differences in the level of foreign investment in CEE banks. According to the 'external demand' logic, one would expect Romania and Ukraine to have registered lower levels of foreign investment because of the poor quality of their banking assets. But there has been more demand for CEE banks than supply, and for good reason. The region came out of communism radically 'underbanked' by industrialized standards, with enormous potential for growth. By the end of 2004, banks with headquarters in Western Europe owned around half of all CEE banking assets, and in that year alone those same banks saw a 15 percent increase in the value of their assets, in large measure because of growth in CEE.[3] Moreover, heightened foreign interest in both Romania and Ukraine corresponded to rationalization of the business environment as well as improved bank balance sheets – developments that stemmed directly from international institutions' advice and conditionality. Thus my own social context argument subsumes the external demand hypothesis: given pent-up demand for CEE banks in Western Europe, a regulatory shift in Romania and Ukraine in favour of international standards was also a decision to attract foreign capital. External demand on its own is insufficient: regardless of consistently strong demand for Slovenian banks, that state has opted to protect high levels of domestic ownership.

Finally, there is the pure conditionality argument. EU conditionality does not explain the variation in foreign ownership levels for two reasons. Although EU laws governing capital mobility and competition policy are relevant to whether and how EU members protect their financial sectors, a proposed law on cross-border takeovers (the Financial Services Action Plan) did not appear until 1999 and was still being transposed in 2006. This did not stop the European Commission from putting pressure on candidate states to privatize their banks with foreign capital, but only Romania did so before accession. Slovenia, by contrast, prevaricated, appeared to relent, only to backtrack in ways that sustained levels of foreign ownership on a par with Ukraine (at less than a third of assets in 2006). While EU membership says nothing about the discrepancy between Slovenia's and Romania's willingness to embrace internationalized ownership, the social context between these states and the EU does.

Bretton Woods conditionality (imposed by the World Bank and the IMF) was often also applied in order to encourage bank privatization. As the evidence here will show, however, states responded differently to similar incentives. Both Hungary and Poland were receptive to Bretton Woods conditionality in the first half of the 1990s whereas Romania and Ukraine were not. The point here is not to argue that conditionality is a weak instrument, but rather to highlight that its variable power is determined by a social context. Where domestic regimes and sectors underwent a sharp break with the past, where domestic actors perceived themselves as subordinate and where the credibility of policies was not in question, international institutions were likely to wield significant authority. Only then would conditionality appear to be 'worth' the costs of compliance.

DISCONTINUITY, STATUS AND CREDIBILITY: EXPLAINING CEE OPENNESS

Discontinuity (H1)

Sectoral and regime discontinuity are the first features of a social context that allow international institutions access to national reform debates. In theory, discontinuity and the resulting uncertainty about reform will lead politicians to seek out foreign advice to gain greater confidence in their own policy choices. For the purposes of this article, I operationalize discontinuity by assessing the durability of both business networks and political leadership through the transition.

In Hungary and Poland, the measure on discontinuity in banking was the strongest of the five cases. The banking sector was discontinuous with the communist era in that price liberalization in both countries was early and comprehensive. Facing free market conditions for the first time, including competition from foreign banks, Polish and Hungarian financiers were relatively open to international financial institution (IFI) advice about how to upgrade their skills, technology and competitiveness. Moreover, political turnover in the transition in both countries resulted in the rise of leaders who had not governed before. Uncertainty over how exactly to preside over major institutional reform of the macro-economy made them susceptible to external advice.

In Poland, the domestic drive to engage foreign advice presented itself in three ways. The Twinning Arrangements, sponsored by the World Bank and the International Finance Corporation (IFC) and launched in 1991, were an outgrowth of a speech by Jeffrey Sachs in which the economist urged Polish banks to pair up with Western ones as a means of upgrading skills and technology and generating Western interest in investing in the sector.[4] A second form of engagement consisted of a Polish bank bail-out plan that requested the financial assistance of the IMF to recapitalize selected Polish financial institutions. Although the IMF ultimately agreed to put $600 million toward the project, it was with the informal condition that Poland privatize six of its remaining state-owned banks by 1996.[5] Until 1993, Poland also supported liberal licensing and market entry laws, allowing foreign banks in particular to enjoy tax relief and flexibility concerning foreign currency holdings and capital mobility (National Bank of Poland 2001: 51). Encouraging competitiveness through market openness was consistent with the range of foreign counsel that Poland was receiving at the time (Bonin *et al.* 1998). Hungary, too, in keeping with strong measures on discontinuity, embraced international institutions' advice. In 1990 and 1991, Hungary adopted liberal licensing laws to encourage competition from foreign banks, legislated limits on state ownership and voting rights in Hungarian banks to 25 percent, and embarked on privatization (see Piroska 2005).

Whereas Poland and Hungary are the most similar cases in terms of the discontinuity variable in the early 1990s, Romania and Slovenia were different. Romanian price liberalization in 1991 was fairly comprehensive (with the exception of some utilities, food and housing prices) so bankers were facing an unfamiliar environment. But the potential access that international institutions would have to the sector based on uncertainty was limited in Romania by regime continuity (the National Salvation Front (FSN) was led by marginalized figures from within Ceauşescu's regime). As a consequence, IFI conditionality failed to elicit compliance: the Romanian governing class simply did not need IFI advice to bolster confidence in its policies. Thus, when the IMF predicated its 1994 stand-by agreement on the drafting of a bank privatization law, and linked subsequent agreements to banking reform, including its 1995 stand-by agreement that called for commercial bank restructuring and the privatization of the Romanian Bank for Development (BRD), Romania failed to comply. That failure led to the World Bank's 1996 Financial and Enterprise Structural Adjustment Loan, which also called for the privatization of the BRD and restrictions on the financing of commercial bank losses by the Romanian central bank (Ghizari 1992: 115, 121; Tsantis 1997: 173, 200), but which Romania also neglected to fulfill. Whereas Poland and Hungary were responsive to IFI counsel and were reluctant to rupture relations with the IMF and the World Bank, Romanian politicians through the first half of the 1990s entered into agreements with which they had no intention of complying or about which they were highly ambivalent.[6]

There was even more economic and political continuity in Slovenia's transition. Slovenia did undertake macro-economic liberalization. But because it had developed strong trading ties to the West under state socialism, the economic transition was not as radical as elsewhere, the transition recession was shorter, and many business networks remained intact (Feldmann 2007). Moreover, although Slovenia did undergo party turnover in the transition that resulted in the Democratic Opposition of Slovenia (DEMOS) taking power, a coalition composed of critics of the state socialist regime, it collapsed in April 1992 less than a year after Slovenia declared independence. The main political force thereafter was the Liberal Democratic Party (LDS) that drew on the nationalist and youth segments of the former state socialist regime, and, apart from six months in 2000, dominated every governing coalition until 2004.

Because of continuity in both the economy and leadership, Slovenia did not seek out external advice to gain confidence in its early policy choices. In contrast to Poland where Jeffrey Sachs was the catalyst for a bank twinning program, his 1992 trip to Slovenia to try to convince politicians there to adopt an IMF-backed privatization plan failed. As one high-level Slovenian politician noted in reference to outside counsel, 'We listened to them, but didn't follow their advice' (quoted in Lindstrom and Piroska 2007: 119).

According to the discontinuity hypothesis, the IFIs should have exercised the least influence over Ukraine's banking reform early in the transition. Not only was there strong continuity in the regime, but sectoral continuity was also bolstered by the fact that price liberalization was initially only slowly implemented and on a stop-and-go basis (see Sochan 1996: 10; Dąbrowski and Antczak 1995: 4). Consistent with what the discontinuity hypothesis would predict, Ukraine's bank reform strategy revealed the least international influence during the 1990s. Two banks remained in state hands while three other banks hived off from the socialist-era monobank were nominally privatized, but to state-owned enterprises, bank managers and employees. Ukraine, in contrast to Poland and Hungary, also maintained restrictions on most kinds of foreign participation in the domestic banking market. There was also little movement towards compliance with international accounting and business standards – itself a symptom of Ukraine's resistance to foreign influence in restructuring the banking sector.

In sum, strong discontinuity in the economy and in leadership, as in Poland and Hungary, corresponded to active engagement with IFIs. Romania, Slovenia and Ukraine were much less susceptible to external influence and, in the case of Ukraine, slow price liberalization and insider privatization of banks left financial institutions beholden to government ministries.

Status (H2)

The status variable assesses the extent to which domestic actors seek international institutions' approbation. I operationalize this variable in terms of regular party turnover or the threat of party turnover (Grzymała-Busse 2002; Vachudova 2005). The status hypothesis suggests that domestic actors are more beholden to international institutions' policy prescriptions when there is a robust opposition with the potential to unseat those in power. Under conditions of political competition and repeated turnover, international institutions not only provide information that potentially exposes the failure of leaders to comply (Vachudova 2005), they also broaden the scope of what political parties compete about as external actors become another constituency to whom politicians must answer. International institutions also gain the ability to confer legitimacy on one set of policies at the expense of another. The status hypothesis thus predicts that international institutions' preferences will act as an anchor, causing political parties to mimic and contest each other on the basis of external actors' advice (or disapproval).

The predictions of the status hypothesis are confirmed for Poland and Hungary. In Poland, political competition had been robust since the outset of transition, continuing with the communist successor parties' surprising electoral victory in 1993. Upon coming to power, the Democratic Left Alliance (SLD) and the Polish Peasant Party (PSL) viewed the diminishing scope for state intervention in the economy with concern. In this connection, they proposed a state-led bank consolidation program, with the end goal being to find domestic buyers who could turn the new banking conglomerates into internationally competitive financial institutions (the details of the plan are outlined in the following section on credibility). In keeping with the status hypothesis, the SLD–PSL coalition abandoned their bank consolidation plans as they discovered how dependent their political reputations were on the approval of international institutions. Indeed, in light of IMF, US Treasury and European Bank for Reconstruction and Development (EBRD) disapproval, the SLD–PSL coalition dramatically changed track, ending their administration with fast-track privatization for a number of Polish banks, soliciting foreign investors as they did so. The socialists in Hungary (MSzP) were similarly responsive to IFI advice, making constructive relations with the Bretton Woods institutions and the EBRD a top priority during their tenure beginning in 1994 (Hanley *et al.* 2002). As ex-communists, complying with international institutions through liberalizing strategies, including the privatization of banks with foreign capital, was one method of remaking their image in the postcommunist era.

Limited party turnover in Romania and Slovenia curtailed international institutions' access to reform debates. The lack of a viable opposition until 1996 in Romania resulted in slower internationalization of the banking sector than in Poland or Hungary. The FSN and its successor parties dominated from 1989 until 1996. Without a viable opposition, EU pre-accession guidelines had little influence on reform and, as we have already seen, Bretton Woods conditionality failed to elicit compliance. After the Democratic Convention of Romania (CDR) came to power in late 1996, however, bank privatization policy changed, largely because this new (if unstable) coalition fashioned its platform to win international approval, in contrast to the FSN. CDR oversaw the privatization of two of Romania's state-owned banks to foreign strategic investors, including the BRD and BancPost. Preparations were also made for Banca Agricola's privatization. Under CDR's leadership, the percentage of banking assets held by foreigners increased from 15.2 percent in 1998 to 43.56 percent two years later (Doltu 2002: 289). Also as the status hypothesis would predict, when the socialists returned to power again in 2000, they continued to pursue bank privatization with foreign capital, much to the West's surprise.[7] Because there was no commensurate threat of party turnover or actual party turnover in Slovenia until 2004, the same year that Slovenia joined the EU, Slovenia had remained relatively immune to international pressure to open up its banking market.

The status variable receives some confirmation in the case of Ukraine, although the effect in terms of soliciting foreign investors was not as dramatic as in Poland, Hungary or Romania. In support of the status hypothesis, political competition intensified in Ukraine with the 1999 presidential race in which Leonid Kuchma portrayed himself as a pro-Western reformer in contrast to Petro Symonenko, the Communist Party candidate who stood against Kuchma in the presidential run-off. Although Kuchma's pro-Western rhetoric during the campaign could be construed as only that – rhetoric – it is notable that in 2000 Ukraine began complying with World Bank recommendations for rationalizing the business environment to attract large-scale foreign investment. Increasing compliance between 2000 and 2004 set the stage for heightened levels of foreign investment in the banking sector after Viktor Yushchenko's victory in the 'Orange Revolution'. Within a short period, foreign ownership of Ukrainian bank assets rose from 10 to 30 percent.

Credibility (H3)

The credibility of policies depends on the normative consistency underpinning them. Normative consistency is measured here in two ways – by observing consensus and practice. Consensus among international actors in favor of privatization was very strong, and when asked to weigh in, international institutions urged internationally competitive tenders. When it came to bank privatization, however, normative consistency in terms of practice was much weaker, particularly at the outset of transition. For although western members of the EU, EBRD, IMF and World Bank were eager to encourage CEE states to open their markets, the lack of substantial foreign ownership in most industrialized states' banks told a different story about what states should maximize (see Table 1 for comparison; see also Johnson (2008) for a similar point about European monetary union). Early in transition, the example set by western states figured in every CEE debate about how to privatize banks, causing friction between domestic reformers and their external advisers, and in some cases limiting international institutions' power to direct outcomes.

In Poland, the most serious bid to break with the liberalizing agenda of the first Solidarity reformers, who had spearheaded the Twinning Arrangements and agreed with the IMF to sell a number of Polish banks before the end of 1996, was the SLD–PSL bank consolidation program, first outlined in 1995 (*Życie Warszawy*, 29 November 1995: 8). Pointing precisely to the fact that industrialized and developing countries in North America, Europe and Asia had protected domestic ownership in banking,[8] the communist successor coalition took a more nationalist approach to commercial bank restructuring (Balcerowicz and Bartkowski 2001). They wanted to commercialize and consolidate six to eight banks into two groups for which the Ministry of Finance would find domestic buyers. Not only would the plan have allowed Poles to control a greater degree of domestic capital allocation, but it would have also potentially given the state more control over the economy. Not sharing these concerns, however, the IMF, EBRD and US Treasury would ultimately dissuade the SLD–PSL coalition from following through on the plan. Slovenia was most similar to Poland in terms of viewing the credibility of competitive international tenders for banks skeptically throughout the transition and beyond. Even in the early 2000s, Slovenian economists arguing against foreign investment in banks pointed explicitly to the fact that foreign penetration in CEE was 'disproportionately high' compared to the EU15 (Lindstrom and Piroska 2007: 122).

Romania's initial reluctance to embrace high levels of foreign investment in banking, like everywhere else, stemmed from the sentiment that 'banks [were] considered to be among the most important, strategic assets of the state' (Tsantis 1997: 201). Hungarians also questioned the wisdom of foreign investment in strategic sectors, for although the first postcommunist government in Hungary (led by the Democratic Forum, MDF) was keen on bank privatization, it envisioned maintaining a strong domestic presence in the sector. In fact, two international deals between 1990 and 1994 fell apart over exactly such concerns: foreign investors wanted a guarantee that if they invested on a small scale in Hungarian banks in the early 1990s, they could ultimately buy larger stakes in the same institutions. The MDF-led government refused to agree (Hjartarson 2004: 10 and 17). But Romania and Hungary share another similarity that does not provide strong support for the credibility hypothesis. After 1994 in Hungary and after 1996 in Romania, neither bank privatization debate evidenced strong concern about disproportionate foreign penetration in a strategic sector. And both countries ended up with very high levels of foreign ownership in banks, at 90 and 80 percent of assets, respectively. Although the growing consistency of the international institutions' message could partly explain the relative lack of debate in the late 1990s and early 2000s,[9] the credibility hypothesis would reasonably predict greater controversy than was manifested.

In keeping with the credibility hypothesis, Ukraine prioritized power over efficiency in its approach to bank privatization, at least until the early 2000s when international institutions' prescriptions about how to rationalize the business environment gained traction. The IMF Standby Agreements of 1995 and 1996, as well as the Extended Fund Facility of 1993, were consistently tied to privatization, but Ukraine failed to fulfill the terms of any of these deals. Lack of compliance with conditionality suggests that the social context did not allow external actors to wield much authority. By the early 2000s, not only had political competition in Ukraine intensified (see previous section on 'status') but international institutions were changing their approach, as well. Rather than focus on the number of privatizations, for example, the IMF shifted its focus to their quality, with particular attention to transparency and foreign access (Elborgh-Woytek and Lewis 2002: 14). Noting that low levels of foreign participation in finance were symptomatic of Ukraine's lagging economic performance, other organizations, including the World Bank, the Organization for Economic Co-operation and Development (OECD) and the US Treasury, all recommended reducing non-payment in the economy, rationalizing the tax structure, improving the financial sector's regulatory framework, ending political protection for weaker banks and limiting arbitrary political interference (see variously: OECD 2001; Roe *et al.* 2001; Brown 2004; Duenwald *et al.* 2005). Research indicated that foreign interest would naturally follow from better business conditions – which it did beginning in late 2004.

As a snapshot of both conflicts over bank privatization and outcomes, the five countries featured here provide strong confirmation of the credibility hypothesis. Where practice in Western Europe was inconsistent with what international institutions were prescribing, one would expect CEE compliance to vary – and indeed it did. However, given the high level of foreign investment across a greater number of CEE countries (see Table 1), the credibility hypothesis looks weaker. Indeed, taking the CEE region overall, the credibility hypothesis is better for predicting the contours of conflict over bank privatization than it is for predicting individual outcomes.

OUTCOMES

The communist successor coalition that took power in Poland in late 1993 initially tried to increase the state's role in the economy through a bank consolidation and domestic sales strategy. The SLD–PSL government dropped the plan in 1996 in response to international pressure, however. Of most immediate concern to Poland's external advisers was the fact that one of the banks slated for consolidation (Bank Przemysłowo-Handlowy) had already been partially privatized, including by the EBRD (15.06 percent). Although Finance Minister Grzegorz Kołodko was inclined to pursue the program despite misgivings in the domestic and international press, he changed course only when he and his deputy, Krzysztof Kalicki, confronted direct pressure from the US Treasury, which in this instance was the last arbiter of IMF and EBRD preferences. In addition to cautioning the government against bank consolidation because it risked sending the wrong signal to foreign investors everywhere (that the communist successors in Poland still harbored central planning instincts), US Treasury officials threatened to withhold the next tranche of bank recapitalization funds, worth $200 million. They argued that state-led bank consolidation was not in the spirit of the IMF's earlier agreement with the post-Solidarity government that six of Poland's state-owned banks be privatized by 1996, and Kołodko dropped the plan accordingly.

Despite the proximity of $200 million in conditionality funds to Poland's abandonment of state-led bank consolidation, the outcome actually highlights the ways in which a social context constitutes the power of conditionality. That it was the social context rather than conditionality taken on its own that contributed to the internationalization of Polish bank ownership is borne out both by facts from the Polish case and by a comparison with Romania.

On the face of it, a transition state would likely prefer to have an additional $200 million than not. However, if money had been the only consideration for the SLD–PSL coalition, it could have marshaled the funds from other sources. They could have refrained from implementing their tax cut, for example, which had only been made feasible by the additional bank privatization and recapitalization funds. Or, given that the Polish parliament had legislated $400 million for adjustment assistance to sensitive enterprises facing restructuring but that the World Bank had agreed to provide those funds instead, the SLD–PSL would have had resources to devote to bank recapitalization. If these alternatives are not persuasive, then consider the fact that Romania over the same period had three separate conditionality agreements linked to bank privatization with the Bretton Woods institutions and fulfilled not one of them (Tsantis 1997: 173, 200).

The difference between Poland and Romania was clearly not the presence or absence of credible conditionality. The difference was in how much the leadership in each country valued constructive relations with external advisers and by extension whether those external advisers had been afforded the power to assign particular meanings to particular policies. The SLD in Poland was highly sensitive to international opprobrium because the first post-Solidarity government had had such a close working relationship with IFIs on account of sharp discontinuity (H1). Moreover, the SLD was a communist successor party in a country where political competition allowed the opposition to use international criticism to undermine the coalition in power (H2). Although communist successors were also governing Romania, they were not similarly susceptible to international opinion because they had governed continuously through the transition and because there was only very weak opposition until late 1996 (H1 and H2).

All measures on the social context changed in the late 1990s in Romania, affording international institutions more access to the country's reform debates. The CDR came to power in late 1996, providing discontinuity in governing personnel (H1) and establishing political competition (H2). As noted in the previous section on the credibility hypothesis, the IFIs and the EU began coordinating their message on bank privatization, even if western practice continued to undermine the preponderant use of foreign capital (H3). As a consequence of Romania's new susceptibility, foreign ownership in banking increased to over 40 percent under the CDR, and when the socialists resumed leadership in 2000, they too embraced international institutions' prescriptions and conditionality. This included preparation and privatization of the Commercial Bank of Romania to the EBRD, the IFC and Austria's Erste Bank in 2004 and 2005. That there was international pressure to embrace internationalization is not in question. Privatization remained a key condition of World Bank and IMF support and Romania was pursuing the earliest possible date for EU accession. But such pressure is unlikely to secure compliance independent of a particular social context. One need only to compare Romanian compliance with the IFIs in the early 2000s to the situation five years earlier to see that conditionality – a feature of both periods – is insufficient on its own to elicit compliance (Tsantis 1997: 200–805). By 2006, foreign ownership in Romania's banking sector had reached over 80 per cent.

Bank privatization and the role of foreign investors in Hungary are largely what the social context would predict, with somewhat less debate after 1994 than one would expect about whether western protection of domestic bank ownership should serve as a model (H3). Sectoral and regime discontinuity (H1) gave international institutions access to Hungarian reform debates during the first postcommunist administration, which undertook liberalization of bank licensing laws and encouraged foreign participation in the banking market. MDF also had a strong commitment to privatization, legislating a 25 percent state ownership or voting rights limit on banks by 1997. But when it came to actually increasing the level of foreign ownership of Hungarian assets, it was the socialists starting in 1994 who enlisted the assistance of the IFIs' that were uniquely qualified to redefine the communist successors' image. The socialists' exploitation of the IFIs power to confer legitimacy is in keeping with what the status hypothesis would predict (H2). By the end of 2002, close to 90 percent of Hungarian banking assets were foreign owned and most of the privatization that produced those levels took place during the socialist administration of 1994–98. When the socialists returned to power in 2002, they again allowed foreigners to buy still larger stakes in the banks that they already controlled.

The measure on discontinuity was the weakest in Ukraine because of delayed price liberalization and continuity in personnel from the communist to the postcommunist regime (H1). The absence of political competition until 1999 and 2000 also limited IFI influence, allowing Ukrainian priorities centred on domestic control to prevail in bank restructuring (H2). The pace of internationalization was increasing by late 2004, however, when Sweden's SEB Group bought 94 percent of Ukraine's Agio Bank. In 2005, Austria's Raiffeisen and France's BNP Paribas bought substantial stakes in Aval and UkrSibBank respectively, two of Ukraine's largest banks. In early 2006, Italy's Banca Intesa purchased another of Ukraine's former state banks, UkrSotsBank (*Kyiv Post*, 15 February 2006). The Orange Revolution of late 2004 no doubt played a role in changing foreign investors' perceptions of Ukraine as an increasingly democratic and western-oriented power. But compliance with IFI prescriptions that would open Ukraine's economy actually started in 2000 when Kuchma began seeking IFIs' assistance to bolster his domestic credibility. In 2001, for example, Ukraine passed the Law on Banks and Banking Activities that eliminated restrictions on foreign investment in the sector. Comparing World Bank assessments, there was little Ukrainian compliance between 1995 and 2000 in connection with a $300 million Financial Sector Adjustment Loan (Roe *et al.* 2001: 4, 33) but much stronger compliance between 2000 and 2005. Whether foreign investment in Ukraine's banking sector would climb above its 2007 level of 30 percent would likely depend on how Ukraine's ongoing political crises would be resolved.

Paradoxically, Slovenia, a liberal democracy, outstanding economic performer, early entrant to the EU and first postcommunist euro adopter, looked more like Romania before 1997 or even Ukraine when it came to opening its banking sector to foreign investment. Strong continuity in the regime and even in the economy as well as the lack of repeated political party turnover between 1992 and 2004 limited the extent to which Slovenians accepted external advice (H1 and H2). In addition, many Slovenians remained deeply affected by the disparity between foreign investment in banks in the East versus the West (H3).

The failure of international institutions to persuade was not for lack of trying. All of the European Commission's annual monitoring reports on Slovenia between 2000 and 2003 were critical of the country's failure to privatize two state-owned banks, in particular NLB and NKBM. The EBRD, the IMF and the World Bank all expressed similar concerns in their own publications and consulting missions, in addition to cautioning about higher than average bank operating costs (from muted market competition) and a risky level of interconnectedness in the financial sector (IMF 2004). It was not that Slovenia refused to do everything the international institutions were asking. In 1999 the government passed legislation that scuttled a previous upper limit on foreign bank ownership, allowed foreign bank branches and subsidiaries to operate, and liberalized capital flows.[10] And by 2001 it even looked like they would privatize NLB and NKBM. In the event, however, the NKBM privatization was cancelled because of domestic political pressure, while the NLB deal was compromised by Slovenia's reluctance to allow the would-be Belgian strategic investor KBC to buy as big a share as it wanted in 2006.[11] In that year foreigners controlled just over 27 percent of Slovenia's banking assets (Bank of Slovenia 2006: 43).

CONCLUSION: BEYOND CONDITIONALITY

This study of conditionality and CEE openness to international institutions' policy prescriptions provides a new interpretation of how information and incentives are constituted in ways that make them 'worth' the costs of compliance. Key to the analysis is the idea that only a narrow social context affords international institutions the power to assign particular meanings to policies. In Poland, Hungary and Romania after 1996, international actors were able to orchestrate a shift in which domestic actors, who began the transition believing that protecting domestic ownership was rational and desirable, ended up embracing policies premised entirely on the efficiency of financial institutions, regardless of power considerations. Looking beyond accession conditionality, there is little reason to think that CEE states will ever be able to revert to national control over banking assets that they have already sold.

Although this article has implications for the power of international institutions globally, the processes through which many CEE states internationalized their banks tell us little about financial sectors in Europe because of forthcoming changes in EU law. For as EU law changes, so, undoubtedly, will the patterns of European compliance. Yet the internationalization of bank ownership as it has transpired in CEE over the last 20 years is more emblematic of that future than the West's long tradition of protecting domestic ownership. The EU and its previous incarnations have long envisioned a fully integrated financial market for the Continent that would bring down costs, increase efficiencies and facilitate cross-border transactions of all kinds. But it is only in the current period – with the directive on takeover bids of publicly traded financial institutions, adopted by the European Parliament in April 2004 and projected for transposition by the member states by May 2006 – that EU law is finally coming to reflect much older European integration aspirations.

NOTES

1 Such efforts began with the 1973 directive on 'The Abolition of Restrictions on Freedom of Establishment and Freedom to Provide Services for Self-employed Activities of Banks and Other Financial Institutions', continued with provisions in the Single European Act of the mid-1980s, the Maastricht Treaty of 1992 concerning monetary union, and finally the Financial Services Action Plan, initiated by the Commission in 1999 (Barth *et al.* 2006).
2 And to the extent that West European states have felt any pressure, they have used their national regulatory authorities to protect domestic ownership of their banks. See *The Economist*, 'Eastern promise', 28 August 1999: 58.
3 Liz Salecka, 'CEE: A land of opportunity', *European Banker*, 18 January 2006: 10.
4 Author's interviews with Anthony Doran and Stefan Kawalec, Warsaw, 1999.
5 Author's interviews with Jan Krzysztof-Bielecki, London, 1999, and Stefan Kawalec, Warsaw, 1999.
6 Author's interviews with Sebastian Vlădescu and Daniel Dăianu, Bucharest, 2004.
7 *European Report*, 'EU/Romania: reluctant reformers chase accession carrot', 22 May 2004.
8 Author's interview with Grzegorz Kołodko, Washington, DC, 2000.
9 The 1999 Accession Partnership with Romania states that from 1998 the European Commission had worked closely with the IFIs and the EBRD to facilitate compliance with pre-accession priorities. The Commission also used data from a range of sources in its annual 'Regular Reports', including from the Bretton Woods institutions (Sasse 2005). Finally, the World Bank and the IMF included in their own publications assessments of how well Romania was doing *vis-à-vis* its EU accession commitments. See, for example, IMF, *Public Information Notice* 06/49, 4 May 2006.

10 'Slovenia – keeping it in the family', *The Banker*, 1 September 2002.
11 For a fuller treatment of these events, see Lindstrom and Piroska (2007). On KBC's pull-out from NLB, see 'Belgian KBC bank reassessing role in Slovene NLB bank is "bad news"', *BBC Monitoring Europe*, 11 May 2006.

REFERENCES

Abarbanell, J. and Bonin, J. (1997) 'Bank privatization in Poland: the case of Bank Śląski', *Journal of Comparative Economics* 25(1): 31–61.
Balcerowicz, E. and Bartkowski, A. (2001) *Restructuring the Development of the Banking Sector in Poland: Lessons to be Learnt by Less Advanced Transition Countries*, Warsaw: Center for Social and Economic Research.
Bank of Slovenia (2006) *Annual Report*, Ljubljana: Bank of Slovenia.
Barth, J.R., Caprio, G. Jr. and Levine, R. (2006) *Rethinking Bank Regulation: Till Angels Govern*, New York: Cambridge University Press.
Bockman, J. and Eyal, G. (2002) 'Eastern Europe as a laboratory for economic knowledge: the transnational roots of neoliberalism', *American Journal of Sociology* 108(2): 310–52.
Bonin, J., Mizsei, K. and Székély, I. (1998) *Banking in Transition Economies: Developing Market Oriented Banking Sectors in Eastern Europe*, Cheltenham: Edward Elgar.
Brown, M. (2004) *Review and Analysis of the Ukrainian Banking Sector*, Washington, DC: United States Treasury.
Cernat, L. (2006) *Europeanization, Varieties of Capitalism and Economic Performance in Central and Eastern Europe*, Basingstoke: Palgrave Macmillan.
Dąbrowski, M. and Antczak, R. (1995) *Economic Transition in Russia, the Ukraine and Belarus in Comparative Perspective*, Warsaw: Center for Social and Economic Research.
Doltu, C. (2002) 'Banking reform in Romania', in Ž. Šević (ed.), *Banking Reforms in South-East Europe*, Cheltenham: Edward Elgar, pp. 285–308.
Duenwald, C., Gueorguiev, N. and Schaechter, A. (2005) *Too Much of a Good Thing? Credit Booms in Transition Economies: The Cases of Bulgaria, Romania and Ukraine*, Washington, DC: International Monetary Fund.
Elborgh-Woytek, K. and Lewis, M. (2002) *Privatization in Ukraine: Challenges of Assessment and Coverage in Fund Conditionality*, Washington, DC: International Monetary Fund.
Epstein, R.A. (2008) *In Pursuit of Liberalism: International Institutions in Postcommunist Europe*, Baltimore, MD: Johns Hopkins University Press.
Epstein, R.A. and Sedelmeier, U. (2008) 'Beyond conditionality: international institutions in postcommunist Europe after enlargement, *Journal of European Public Policy* 15(6): 806–25.
Feldmann, M. (2007) 'The origins of varieties of capitalism: lessons from postsocialist transition in Estonia and Slovenia', in B. Hanké, M. Rhodes and M. Thatcher (eds), *Beyond Varieties of Capitalism*, New York: Oxford University Press, pp. 328–50.
Ghizari, E.I. (1992) 'Banking reform in Romania', in D.M. Kemme and A. Rudka (eds), *Monetary and Banking Reform in Postcommunist Economies*, New York: Institute for East-West Security Studies and Westview Press, pp. 115–22.
Grzymała-Busse, A. (2002) *Redeeming the Communist Past: The Regeneration of Communist Parties in East Central Europe*, New York: Cambridge University Press.
Hanley, E., King, L. and János, I.T. (2002) 'The state, international agencies, and property transformation in postcommunist Hungary', *American Journal of Sociology* 108(1): 129–67.

Hjartarson, J. (2004) 'Foreign banks, domestic networks and the preservation of state capacity in internationalized financial sectors: a study of two transition economies', unpublished manuscript.
International Monetary Fund (2004) *Republic of Slovenia: Financial System Stability Assessment Update, including Reports on the Observance of Standards and Codes on the Following Topics: Banking Supervision and Insurance Supervision*, Washington, DC: International Monetary Fund.
Johnson, J. (2008) 'The remains of conditionality: the faltering enlargement of the euro zone', *Journal of European Public Policy* 15(6): 826–41.
Kelley, J. (2004) *Ethnic Politics in Europe: The Power of Norms and Incentives*, Princeton, NJ: Princeton University Press.
Lindstrom, N. and Piroska, D. (2007) 'The politics of privatization and Europeanization in Europe's periphery: Slovenian banks and breweries for sale?', *Competition & Change* 11(2): 115–33.
National Bank of Poland (2001) *Summary Evaluation of the Financial Situation of Polish Banks*, Warsaw: National Bank of Poland.
OECD (2001) *Ukraine Investment Policy Review: The Legal and Institutional Regime for Investment: Assessment and Policy Recommendations*, Paris: Organization for Economic Co-operation and Development.
Piroska, D. (2005) 'Small post-socialist states and global finance: a comparative study of the internationalization of state roles in banking in Hungary and Slovenia'. Ph.D. dissertation, Department of Political Science, Central European University.
Roe, A., Forgacs, K., Olenchyk, A., Peachey, S., Prigozhina, A., Vlasenko, Y. and Zhyliaev, I. (2001) *Ukraine: The Financial Sector and the Economy*, Washington, DC: World Bank.
Sasse, G. (2005) 'EU conditionality and minority rights: translating the Copenhagen criteria into policy', *EUI Working Paper*, RSCAS No. 2005/16.
Schimmelfennig, F. (2005) 'Strategic calculation and international socialization: membership incentives, party constellation, and sustained compliance in Central and Eastern Europe', *International Organization* 59(4): 827–60.
Sedelmeier, U. (2008) 'After conditionality: post-accession compliance with EU law in East Central Europe', *Journal of European Public Policy* 15(6): 806–25.
Shields, S. (2003) '"Charge of the right brigade": transnational social forces and the neoliberal configuration of Poland's transition', *New Political Economy* 8: 225–44.
Sochan, P. (1996) *The Banking System in Ukraine*, Warsaw: Center for Social and Economic Research.
Tsantis, A. (1997) 'Developments in the Romanian banking sector', in *The New Banking Landscape in Central and Eastern Europe*, Paris: Organization for Economic Co-operation and Development, pp.167–216.
Vachudova, M.A. (2005) *Europe Undivided: Democracy, Leverage, and Integration after Communism*, New York: Oxford University Press.

Out-liberalizing the EU: pension privatization in Central and Eastern Europe

Mitchell A. Orenstein

INTRODUCTION

The pension privatization trend that swept Central and Eastern Europe (CEE) between 1998 and 2004 presents a conundrum when viewed from the perspective of European Union (EU) enlargement. While these reforms took place during the EU accession process, the EU did not use its formidable membership conditionality to impose them on CEE accession states. Quite the contrary, Ferge and Juhász (2004: 234) show that the EU played an 'unduly modest role in shaping CEE social policy during the enlargement,' and little to no role in reforming pension systems in the region (see also Deacon 2000; Vaughan-Whitehead 2003, 152–6; Potůček 2004). Therefore, the rise of pension privatization in CEE cannot be attributed to the 'active leverage' of the EU (Vachudova 2005). The trend towards full or partial replacement of pay-as-you-go pension systems with ones based on private individual pension savings accounts (what I term 'pension privatization') was seen by many experts as an explicit rejection of the European social model and an 'Americanization' of social policy (Ferge and Juhász 2004: 249; Bohle and Greskovits 2006; O'Dwyer and Kovalčík 2007: 4). The question that arises is: if the EU did not demand pension privatization, why did so many CEE countries adopt it just before and during the accession process?

This paper explores the major causal explanations for pension privatization in CEE and argues that this trend was set in motion by a transnational policy campaign led by the World Bank and the the United States Agency for International Development (USAID). It is therefore a case that looks beyond conditionality insofar as there were no explicit EU rules (Epstein and Sedelmeier 2008). For the most part, this campaign relied on norms-teaching and persuasion rather than on hard conditionality. It found fertile ground in CEE for a number of reasons, one of which was that pension privatization differed from EU social policy norms. CEE states did not seek to replicate EU pension systems, but to surpass them by adopting more 'modern' policy advice from the World Bank and USAID. Pension privatization enabled CEE states to signal the rise of a more liberal approach to social welfare issues in the centre and east of the continent.

These findings have substantial implications for the study of Europeanization. First, they suggest that the EU has collaborated with other transnational actors to pursue policy change in new accession states, surrendering some control of the policy agenda in the process. Second, they show that in at least some issue areas, under some conditions, persuasion, rather than conditionality, can be a powerful mechanism of transformation (though see Sasse 2008 and Schimmelfennig 2008 for different findings). Third, they illustrate that an important driver of CEE state policy during the accession process has been the desire to out-liberalize the EU. Out-liberalizing the EU makes sense for two reasons. First, CEE states stand to gain from economic liberalization because they are relatively low-wage, low-cost production zones within the EU. Economic liberalization, by reducing labor costs, fits with their overall development strategy. Second, relatively weak CEE states see out-liberalization as an opportunity to exert political-economic leadership within the EU. By distinguishing themselves as leaders in economic reform, they increase their prominence as members of that group of EU states that wishes to push the EU towards a more liberal economic model. In short, while conditionality has been emphasized as the dominant dynamic of the accession process, it has not been the only game in town. As the impact of conditionality diminishes in coming years, the dynamic of out-liberalization is likely to increase in importance, forcing policy changes throughout the EU.

PENSION PRIVATIZATION

Before exploring causal explanations for the adoption of pension privatization, it is important to describe what pension privatization consists of and how widespread it has become in CEE states. The trend towards pension privatization began in Chile, which in the early 1980s fully replaced its traditional, pay-as-you-go type pension system with one based on privately managed, individual pension savings accounts. In pay-as-you-go pension systems, current taxpayers pay for the retirement benefits of current retirees via a state social security administration. In funded individual-account systems, like the Chilean one, individuals receive a retirement benefit that depends on the amount they have invested in their individual accounts over a lifetime of work and the rate of return on investment minus fees.[1] The fund is managed not by a social security agency but by a private investment company in most cases and is used at the end of the working life to pay for retirement income. Most funds are typically invested in-country, in stocks and government bonds, though a small percentage may be invested abroad. Thus, the means of financing and administration of pension privatization and social security type systems differ greatly. They also differ in their distributive consequences. Whereas many (though not all) pay-as-you-go pension systems redistribute income from wealthier to poorer pensioners, personal private pensions individualize risk and returns. Often, countries seek to combine the benefits of both systems, for instance by partially rather than fully replacing their existing pay-as-you-go system with one based on individual accounts. Therefore, the differences between actual country systems may not be as great as a side-by-side comparison of pay-as-you-go and private, funded systems may suggest. However, the shifts to funding and to individual accounts constitute major changes in pension regulation that have substantial distributive consequences. As a result, they are always controversial both in developing and developed countries.

Nearly 30 countries around the world have adopted pension privatization, mostly since the early 1990s, a remarkable number in such a short time period (see Orenstein 2003 for a comparison of the spread of pension privatization with that of first pension systems since 1889). Twelve of these are countries of CEE and the former Soviet Union. Aside from Latin America, where the pension privatization trend had its start, CEE has been the region of the world most amenable to these reforms. Table 1 provides a list of all countries adopting pension privatization. CEE countries are indicated in bold type.

Table 1 divides reforming countries into three distinct types. Substitutive reforms are those that fully replace social security type systems with ones based on individual, funded pension savings accounts. Mixed reforms, the most common type in CEE states, partially replace the former social security type system with individual accounts. Participants contribute to both a scaled down pay-as-you-go system and to individual pension savings accounts. Parallel reforms also maintain both systems, but allow individuals to choose whether to participate in the individual pension savings account system or not. In CEE mixed systems, it is common for approximately one-third of total contributions to be allocated to pension savings accounts, with the rest going to support the social security type system (European Commission 2003a; Holzmann and Hinz 2005). Though less radical than full substitution, mixed reform still represents a sizable shift in the method of pension financing and retirement outcomes.

Table 1 Types of pension privatization worldwide

Substitutive	Mixed	Parallel
Chile 1981	Sweden 1994	UK 1986
Bolivia 1997	**Hungary 1998**	Peru 1993
Mexico 1997	**Poland 1999**	Argentina 1994
El Salvador 1998	Costa Rica 2001	Colombia 1994
Kazakhstan 1998	**Latvia 2001**	Uruguay 1996
Dom. Rep. 2001	**Bulgaria 2002**	**Estonia 2001**
Nicaragua 2001	**Croatia 2002**	**Lithuania 2002**
Kosovo 2001	**Macedonia 2002**	
Nigeria 2004	**Russia 2002**	
Taiwan 2004	**Slovakia 2003**	
	Romania 2004	
	Uzbekistan 2004	

Sources: Orenstein (2000); Madrid (2003); Müller (2003); Fultz (2004); Palacios (2003); Holzmann and Hinz (2005); Becker et al. (2005); and web resources from World Bank, Inter-American Development Bank (IDB), and USAID.

EXPLAINING PENSION PRIVATIZATION

Europeanization and conditionality

In contrast to other policies adopted in CEE during the accession process, pension privatization cannot be explained by EU active leverage. Many prominent analyses of enlargement show that the 'asymmetric interdependence' (Vachudova 2005) of Western and Eastern Europe and the vast power disparities between the two sides forced CEE states to comply with EU policies through the application of membership conditionality. Moravcsik and Vachudova (2003) argue that CEE accession states need the West European states more than West Europe needs them, and that therefore CEE states have been consistently weaker in membership negotiations. Indeed, these negotiations were barely worthy of the name, since little negotiation took place. Rather, CEE states received the positions of the EU and were asked to make haste to comply. Jacoby (2004, 2008) has used the image of a 'priest and penitent' to describe this impression of the accession process. Humble CEE countries approached the EU as a sinner approaches a priest, hoping for forgiveness for poor policies and advice on how to come closer to the divine. Similarly, Cameron (2003) writes that 'new members will be re-created as states' in the EU accession process, emphasizing the 'transformative power of the EU' (Grabbe 2001). During the accession process, CEE legislatures were forced to adopt dozens of laws with little or no debate in order to comply with EU regulation in numerous areas of policy.

A new literature has emerged that inquires into the 'Europeanization' of CEE and the extent of compliance with the directives of the EU. In this literature, the major emphasis has been placed on conditionality and coercion as tools of influence (Schimmelfennig and Sedelmeier 2004), though some authors also discuss normative suasion as a means that the EU has used to exert influence. Moravcsik and Vachudova (2003) emphasize that membership conditionality has been by far the most powerful tool of the EU in its efforts to gain compliance from CEE new member states. Kelley (2004) shows that conditionality combined with normative appeals have been influential, but that norms alone are rarely enough to encourage compliance with EU minority policies.

Pension privatization, however, does not conform to patterns of 'Europeanization' of either the norms-based or coercive variants. First, as mentioned above, the EU did not attempt to exercise much coercion or even normative influence in CEE pension reforms (Deacon 2000; Potůček 2004: 263). As opposed to other areas of social policy (Sissenich 2007), the EU had no strong or coordinated stance on pension reform in CEE. The EU did not attach hard conditions to the form of pension reform. Consultants hired under the PHARE program to support pension reform efforts in CEE states sometimes opposed pension privatization (as in Hungary, see Orenstein 2000) and sometimes supported it. Deacon suggests that individual consultants were given wide latitude to set their own policy advice (Deacon 2000: 159). In short, pension privatization in CEE states cannot be explained by EU policy conditionality. There was none.

Beyond conditionality

If the EU did not use conditionality to press pension privatization on CEE states, why did so many CEE states adopt it concurrently with the accession process? Any explanation of the pension privatization trend needs to explain this spatial and temporal clustering (Weyland 2005). Scholars propose a number of different explanations. First, they emphasize economic or demographic conditions that facilitated the adoption of pension privatization or made it more appealing. Second, they emphasize the role of domestic political conditions that have favored these reforms. Third, they emphasize the role of non-EU transnational actors on CEE reforming countries. This section explores these competing explanations and argues that while each of these explanations has merit, the rise of pension privatization in CEE cannot be explained without reference to the international campaign for their adoption launched by the World Bank in 1994.

Economic and demographic factors

Some analysts suggest that economic and demographic conditions have made pension privatization particularly desirable or necessary in CEE. In particular, it has been argued that many countries, including those in CEE, face a demographic crisis that will negatively affect pension system finances over the coming years (World Bank 1994; James 1998). As populations in Europe age, the proportion of pension system contributors to beneficiaries decreases.

In order to maintain the same pension levels, payroll taxes and retirement ages need to rise. Otherwise, benefits will have to be cut. Changing to a funded pension system under which each individual relies on his or her own lifetime contributions to fund retirement savings can also reduce reliance on state pension systems and ease their financial crisis. From the perspective of the state budget, privatization relieves governments of a large and (for the foreseeable future) ever-increasing fiscal burden (James 1998; James and Brooks 2001).

While demographic aging is no doubt an important background condition explaining the emerging crisis in pension system finance, it provides only a partial explanation for the rapid spread of pension privatization itself. Pension privatization is not the most obvious solution to fiscal pressures resulting from demographic aging. While pension privatization can help to ameliorate the fiscal effects of an emerging demographic crisis in the long run, in the short and medium run it actually increases pressure on the government budget. This is because, in the transition to a private pension system, the state must continue to pay current pensioners while diverting a part of payroll tax contributions to private, individual accounts. As a result, the government must borrow money to offset these contributions to individual accounts. Yet governments are often expected to respond to short-term, rather than long-term pressures.

Second, empirically, if countries adopted pension privatization in order to stave off a demographic crisis, one would expect to see these reforms adopted primarily in countries most imminently facing such a crisis, i.e. in demographically older countries. However, pension privatization has been enacted in a wide variety of countries with different demographic profiles, ranging from older Baltic countries to younger ones such as Poland (and throughout Latin America). Some of the demographically oldest countries in the world are in Western Europe, but few West European countries have privatized their pension systems, in part because of transition costs. While the possibility of a demographic fiscal crisis may help to explain the propensity to adopt pension privatization in CEE, it does not provide a sufficient explanation for this trend. A demographic crisis can be dealt with in a number of other ways, such as by enacting a phased increase in the retirement age and otherwise reforming existing social security type pension systems (Barr 2005).

Domestic political factors

Another common set of explanations for the adoption of pension privatization is domestic political factors. First, scholars have emphasized the weakness of the political and social backing for communist-era pension systems. This lack of political support arguably provided an opportunity for radical change. Second, O'Dwyer and Kovalčík (2007: 5) note the weakness of CEE party systems and suggest that second-stage economic reforms like pension privatization are more likely in countries with high levels of party volatility and political instability. 'What stands out about the second-generation reformers is the following. They have been parliamentary democracies with weak executives. They have chaotic party systems, whose under-institutionalization weakens vertical accountability between government and voters.' Others have argued that as trade unions and left parties have declined in power, existing pension systems have become more vulnerable to change. Likewise, Brooks (2005) posits that countries with more concentrated political power and fewer veto points are more likely to reform. CEE countries appear to be more likely to adopt radical economic reforms because of relatively weak democratic processes.

Domestic political factors help to explain the propensity to reform in CEE, but like demographic factors they cannot explain the exact nature of the pension privatization trend or its timing. According to theory, domestic political conditions were amenable to reform since 1990 in CEE. Why did pension privatization take place only after 1998? A careful investigation of pension reforms in CEE countries reveals that nearly all countries in the region indeed reformed their pension systems soon after 1990 without adopting pension privatization (Orenstein 2000). Instead, most countries increased payroll taxes and reduced benefits in a fairly ad hoc manner. They did not initially enact or in most cases even consider pension privatization. This suggests that while domestic politics can help to understand why pension shifts were possible, they cannot explain the direction of these changes.

Social learning

In order to explain the exact nature and timing of pension privatization in CEE, rather than a general propensity to reform, it is necessary to consider external social learning factors. There are two variants: non-hierarchical and hierarchical social learning. Weyland (2005) exemplifies the non-hierarchical explanation. Weyland suggests that the reason why policy-makers have adopted these reforms is that when faced with the demographic, economic, and political factors that together constitute a pension system 'crisis,' they have tended to look to neighboring countries for solutions. This helps to explain why neighboring countries adopt similar reforms at around the same point in time. However, Weyland's argument, which was developed to explain the Latin American countries, misses some important features of the CEE experience. First, whereas in Latin America, there was a clear regional reform example, Chile, in CEE there was none, at least not prior to 1998. Where did the CEE first movers, Poland and Hungary, find their inspiration? To answer this question, one must address the role of transnational actors in CEE pension reforms.

Transnational policy campaign

Pension privatization came to CEE as part of a transnational policy campaign led by the World Bank but with additional participation from a host of international, bilateral, multilateral, and independent transnational organizations. USAID was particularly influential in CEE, providing extensive resources to reforming countries for planning and implementation over multiple years. The Organization for Economic Cooperation and Development (OECD) supported these reforms as well through conferences, technical support, and training. These efforts were complemented by those of independent reform entrepreneurs such as José Piñera, the Labour Minister who first implemented private accounts in Chile. Piñera has spent many years advising CEE politicians on pension privatization, through individual meetings with leaders such as Vladimir Putin and much longer, more involved consultation with reform designers in Croatia, for instance. Piñera attests to being involved at some level in most CEE reforming countries (author interview, 2006).

Piñera's work in Slovakia has been extensively documented in a book published by the F.A. Hayek Foundation in Bratislava, part of a worldwide network of liberal think-tanks (Oravec 2006: 28–43). Piñera arranged a four-day visit to Slovakia together with the F.A. Hayek Foundation just as the idea of pension reform came to the political agenda in Slovakia. During his visit, he gave the annual lecture of the Foundation, attended an international conference on pension reforms organized by the Foundation, attended the presentation of the Hayek Foundation's reform proposal, which Piñera had advised on, and made several TV appearances and visits with politicians from various parties. Piñera is a deeply influential and charismatic public speaker and his visit made a strong impact on publicity and on politicians in support of pension privatization (Oravec 2006: 32). Piñera continued to advise his local contacts from afar as they made crucial decisions about the pension reform agenda. He returned to Slovakia for an additional visit at a critical point in the legislative balance, helping to tip legislators in favor of his preferred reform design. This appears to be a typical example of his work in many CEE countries.

While Piñera had been active in promoting pension privatization in Latin America and other countries outside of CEE since the early 1980s, the transnational campaign for pension privatization received a major boost in 1994 with the publication of the World Bank's report, *Averting the Old Age Crisis* (World Bank 1994). This report was commissioned by Chief Economist Larry Summers under the direction of research director Nancy Birdsall. Led by economist Estelle James, the *Averting* project gathered together a core group of World Bank economists who later formed the kernel of the Bank's policy advisory group on pensions. Prior to *Averting*, pensions had not been a core area of the Bank's work. However, with the transition in CEE and demographic aging in other parts of the developing world, the Bank decided to put greater emphasis on pension systems, given their large fiscal ramifications. Most OECD countries, for instance, spend between 5 and 15 percent of gross domestic product (GDP) on pensions. Developing countries tend to spend less, though CEE countries generally fall in the OECD range. Poland and Slovenia have been at the high end of the OECD range.

The reform model advanced in *Averting* represented a substantial innovation in pension reform thinking. It promoted what it termed a 'multi-pillar' approach to pension systems, incorporating a basic, redistributive state system, a second pillar based on individual pension savings accounts, and a third, voluntary occupational system. This departed from the Chilean model, insofar as it did not call for a complete replacement of previous social security type systems, but rather a reduction in them, carving out space for private, individual accounts. These accounts were argued to be the best way to provide an income-related benefit. In addition, funded accounts were said to provide a pool of investment capital for developing countries, creating a spur to economic growth that would help all people, including retirees, over time. *Averting* signaled the launch of a major transnational campaign for pension privatization, fueled by the tremendous legitimacy, international presence, and substantial resources of the World Bank.

The World Bank began vigorously promoting its multi-pillar model in CEE starting in 1994. Prior to that date, there is little evidence that CEE countries considered pension privatization. The only instance of a CEE government even considering funded accounts took place in 1991 in Poland, where the director of the social security administration, ZUS, wrote a brief proposal for a funded pension system in Poland. Interestingly, this proposal was quashed by the World Bank social policy specialist in Poland at the time, Nick Barr, a renowned pension economist. Barr had been hired to work on pension issues in CEE and opposed private pensions (see Barr 2005). The fact that World Bank opposition to reform in Poland prevented these reforms from going ahead attests to just how important World Bank support was to the implementation of these reforms in later years. World Bank and other international support was a necessary condition for the spread of pension privatization in CEE.

World Bank and USAID support for pension privatization in Poland and Hungary was particularly intensive. As in other countries in CEE, the World Bank provided training and recruitment sessions for government officials interested in pension privatization at locations in Washington DC, Harvard and Oxford Universities. These seminars acquainted leading pension officials with information and norms supportive of pension privatization. In addition, the World Bank and USAID funded government reform teams who undertook to plan reforms in particular countries, providing resources that enabled them to make pension privatization a serious priority. In Poland, the World Bank released one of its key pension reform advisers, Michał Rutkowski, to work for the Polish government as head of the office of the plenipotentiary for pension reform, the key office charged with formulating reform proposals. In Hungary, the World Bank seconded two high-level employees to work for periods of six months or more with the Hungarian inter-ministerial working group planning reform. These officials were involved in a detailed manner with the discussion within the government and with stakeholders outside the government in reform negotiations. Ferge and Juhász (2004: 244) go so far as to say that the World Bank, 'forced its "multi-pillar" system onto the agenda' in Hungary. USAID provided funding for public relations campaigns to ensure diffuse public support for reform. This included training a cadre of journalists to understand pension privatization issues and sending journalists and parliamentarians on study trips to Latin America to learn about the benefits of pension privatization. USAID further provided several years of technical assistance for reform implementation, helping to establish regulatory agencies and regulations for the control of pension fund managers.

Technical and policy assistance from a range of transnational policy actors was a necessary factor for reform in CEE reforming states. Reforms in particular countries also responded to domestic interest group pressures and political conditions. However, these reforms would not have happened throughout CEE without the well-organized transnational policy campaign led by the World Bank, but including other agencies and individuals as partners, including USAID, the OECD, the International Monetary Fund (IMF), and individual consultants and policy entrepreneurs. Transnational actors helped to put pension privatization on the reform agenda in CEE countries and provided the resources for governments to follow through with the development and implementation of reform programs.

EU tacit support

While the EU did not take direct part in the transnational campaign for pension privatization in CEE, it did play an indirect role. Transnational actors tend to coordinate with one another (Orenstein 2008) and it was only natural that officials of the World Bank and the OECD consulted with the EU as they pursued pension privatization in CEE states. The EU considered these reforms and debated them in top policy circles. Ultimately, the EU did not take a definitive stance on pension privatization, disappointing many who would have liked to see the EU promote a European social model that would oppose pension privatization (Deacon 2000: 159; Ferge and Juhász 2004; Vaughan-Whitehead 2003). Instead, the EU took a passive approach that reflected differences of opinion within the EU. However, passivity differs from neutrality. In this case, the EU did not impose conditionality for pension reform, but by staying out of the way, it left the pensions field open to the transnational campaign organized by the World Bank.

Internal EU debates on pension privatization are reflected in several documents produced during the accession process. In particular, the 2001 Economic Policy Committee 'Report on Budgetary Challenges Posed by Ageing Populations' argued for increased reliance on private pensions in the EU (EPC 2001). This report was endorsed by the powerful Economic and Financial Affairs (ECOFIN) Council. In the same year, the Social Protection Committee 'Report on the Future Evolution of Social Protection' (SPC 2001) called for further modernization of pension systems in the EU and indicated a role for pension privatization, without advocating any particular reforms. This latter document became the basis for further discussions among member states within the context of the open method of coordination (OMC) on pensions and was later published in a modified form as a Joint Commission/Council Report on Adequate and Sustainable Pensions (European Commission 2003b).

The joint report on adequate and sustainable pensions reflected a compromise between the Economic Policy and Social Protection Committees' position on a number of issues, including the role of pension privatization (Nanz and de la Porte 2004; Schludi 2003). The word 'adequate' seems to represent the social side and the word 'sustainable' the economic one. The joint report noted that private funding of pensions can reduce 'pressures for public expenditure increases' in the face of demographic aging and thus help to improve financial sustainability (European Commission 2003b: 8). The report also noted the severe problems of West European pension systems and called for 'modernization' of pension arrangements, though it stopped short of advocating any single model of reform.

In effect, by not coming out against the transnational campaign for pension privatization, the EU lent it tacit support. The Economic Policy Council and ECOFIN were well aware that the World Bank had launched this campaign in CEE states. By making comforting noises in Brussels and preventing the EU from explicitly opposing it, they created the impression that the EU would accept CEE countries which adopted pension privatization. This conclusion is reinforced by evidence that the EU coordinated its (in)action with the World Bank. According to an official World Bank document entitled, 'European Union accession and the World Bank' (World Bank 2004), the World Bank during the accession process 'helped the EU8 in modernizing social services and meeting other development goals. Although not governed by the *acquis*, the World Bank's support in these areas was closely coordinated with the EU Commission.' Both World Bank and USAID officials clearly interpreted the EU stance as being broadly supportive of their pension privatization efforts (interview with Denise Lamaute, pension team leader, USAID).

Interviews with government leaders in Slovakia provide further insight into the relation between the EU and World Bank in pension privatization in CEE states. Slovakia privatized its pension system in 2003 as part of a wave of neoliberal economic reforms undertaken by Finance Minister Ivan Mikloš. According to the chief economic adviser to the Finance Minister responsible for pension reform, Martin Bruncko, the EU exerted no direct influence on pension privatization in Slovakia. It was an important background force, since its conditionality had helped to oust the government of Vladimir Mečiar and make possible the liberal economic policies of the Dzurinda government that followed. However, the EU gave no specific advice on pension reform nor was it seriously considered in government efforts to prepare the reform. Instead, Slovakia based its pension privatization model on the advice of the World Bank and the OECD, which had prepared a set of pension reform recommendations for Slovakia in 2001–02. The IMF also helped with pension projections (interview, June 13, 2007). According to Peter Golias, a member of the Slovak government working group for pension reform, the World

Bank played a major role in Slovakia's reform, producing econometric models of the costs of reform. World Bank officials Augusto Iglesias and Hermann von Gersdorff stayed for several months in Slovakia to work on all aspects of pension reform planning, legislation, and implementation. The World Bank also provided financing for the Slovak government's pension reform working group (interview, June 13, 2007). State Secretary of Labor Miroslav Beblavy confirms that the EU had no direct influence on pension privatization in Slovakia beyond trying to enforce the Maastricht criteria for public finance. He went so far as to say that the 'EU is a content neutral organization' in labor market and social policy (interview, June 14, 2007). However, inaction should not be confused for neutrality. By staying out of the way, the EU gave a green light to pension privatization in CEE states during the accession process.

In this way, pension privatization can be seen as an example of EU 'passive leverage' on CEE (Vachudova 2005). Just by being there, the EU exerted a subtle (and for some officials unintentional) influence on CEE states to adopt pension privatization, a policy that was expected to help CEE countries compete economically within the EU.

OUT-LIBERALIZING THE EU

Pension privatization in CEE states can be explained by a combination of factors. Economic transition, demographic trends, and political instability created unusually favorable conditions for radical economic reform. This made CEE fertile ground for a transnational policy campaign led by the World Bank starting in 1994. Once several leading CEE states adopted pension privatization in 1998, others quickly followed suit. The EU supported the transnational campaign for pension privatization by staying out of the way while the World Bank took the lead.

Yet the question still remains, why did CEE states feel that pension privatization was a worthwhile policy innovation at a time of EU accession? It could be argued that CEE states had enough on their agendas with passing the large quantity of legislation required to enact the *acquis communautaire*. Why did they feel compelled to add to this agenda by adopting radical pension reforms at the same time?

To explain the relation between EU accession and the adoption of pension privatization in CEE, one additional factor needs to be considered: the fit between pension privatization and the liberal economic development strategies adopted by governments in CEE since 1989 (Orenstein 2001). Since 1989, economic policy in CEE states has been dominated by liberal governments which come to power periodically determined to enact reforms that will wipe out all traces of communism and significantly liberalize the economic environment. At the time of EU accession, CEE liberals (such as Czech President Vàclav Klaus) expressed concerns that EU accession would require a re-regulation of the economy that might conflict with their goals of economic liberalization. While

CEE liberals came to accept EU accession, they did so with the hope of pushing the EU as a whole towards a more liberal policy regime.

Pension privatization was attractive for CEE government leaders not because it conformed to an EU model, but because it helped to distinguish CEE states as policy leaders in economic liberalization. CEE states were attempting to out-liberalize the EU. They had two motives for this. First, pension privatization enabled CEE states to cope with demographic aging in a way that signaled their commitment to a liberal economic environment and to low labor costs, an important feature of these countries' comparative advantage within and outside the EU. Like other second-stage reforms, pension privatization was intended to make Central European markets more attractive and to tap 'investment flows opened up by accession to the European Union' (O'Dwyer and Kovalčík 2007: 4). Second, out-liberalizing the EU also promised to turn CEE states from poor cousins into respected policy leaders at a time when the rest of the EU was failing to implement the Lisbon agenda on economic reform. For weak CEE states humiliated by the process of accession, out-liberalization created an opportunity to strengthen their hands within the EU.

Pension privatization fit closely with CEE liberal reformers' preferred economic development strategy. It is no secret that CEE states have pursued a low-wage, low-cost development strategy since 1989, seeking to become low-cost production hubs benefiting from inclusion in the EU. This strategy has netted substantial rewards in terms of inward investment and high growth rates in recent years. In just one instance, Nokia in 2008 decided to move one of its major mobile phone production facilities out of Bochum, Germany, laying off 2,300 workers, and creating a new 60 million euro plant that could employ as many as 3,500 workers in Cluj, Romania (*Financial Times*, January 15, 2008: 20). Wages in Romania are approximately one-tenth of those in Germany. In order to maintain low labor costs, CEE states have liberalized their formerly highly regulated labor markets to a much greater extent than most countries in Western Europe. CEE states are now not only cheaper, but also considerably more liberal in terms of hiring, firing, work conditions, inward investment (Epstein 2008), and safety regulation (Crowley 2006).

Pension privatization provided CEE liberals with an opportunity to signal a good business climate and economic liberalism in an area that has a substantial impact on labour costs. CEE states sent a strong signal to investors that they were working to prevent the rapid growth of non-wage labor costs. It did not matter that these reforms were not tried and tested in Western Europe. The point was to enact reforms that would differ from the high-labor-cost strategies of West European countries.

Furthermore, CEE government officials saw pension privatization and other liberal reforms as an opportunity to exert policy leadership within the EU. Committed to a more liberal policy agenda than is the norm in the EU, CEE liberals have sought to influence EU policy, in part by enacting liberal reforms at home. These reforms then influence the EU in several ways, through public information, by putting pressure on labor costs in Western Europe, and through policy discourse. As one example, chief adviser Martin Bruncko notes that Slovakia's adoption of the flat tax (at the same time as pension privatization) has had an impact on other EU states. He points out that corporate tax rates began to drop more sharply in Europe with the advent of the 19 percent flat tax in Slovakia and that pension reforms in Central Europe bolstered the confidence of liberals within other EU governments (interview, June 13, 2007). Vladimir Dlouhy, former Economy Minister of the Czech Republic now working for Goldman Sachs, also said that 'we believed that the EU would change' as a result of the accession of the new Central European member states, pushing it in a more liberal direction. However, he opined that this 'didn't happen ... a big disappointment for me' (interview, June 26, 2007). Yet CEE liberals continue to try. Liberal reforms help to make CEE states more attractive for inward investment and push the rest of the EU towards further liberalization. This can result in greater recognition of CEE states as reform leaders and increase their status in ways that are important for economic development, national stature and security.

This pattern of behavior presents a very different model of EU influence on CEE state policy than that posited by most of the literature on accession. Rather than CEE states being forced to more or less implement EU directives under threat of coercion, the case of pension privatization suggests that CEE countries have responded to EU accession by seeking out policy initiatives that allow them to distinguish themselves from EU norms and gain comparative advantage in areas where they have room to maneuver outside the *acquis*.

IMPLICATIONS: COOPERATION, PERSUASION, AND COMPARATIVE ADVANTAGE

The dynamics of pension privatization in CEE states have had little to do with EU conditionality. The EU, without strong *acquis* in this area, left the field of pension reform assistance in CEE states in the hands of a campaign led by the World Bank. This raises some interesting questions about the ways that the EU has cooperated with other transnational actors during the accession process.

As in several other areas of policy, the EU effectively delegated its authority to other actors and left them to pursue their programs of policy advice relatively independently during the accession process. Vachudova (2008), looking at different policy areas, interprets this to mean that the EU has effectively bolstered the effectiveness of other transnational actors during the accession process. CEE states may follow the advice of the Council of Europe or the Organization for Security and Cooperation in Europe (OSCE) High Commissioner, but only because the EU's membership conditionality says that they must. However, the case of pension reform is different. Here, the EU did not enforce any strong conditionality. Instead, the EU Commission deferred to the World Bank, OECD, and USAID and allowed them to pursue their campaign for pension privatization, agreeing that such reforms would not compromise membership, though they were not required. Further comparative research is needed on the ways that the EU coordinates with other transnational actors in policy reform and the impact that this may have in the absence of membership conditionality.

In a separate study (Orenstein 2008), I hypothesize that transnational actors, including the EU, often lack the resources to regulate and monitor the wide (and often increasing) areas of their authority. Therefore, they coordinate where possible with other organizations in the pursuit of broader transnational campaigns. This coordination is dictated by resource constraints and governed by 'donor conferences' and other informal methods of coordination. It allows for a division of labor between transnational actors committed to broad policy campaigns. However, it also means that transnational actors are forced to rely on other organizations within their sphere of behavior and delegate substantial authority to them in goal-setting, strategy, and tactics.

In addition to considering the ways that transnational actors collaborate with one another, this study suggests that conditionality is far from the only manner in which transnational actors have affected policy in CEE states during the accession process. The World Bank-led coalition succeeded largely through the mechanism of persuasion, devoting enormous resources to policy studies, recruitment of officials, and other means of convincing CEE states to adopt pension privatization. While there are undoubtedly many conditions and policy areas in which persuasion may not work, the success of the campaign for pension privatization suggests that persuasion should not be discounted as a method of influence.

Influence through persuasion does not operate the same way as influence through conditionality. Conditionality can provide better chances to get recalcitrant officials to comply with transnational actor agendas in a shorter period of time. Persuasion strategies may work better when domestic officials are more predisposed to being persuaded, for instance because they share a similar liberal outlook (Johnson 2008). Therefore, campaigns of persuasion may take a longer period of time. Transnational actors may have to have the resources to wait until liberal-oriented governments come to power and then press their advantage through 'windows of opportunity' for liberal policy innovation. But the success of the campaign for pension privatization in CEE states suggests that this can be done effectively. High-profile policy reforms in neighboring states can also be a highly effective means of persuading policy-makers to comply with transnational actor agendas as countries try not to be left behind.

This brings us to the issue of policy competition. I have presented some evidence to suggest that part of the reason for the adoption of pension privatization in CEE states has been a policy dynamic driven by competitiveness pressures. CEE states seek to distinguish themselves by economic liberalism, signaling a positive climate for inward investment. Pension privatization adds to this image of economic liberalism because these reforms are promoted by the World Bank and allied organizations, and helps to distinguish CEE states from Western Europe. It also helps CEE states to pursue its low-wage, low-cost development strategy within the EU.

It will be interesting to observe over the coming decade the extent to which CEE states are able to exert policy leadership within the EU by following avant-garde policies of economic liberalization. By adopting more liberal economic policies, it is possible that CEE states will push other EU members towards greater market liberalization. This effect has already been visible in the accelerated drive to cut corporate income taxes, and it may become more visible in pension reform through the impact of the OMC. As CEE states achieve and possibly maintain high levels of economic growth in coming years, their liberal policies may gain credence and be emulated, at least in part, by older EU member states.

While the EU accession process often looked like a forceful imposition of *acquis* legislation under the threat of membership conditionality, in the area of pension reform, CEE countries adopted policies that are largely outside of EU practice and represent the forefront of liberal economic policy-making. As membership conditionality ends, this dynamic of competitive out-liberalization may become more influential as a driver of policy throughout the expanded EU.

NOTE

1 Note that the government of Michelle Bachelet launched an effort to revise the Chilean pension system in 2006 to provide greater protection for the poor and those with shorter working histories. While the proposed changes are significant, current plans do not involve a dismantling of the private pension fund system or a return to a pay-as-you-go social security type system.

REFERENCES

Barr, N. (ed.) (2005) *Labor Markets and Social Policy in Central and Eastern Europe: The Accession and Beyond*, Washington, DC: The World Bank.

Becker, C.M., Seitenova, A. and Urzhumova, D. (2005) 'Pension reform in Central Asia: an overview', *PIE Discussion Paper Series*, Tokyo: Hitotsubashi University.

Bohle, D. and Greskovits, B. (2006) 'Capitalism without compromise: strong business and weak labor in Eastern Europe's new international industries', *Studies in Comparative International Development* 41(1): 3–25.

Brooks, S.M. (2005) 'Interdependent and domestic foundations of policy change: the diffusion of pension privatization around the world', *International Studies Quarterly* 49: 273–94.

Cameron, D. (2003) 'The challenges of accession', *East European Politics and Societies* 17(1): 24–41.

Crowley, S. (2006) 'East European labor and the challenge to Europe's "social model"'. Paper presented at the annual meeting of the American Political Science Association, Philadelphia, PA, August 31.

Deacon, B. (2000) 'Eastern European welfare states: the impact of the politics of globalization', *Journal of European Social Policy* 10, 146–61.

Economic Policy Committee (2001) 'Report on Budgetary Challenges Posed by Ageing Populations: the Impact on Public Spending on Pensions, Health and Long-Term Care for the Elderly and Possible Indicators of the Long-Term Sustainability of Public Finances', Brussels: European Commission.

Epstein, R.A. (2008) 'Transnational actors and bank privatization', in M.A. Orenstein, S. Bloom and N. Lindstrom (eds), *Transnational Actors in Central and East European Transitions*, Pittsburgh: University of Pittsburgh Press.

Epstein, R.A. and Sedelmeier, U. (2008) 'Beyond conditionality: international institutions in postcommunist Europe after enlargement', *Journal of European Public Policy*, 15(6): 795–805.

European Commission (2003a) *Social Protection in the 13 Candidate Countries: A Comparative Analysis*, Brussels: Directorate-General for Employment and Social Affairs Unit E.2.

European Commission (2003b) *Adequate and Sustainable Pensions: Joint Report by the Commission and the Council*, Brussels: Directorate-General for Employment and Social Affairs Unit E.2.

Ferge, Z. and Juhász, G. (2004) 'Accession and social policy: the case of Hungary', *Journal of European Social Policy* 14, 233–51.

Financial Times (2008) 'Nokia to shift German jobs to Romania', January 15.

Fultz, E. (2004) 'Pension reform in the EU accession countries: challenges, achievements, and pitfalls', *International Social Security Review* 57(2): 3–24.

Grabbe, H. (2001) 'How does Europeanization affect CEE governance? Conditionality, diffusion and diversity' *Journal of European Public Policy* 8(6): 1013–31.

Holzmann, R. and Hinz, R. (2005) *Old Age Income Support in the 21st Century: An International Perspective on Pension Systems and Reform*, Washington, DC: The World Bank.

Jacoby, W. (2004) *The Enlargement of the European Union and NATO: Ordering from the Menu in Central Europe*, Cambridge: Cambridge University Press.

Jacoby, W. (2008) 'Minority traditions and postcommunist politics: how do IGOs matter?', in M.A. Orenstein, S. Bloom and N. Lindstrom (eds), *Transnational Actors in Central and East European Transitions*, Pittsburgh: University of Pittsburgh Press.

James, E. (1998) 'The political economy of social security reform: a cross-country review', *Annals of Public and Comparative Economics* 69(4): 451–82.

James, E. and Brooks, S.M. (2001) 'The political economy of structural pension reform', in R. Holzmann and J.E. Stiglitz (eds), *New Ideas about Old Age Security: Toward Sustainable Pension Systems in the 21st Century*, Washington, DC: The World Bank.

Johnson, J. (2008) 'Two-track diffusion and central bank embeddedness: the politics of euro adoption in Hungary and the Czech Republic', in M.A. Orenstein, S. Bloom and N. Lindstrom (eds), *Transnational Actors in Central and East European Transitions*, Pittsburgh: University of Pittsburgh Press.

Kelley, J. (2004) *Ethnic Politics in Europe: The Power of Norms and Incentives*, Princeton, NJ: Princeton University Press.

Madrid, R.L. (2003) *Retiring the State: The Politics of Pension Privatization in Latin America and Beyond*, Stanford, CA: Stanford University Press.

Moravcsik, A. and Vachudova, M. (2003) 'National interests, state power, and EU enlargement', *East European Politics and Societies* 17(1): 42–57.

Müller, K. (2003) *Privatising Old-Age Security: Latin America and Eastern Europe Compared*, Aldershot: Edward Elgar.

Nanz, P. and de la Porte, C. (2004) 'The OMC – a deliberative-democratic mode of governance? The cases of employment and pensions', *Journal of European Public Policy* 11(2): 267–88.

O'Dwyer, C. and Kovalčík, B. (2007) 'And the last shall be first: Party system institutionalization and second-generation economic reform in postcommunist Europe', *Studies in Comparative International Development* 41(4): 3–26.

Oravec, M. (2006) *The Story of the Creation of Personal Retirement Accounts in Slovakia*, Bratislava: F.A. Hayek Foundation.

Orenstein, M.A. (2000) *How Politics and Institutions Affect Pension Reform in Three Postcommunist Countries*, World Bank Policy Research Working Paper 2310, Washington, DC: The World Bank.

Orenstein, M.A. (2001) *Out of the Red: Building Capitalism and Democracy in Postcommunist Europe*, Ann Arbor: University of Michigan Press.

Orenstein, M. (2003) 'Mapping the diffusion of pension innovation', in R. Holzmann, M. Orenstein and M. Rutkowski (eds), *Pension Reform in Europe: Process and Progress*, Washington, DC: The World Bank.

Orenstein, M. (2008) *Privatizing Pensions: The Transnational Campaign for Social Security Reform*, Princeton, NJ: Princeton University Press.

Palacios, R. (2003) *Pension Reform in the Dominican Republic*, Social Protection Discussion Paper 0326, Washington, DC: The World Bank.

Potůček, M. (2004) 'Accession and social policy: the case of the Czech Republic', *Journal of European Social Policy* 14(3): 253–66.

Sasse, G. (2008) 'The politics of EU conditionality: the norm of minority protection during and beyond EU accession', *Journal of European Public Policy* 15(6): 842–60.

Schimmelfennig, F. (2008) 'EU political accession conditionality after the 2004 enlargement: consistency and effectiveness', *Journal of European Public Policy*, 15(6): 918–37.

Schimmelfennig, F. and Sedelmeier, U. (2004) 'Governance by conditionality: EU rule transfer to the candidate countries of Central and Eastern Europe', *Journal of European Public Policy* 11(4): 661–79.

Schludi, M. (2003) 'Chances and limitations of 'benchmarking' in the reform of welfare state structures – the case of pension policy', Paper presented at the Amsterdams Instituut voor ArbeidsStudies, May 8. Accessed online at: http://eucenter.wisc.edu/OMC/Papers/Protection/schludi.pdf

Sissenich, B. (2007) *Building States without Society: European Union Enlargement and the Transfer of EU Social Policy to Poland and Hungary*, Plymouth: Lexington Books.

Social Protection Committee (2001) 'Adequate and Sustainable Pensions: A Report by the Social Protection Committee to the Gothenburg European Council on the Future Evolution of Social Protection', Brussels: European Commission.

Vachudova, M. (2005) *Europe Undivided*, Oxford: Oxford University Press.

Vachudova, M. (2008) 'The European Union: the causal behemoth of transnational influence on postcommunist politics', in M.A. Orenstein, S. Bloom and N. Lindstrom (eds), *Transnational Actors in Central and East European Transitions*, Pittsburgh: University of Pittsburgh Press.

Vaughan-Whitehead, D. (2003) *EU Enlargement versus Social Europe? The Uncertain Future of the European Social Model*, Cheltenham: Edward Elgar.

Weyland, K. (2005) 'Theories of policy diffusion: lessons from Latin American pension reform' *World Politics* 57(2): 262–95.

World Bank (1994) *Averting the Old Age Crisis: Policies to Protect the Old and Promote Growth*, Oxford: Oxford University Press.

World Bank (2004) 'European Union accession and the World Bank'. Accessed at: http://lnweb18.worldbank.org/eca/eca.nsf/66d6f5004ed085ca852567d10011a8b8/b8c2e0cb892bc86e85256e7b007150e8?OpenDocument (January 16, 2008).

EU political accession conditionality after the 2004 enlargement: consistency and effectiveness

Frank Schimmelfennig

INTRODUCTION

Enlargement is often claimed to be the most successful foreign policy of the European Union (EU). It is considered to have contributed to democratic consolidation, respect for human rights, minority protection, conflict resolution, and stability in Eastern Europe. The EU's political accession conditionality has been the cornerstone of this success. By making a highly attractive external incentive – the benefits coming with membership – conditional on democracy, human rights, and peaceful conflict management, the EU has induced its would-be members to conform to these political norms. There is widespread agreement in the literature that a credible conditional EU membership perspective is indeed a necessary condition for the EU to bring about substantial domestic change. In order to be effective, however, EU conditionality has to fall on fertile domestic ground. In particular, when the political costs of compliance are high for the target government, that is, when fulfilling EU conditions threatens the survival of the regime or the government, even credible membership incentives prove ineffective.

In light of these findings, recent developments in the EU and its neighbouring countries give reason to doubt whether the EU will be able to continue this successful policy into the future (see also Epstein and Sedelmeier 2008). First, the EU is reluctant to extend a membership perspective to further countries. According to its 2006 enlargement strategy, the EU will be 'cautious about assuming any new commitments' (Commission 2006). In addition, even existing commitments to Turkey and the Western Balkans have come under pressure from relevant member states. After 2004, 'enlargement fatigue' has been seen as the prevailing mood in Brussels, in many member state capitals, and among EU citizens. The emphasis on 'integration capacity', the exit options contained in the EU's Negotiating Framework for accession negotiations with Turkey, and the fact that future enlargements may be put to a referendum in France and possibly other countries (such as Austria in the case of Turkish membership) seem to indicate that new candidates for membership face more uncertainty and higher hurdles than previous applicants. These developments are likely to reduce the credibility of the membership perspective on which the effectiveness of EU political conditionality has been based in the past. Finally, the grave domestic political problems of most of the remaining non-member countries in Eastern and South-eastern Europe (including the legacies of ethnic conflict and widespread corruption) call into question their ability and willingness to fulfil the conditions, even if the EU was open to admitting them in principle. Recent events confirm the strains and frictions: the start of accession negotiations with Croatia was postponed for half a year in 2005; accession negotiations with Turkey were partially suspended in December 2006; and association negotiations with Serbia were frozen between May 2006 and June 2007.

This article examines whether the EU's political accession conditionality and the conditions of its impact have changed in recent years. Does the EU still link progress toward accession consistently with progress toward democratic consolidation, or does it discriminate against those countries that still remain outside the EU? Have the recent problems in accession conditionality been caused by a change in EU policy or can they be attributed to unfavourable domestic conditions in the target countries? Finally, on a more theoretical level, does recent evidence cast doubt on or confirm our knowledge of EU political accession conditionality and the conditions of its impact?

The results are twofold. On the one hand, I show that EU enlargement policy has remained consistently linked to compliance with basic democratic norms in the target countries. The EU has thus not discriminated against the latecomers of democratization. On the other hand, however, the legacy of ethnic conflict in the former Yugoslavia and Cyprus creates domestic obstacles to effective political conditionality. EU conditions such as co-operation with the International Criminal Tribunal for the former Yugoslavia (ICTY) at The Hague and between the ethnic groups in Bosnia-Herzegovina, the future status of Kosovo, and Turkey's recognition of the Republic of Cyprus are related to issues of national identity that put potentially high political costs of compliance on the target governments and have been responsible for the recent problems in the enlargement process. Whereas these legacies do, indeed, complicate enlargement and reduce the effectiveness of political accession conditionality, their effects highlight the continuing relevance of credible membership incentives and domestic political costs and are thus consistent with established theory.

The remainder of the article is organized as follows. In the next section, I present propositions on the conditions of effective political conditionality that are informed by recent research on eastern enlargement and that will serve as guiding hypotheses for the subsequent empirical study. The following two sections analyse the normative consistency of the EU's political accession conditionality by studying the eligibility of non-member countries and discrimination in the EU's enlargement policy. Subsequently, I analyse the conditions of effectiveness in three recent problematic cases of political conditionality: Croatia, Serbia, and Turkey.

EU POLITICAL CONDITIONALITY: CONDITIONS OF SUCCESS

Recent research has generated a rich body of empirical studies on the use and effects of EU political conditionality in Central and Eastern Europe as well as other neighbouring countries such as Cyprus and Turkey. It has also produced quite consistent findings regarding the conditions of success (see Kubicek 2003; Kelley 2004; Pridham 2005; Schimmelfennig and Sedelmeier 2005; Vachudova 2005; Schimmelfennig et al. 2006). Most generally, the effectiveness of political conditionality depends on an interaction of international (EU) and domestic factors.

On the part of the EU, the size and kind of international incentives for compliance are crucial, and nothing short of a credible conditional accession perspective has proven effective. Non-material incentives and mechanisms of social learning such as imitation, persuasion, or social influence do not generally overcome domestic resistance against the adoption of democratic and human rights norms. Even material incentives below the threshold of EU membership – such as financial aid or association agreements – are too weak (Kelley 2004; Vachudova 2005; Schimmelfennig et al. 2006). In addition, accession conditionality has to be credible in two ways: target states need to be certain that they are rewarded with significant steps toward accession (soon) after complying with the EU's political conditions – and that they will be excluded from EU membership otherwise.

In other words, credible conditionality requires normative consistency (see also Johnson 2008). First, and in line with Article 49 of the Treaty on European Union (TEU), the EU ought to offer a general membership perspective to 'any European state' adhering to the fundamental political 'principles of liberty, democracy, respect for human rights and fundamental freedoms, and the rule of law norms' (Article 6, TEU). In making its enlargement decisions, then, the EU ought to be guided only by the democratic and human rights performance of the target countries and it ought not to discriminate against any country either positively or negatively on the basis of other considerations.[1]

Credible accession conditionality, however, is only a necessary but not a sufficient condition of EU success. It has to be accompanied by favourable domestic conditions. In her analysis of ethnic politics in Central and Eastern Europe, Kelley finds that 'authoritarian leadership or strong nationalist opposition in parliament decreases and sometimes even blocks institutional success' (2004: 175). Vachudova shows that, for 'illiberal ruling elites in Romania, Bulgaria, and Slovakia, complying with EU membership requirements was too costly, undermining their hold on power' (2005: 4). Likewise, the comparative analysis of Schimmelfennig, *et al.* revealed that domestic political adaptation costs threatening the security or integrity of the state, or the survival of the regime or the government, were an obstacle to compliance even in the presence of credible membership incentives. Only in the final phases of negotiations on opening or concluding accession talks ('the endgame') did governments comply even in the face of substantial but short-term domestic power costs (2006: 10, 239–40).

In sum, then, *the success of political conditionality depends on (i) the conditional offer of EU membership to the target government; (ii) the normative consistency of the EU's enlargement decisions; and (iii) low political compliance costs of the target government.* This hypothesis is in line with the external incentives model of conditionality and Europeanization (Schimmelfennig and Sedelmeier 2005).

For the analysis of current EU political accession conditionality, it follows that the institutional status of the remaining European non-member states with the EU will be upgraded as they improve liberal democracy and that they will be allowed to join once they develop into consolidated democracies. Latecomers will not be discriminated against, but treated according to the same liberal-democratic standards as earlier applicants for membership. Accordingly, a slowdown or stop of EU institutional expansion would have to be attributed to a lack of normatively eligible non-member countries or high political costs of compliance for the target governments – and not to a change in EU policy. In order to see whether these expectations are correct, the first step is to establish the eligibility of non-member countries.

ELIGIBILITY OF NON-MEMBER COUNTRIES

Eligibility is defined by the enlargement rules of the EU. Countries that are both European and democratic and are not yet integrated into the EU are classified as eligible. An analysis of eligibility thus requires operationalizing 'Europe', 'democracy', and 'integration'.

The limits of 'Europe' have never been clearly set by the EU – at least not in the East. The participants of the European Neighbourhood Policy (ENP) can serve as a starting point for excluding countries unlikely to fit under the EU's current definition of Europe. First, considering the EU's 1987 rejection of Morocco's membership application on the grounds that Morocco was not a

European country, the ENP countries of Northern Africa and the Middle East can be excluded as a whole. Second, I disregard the three countries of the Caucasus, which were initially not even admitted to the ENP. This leaves us with Belarus, Ukraine, and Turkey as the easternmost countries of the EU's 'Europe'. For these countries, there is at least a debate in the EU about whether they belong to Europe and ought to have a membership perspective. Excluding finally those countries from the analysis that have decided against becoming members, although the EU would have accepted them long ago (Iceland, Norway, and Switzerland), leaves us with 21 European countries from 1990 or the year of their independence (see Appendix 1).

To measure democracy, I use the annual ratings of political rights and civil liberties by Freedom House.[2] Although this measure is not without methodological problems (Munck and Verkuilen 2002), it has three attractive features. First, Freedom House provides up-to-date ratings for all countries concerned, which is important for studying recent developments in EU political conditionality. This is not the case for other measures. Second, the combination of political rights and civil liberties in Freedom House scores comes conceptually close to the 'liberal democracy' in the EU's constitutive norms. Third, it provided a good fit for the EU's earlier eastern enlargement decisions (Schimmelfennig 2003: 99–108).

This still leaves the threshold problem open. Freedom House does not classify countries into democracies and non-democracies but into 'free', 'partly free', and 'not free' countries. Free countries score 2.5 or better on the Freedom House scale from 1 (best) to 7 (worst). 'Free' can be translated as 'liberal democracy' whereas the upper tier of 'partly free' countries represents electoral democracies.[3] For this study, I not only define 'free' European countries as eligible but also those with a score of 3, that is, electoral democracies on the verge of becoming liberal democracies. I thus give the benefit of the doubt regarding eligibility to the non-member countries and not to the EU.[4]

As to the integration threshold, the analysis focuses on two major events: the decision to open association negotiations (for Europe Agreements and for Stabilization and Association Agreements) and the decision to open accession negotiations. These are the main political enlargement decisions. It is in the run-up to these decisions, and ahead of the decision to open accession negotiations in particular, that the European Commission's reporting focuses on the political conditions and the member states enter into a general debate on the merits of a country as a future member of the Union. In sum, any European country that has a Freedom House rating of 3 and has not yet entered into association or accession negotiations with the EU is eligible.

Figure 1 shows the development of the number of eligible countries for association and accession.[5] The first finding is that of a saturation effect. Since the number of European countries is finite, with each start of association and accession negotiations the number of non-associated European countries and the number of European countries that have not yet started accession negotiations decrease unless new states become independent (see the dashed lines in Figure 1). Out of the 21 countries in the pool, only eight have not yet opened accession negotiations and only four have not yet opened association negotiations. This saturation effect has to be taken into account when analysing the number of eligible countries and EU policy. Even without a change in EU policy, the saturation effect necessarily results in a decrease of eligible countries and a slowdown of enlargement. In 2006, only Montenegro and Ukraine were left as eligible for association. In addition, Albania and Macedonia were eligible for opening accession negotiations.

The ratio of eligible countries to the pool of remaining European non-associated or non-member countries controls for the saturation effect (see Figure 2). Both figures reveal two waves of eligibility, which correspond to the two waves of democratization in the region. Association negotiations with the early democratizing countries (mainly the Central European and Baltic countries) ended in the mid-1990s; accession negotiations with these countries started in 1998 and 2000. As a result, the number of eligible countries decreased strongly. However, the second wave of revolution and reform (including countries such as Croatia, Serbia, Turkey, and Ukraine) has led to a new increase in eligibility. As Figure 2 shows, the ratio of countries eligible for association is currently similar to (and even slightly higher than at) the beginning of the eastern enlargement process. As to accession, the eligibility ratio is as high as before the 1997 decision to enlarge. That is, as far as the target countries and their state of democratization are concerned, the potential for further enlargement is in

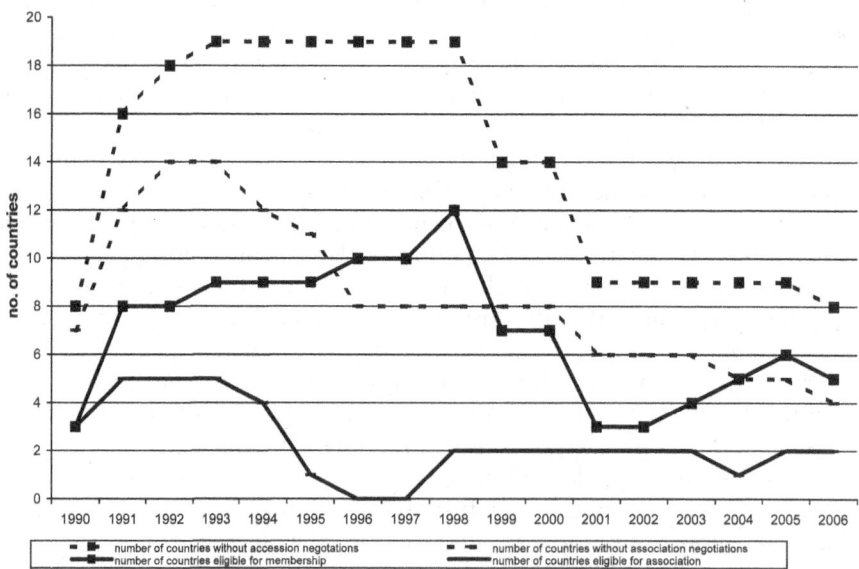

Figure 1 Eligible countries in EU enlargement

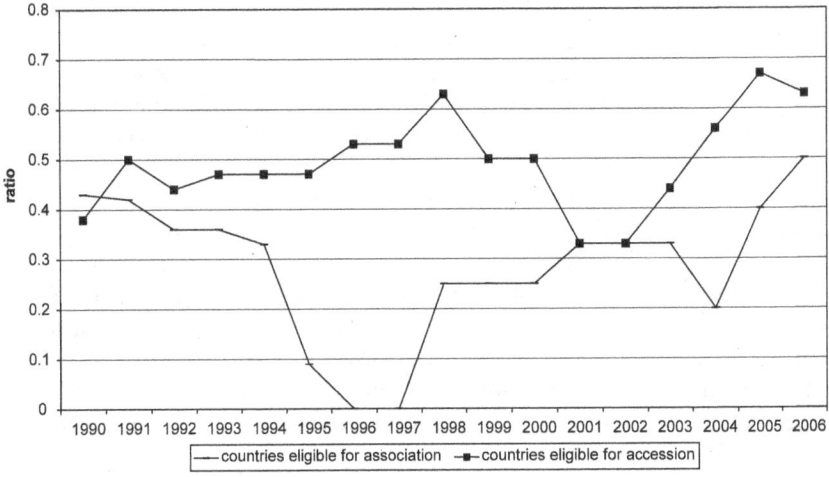

Figure 2 Eligibility ratios in EU enlargement

relative terms as high as in the 1990s. How has the EU then dealt with the second wave of eligible countries? Does it discriminate the latecomers in comparison with the frontrunners?

DISCRIMINATION IN EU POLITICAL ACCESSION CONDITIONALITY

In order to analyse discrimination, I will first specify a baseline model of non-discriminatory enlargement decisions. The main ingredient for this model is eligibility. In addition, a realistic assessment of discrimination needs to take into account the EU decision-making process. Once a country has crossed the threshold to democracy, the EU needs time to assess the political change and its stability, and to prepare the decision to start negotiations. Moreover, the EU has an established sequence of institutional relationships with third countries. That is, the start of accession negotiations is regularly preceded by some form of association agreement. In sum, in addition to a democracy threshold, the baseline model needs to specify a time lag.

There are two plausible ways of constructing the baseline model. Theoretical specification would start from the normative standards of the EU and theoretical considerations on the EU decision-making process. By contrast, empirical specification starts from how the EU has normally behaved in its enlargement decisions. Since the main goal of the analysis is to see whether the EU has changed its policy and treats recent applicants differently, empirical specification is advisable. However, while I did not introduce any restrictions for the length of the time lag, I stipulated that the democracy threshold not fall below the value of 3 according to the Freedom House scale. With this restriction, I optimized the baseline model so that it would result in the lowest number of discriminations possible. This 'best fit' model reflects average actual EU practice and permits us to detect those cases that deviate from normal behaviour.

The best fit resulted from a model using a Freedom House score of 3 and a time lag of two years between attaining this score and the opening of association negotiations and between the entry into force of association and the opening of accession negotiations.[6] Thus, if association negotiations start with a country scoring worse than 3 or earlier than two years after the country has achieved this rating, or if accession negotiations start earlier than two years after association, this is a case of positive discrimination. Alternatively, if a country has attained a Freedom House rating of 3 or better and is not invited to association negotiations two years later (or to accession negotiations two years after association), it is being negatively discriminated against. Figure 3 shows the number of discriminated countries relative to the number of European countries not yet participating in association or accession negotiations.

First, discrimination again mirrors the two waves of transition in Eastern Europe. Discrimination in association negotiations (lines 1 and 2 in Figure 3) was present for the first wave from 1990 to 1995 and for the second wave from 2000 onwards (with interruptions in 2002 and 2004). Discrimination in accession negotiations (lines 3 and 4) was followed by a five-year delay: first from 1996 to 1999 and then from 2005 onwards. Put positively: within five years, both positive and negative discrimination ended for the early democratizing countries in Eastern Europe. On the one hand, the EU stopped negative discrimination by inviting eligible countries (even if belatedly). On the

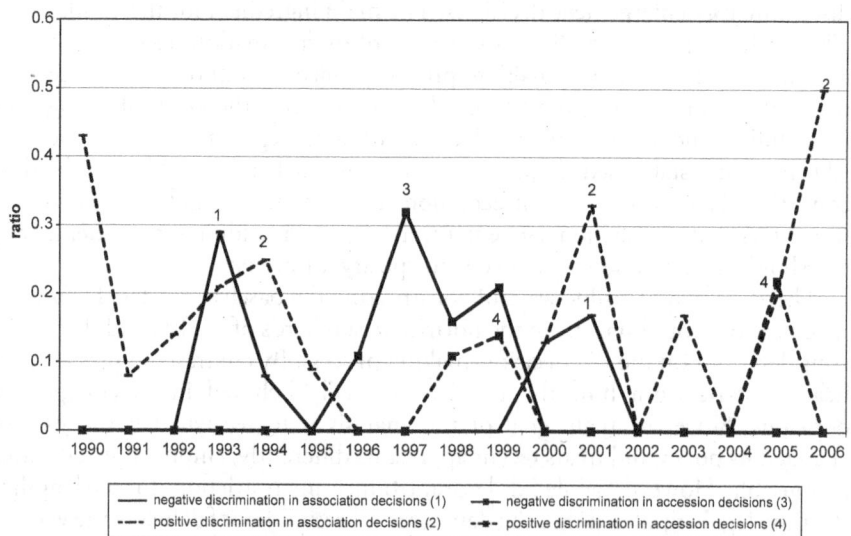

Figure 3 Discrimination in EU enlargement policy

other hand, countries that had been invited to association without meeting the standard further consolidated or stabilized democracy.[7]

Second, whereas positive discrimination was more widespread in the association process, negative discrimination has been more pronounced in accession. This can be explained by the higher costs of accession as compared to association, which made the member states more reluctant to open negotiations. Finally, it is striking that, according to the baseline model, there has not been any negative discrimination (the solid lines in Figure 3) against non-member countries after 2001. As far as accession negotiations are concerned, negative discrimination ended with the 1999 decision of the European Council in Helsinki to open accession negotiations with the remaining five associated Central and Eastern European countries. By contrast, positive discrimination (the dashed lines in Figure 3) visibly increased after 2001.

Thus, in contrast to what the current debate suggests, latecomers in the transition process have not been treated worse by the EU than the frontrunners. In 2006, Bosnia-Herzegovina and Montenegro were positively discriminated against, because association negotiations had been opened, although Bosnia-Herzegovina had not attained the democracy threshold and although Montenegro had just become independent. It would, however, be wrong to jump to the conclusion that latecomers are systematically given preference. The situation is similar to the early 1990s and the years after 2006 are likely to produce cases of negative discrimination again. Finally, even in the cases of positive discrimination, the EU has on average adhered to its democratic standards (operationalized here as a minimum rating of 3).

Table 1 EU enlargement decisions and democracy in the applicant countries

Year	Association negotiations	Association treaty	Accession negotiations	Accession treaty
1990	2			
1991		2		
1992	3.25			
1993		2.75	1	
1994	2.3			1
1995	1.5	1.8		
1996		1.5		
1997			1.4	
1999			1.7	
2000	3			
2001		3		
2003	3			1.35
2005	3		2.5	1.75
2006	3	3		
Average	2.6	2.3	1.5	1.3

These conclusions also follow from Table 1. It compares the mean Freedom House scores for those countries that started association or accession negotiations, or signed association or accession treaties, in a given year (1 is the best and 7 is the worst score). Whereas the table shows that the EU's democracy standards become, on average, more demanding as integration progresses from the opening of accession negotiations to the signing of the accession treaty, and that the EU has not gone below an average of 3, it also reveals that, in recent enlargement decisions, the EU has accepted countries whose average state of liberal democracy was lower than that of earlier candidates – with the exception of 1992. In sum, the analysis suggests so far that the EU's political accession conditionality has been normatively consistent on the whole. Positive and negative discrimination have only occurred temporarily and have not affected any particular country or group of countries in particular.

PROBLEMATIC CASES: CROATIA, SERBIA, TURKEY

How does this general analysis fit with the recent drawbacks in eastern enlargement: the postponement of accession negotiations with Croatia in 2005, the suspension of association negotiations with Serbia between 2006 and 2007, and the partial freezing of accession negotiations with Turkey in 2006? As shown above, these events cannot be attributed either to a worsening of the general state of democracy in the non-member countries (the Freedom House ratings remained unchanged) or to negative EU discrimination (the opening of accession negotiations with Turkey has even been a case of positive discrimination in comparison with general EU practice since 1990). I contend that the recent problems have to do with a particular set of EU conditions that are related to specific historical legacies of ethnic conflict in these countries and cause potentially high political costs to the target governments owing to nationalist mobilization.

The recent drawbacks are not directly related to democratic institutions, political rights, or civil liberties, and are therefore not captured by the general analysis. In the cases of Croatia and Serbia, the EU made the opening and continuation of negotiations conditional on the governments' co-operation with the ICTY to capture and extradite suspected war criminals: in particular Generals Gotovina (Croatia) and Mladic (Serbia). In the case of Turkey, the partial suspension of negotiations resulted from Ankara's refusal to implement the 2005 Additional Protocol to its association agreement with the EU, which would have extended the customs union to the Republic of Cyprus (RoC) and given ships and aircraft coming from Cyprus free access to Turkish ports and airports. To be sure, these conditions do not constitute a normative inconsistency as such: the recognition and equal treatment of all member states is a fundamental rule of the EU; in addition, coming to terms with war crimes has been a condition of intensified EU co-operation with the Western Balkans since the 'Regional Approach' of 1996, and can be justified as an important step toward democratic consolidation. Such problems simply did not exist in the countries that joined in 2004 and 2007.

What unites these issues is their high symbolic value for national identity and the fact that they potentially cause high domestic political costs to any government complying with EU demands. The generals are regarded as national heroes by many Croats and Serbs. Their indictment represents a challenge to the conviction that their nations fought a just war and were victims rather than perpetrators; extraditing them appeared tantamount to admitting war guilt. In Turkey, the recognition of the (Greek Cypriot) RoC is intricately linked to the fate of the Turkish community in the north of the island. In the Kemalist establishment, the 'Turkish Republic of Northern Cyprus' has traditionally been regarded as an indispensable part of the Turkish motherland. Unilateral concessions to the RoC are widely seen as a sellout of fellow Turks and essential Turkish national interests.

Among the new member states, a similar constellation existed in Estonia and Latvia, where the consolidation of democratic institutions went hand in hand for a long time with a refusal to heed the calls of international organizations to liberalize the naturalization and strengthen the rights of the 'Russian-speaking minority'. In particular, the public use of the Russian language still proved controversial when the EU had already committed itself to accession negotiations with the two Baltic countries and the promise of membership was thus highly credible. Yet, political costs for the target governments were high, too, because parliaments blocked compliance, passed laws in defiance of the international community, and threatened to withdraw their support from the government. In 1999, Latvian Prime Minister Kristopans even resigned over the conflict with parliament on the minority issue. In the end, however, these political costs could be overcome when the opening or closing of accession negotiations was imminent and if nationalist beliefs were balanced by a strong identification with the Western or European international community. Under this condition, governments or key players in government were ready to pay the price of short-term political losses in return for immediate and long-term gains (Schimmelfennig *et al.* 2006). How did these conditions play out in the cases of Croatia, Serbia, and Turkey?

Croatia

In December 2004, the European Council decided to open accession negotiations with Croatia in March 2005. The only remaining obstacle was full co-operation with the ICTY. In particular, the EU expected the Croatian government to assist the ICTY in arresting General Ante Gotovina. In March 2005, the EU followed ICTY Chief Prosecutor Carla Del Ponte in concluding that Croatia was not fully co-operating and postponed the opening of accession negotiations. Yet it also adopted a negotiating framework so that accession talks could begin as soon as full co-operation was established.

Thus, Croatia was in an endgame of highly credible political conditionality: the ultimate prize of accession negotiations was in reach; compliance on the national identity issue was the last remaining stumbling block; and the EU had demonstrated its resolve to sanction non-compliance. However, the extradition of Gotovina was a highly unpopular issue. Mass protests accompanied the demands of the EU. After the postponement of accession negotiations, more than 80 per cent of Croats continued to view Gotovina as a war hero rather than a criminal and opposed delivering him to The Hague. At the same time, support for EU membership fell to under 40 per cent after strong majorities in previous years.[8]

In addition, Croatia had been governed since 2003 by a minority coalition under the leadership of the Croatian Democratic Union (HDZ), the party that was ruling Croatia under the leadership of General Tudjman when General Gotovina committed the alleged war crimes. Although Prime Minister Ivo Sanader had rejuvenated the party during the opposition years from 2000 to 2003, distanced himself from the extreme nationalists, positioned the HDZ as a pro-European party of the centre-right, and thus paved the way to regaining power, co-operation with the ICTY and the EU on war crimes issues remained unpopular. Voicing the discontent, Branimir Glavas, who had been instrumental in securing the right-wing flank of the party up to the present, broke ranks with Sanader in May 2005. These developments reduced the popularity of the prime minister and his power base in the party and in parliament but did not directly threaten his political survival or that of his government. Political costs therefore remained moderate. Finally, identification with the West and the EU was strong in the government and in parliament. Sanader had modernized his party on a pro-European platform and declared EU and North Atlantic Treaty Organization (NATO) accession to be the top foreign policy goals of his term.

In October 2005, Gotovina was still at large, and so it came as a surprise when Del Ponte testified that Croatia was now fully co-operating with the ICTY, thereby opening the door to accession negotiations. Many observers initially suspected that the EU had exercised political pressure on Del Ponte or that the positive decision for Croatia was merely a concession to Austria in return for its acquiescence to opening accession negotiations with Turkey. However, after Gotovina was arrested in Tenerife in December 2005, it became clear that Del Ponte's positive assessment resulted from the fact that Gotovina had indeed already been located in October and that the Tribunal had received crucial information from the Croatian intelligence services. The postponement of accession negotiations demonstrated that the EU was serious about its preconditions and persuaded the government to comply with an unpopular demand in a constellation of strong identification with the EU, moderate costs to the government, and high incentives in close reach. In addition, the fact that Gotovina could be arrested outside of Croatia and did not have to be extradited by Croatian authorities reduced the domestic political pressure and costs significantly (Freyburg 2006). The Croatian case thus confirms the findings from the Baltic cases.

Serbia

The Serbian government was faced with the same unpopular EU demand. After complaints by Carla Del Ponte that Serbia's co-operation had deteriorated since the EU had opened stabilization and association talks in late 2005, the EU threatened to interrupt negotiations if Mladic was not arrested and extradited by the end of March 2006. New guarantees by the Serbian government persuaded the EU to give Serbia another deadline, but when Mladic was still at large at the beginning of May, the EU decided to suspend the Stabilization and Association Agreement (SAA) negotiations until Serbia co-operated fully with the ICTY.

The conditions of the Serbian case differ in several respects from those of the Croatian case. First, there were fewer incentives: the EU suspended association rather than accession talks. Although the SAA is an indispensable milestone on the way to membership, it was not the same endgame as in the case of Croatia and the Baltic countries. Second, in contrast to Prime Minister Sanader of Croatia, Serbian Prime Minister Vojislav Kostunica had not broken with traditional Serbian nationalism and continued to cater to the nationalist-conservative spectrum of the electorate. He denounced the ICTY as an anti-Serbian, 'American' court with doubtful legal standing and protested about the extradition of Milosevic to The Hague. Although he did not go as far as the Radical Party or the Socialist Party of former President Milosevic in advocating an anti-Western partnership with Russia, his identification with the EU has at best been neutral – a matter of perceived necessity rather than political belonging (Schimmelfennig et al. 2006: 89–90). Third, rather than establishing a democratic and Western-oriented coalition with the Democratic Party (DS) after the elections of 2004, Kostunica's Democratic Party of Serbia (DSS) chose to form a minority government, which was dependent on the backing of the Socialist Party in parliament. This considerably reduced Kostunica's room for manoeuvre in making concessions to the EU – even if he had been prepared to do so. Thus, the political costs of compliance can be considered high in terms of vote-seeking and coalition politics. In sum, the reduced incentives, the less positive identification with the West, and the higher political costs over-determine the difference in the Serbian and Croatian responses to EU conditionality.

Yet the change in government in 2007 helps to reduce the points for explanation. After almost three months of tough negotiations, the DSS finally agreed to form a government with the pro-reform and pro-EU DS and G17+ parties, in which Kostunica (DSS) would remain prime minister but cede control over the security services to President Boris Tadic (DS). The new coalition not only increased the identification of the government with the EU but also reduced the political costs of co-operating with the ICTY. It immediately strengthened its efforts to capture suspected war criminals, helped to arrest General Zdravko Tolimir (number three on the ICTY list after Karadzic and Mladic), and was praised by Carla Del Ponte. In mid-June, the SAA negotiations were resumed.

Turkey

On Cyprus, an uneasy last-minute compromise paved the way for opening accession negotiations with Turkey in 2005. On the one hand, Cyprus gave up its demand for early international recognition by Turkey. On the other hand, Turkey promised to implement the 'Additional Protocol' before the end of 2006. On 20 November 2006, the EU set a firm deadline to comply before the end of the month but Turkey continued to demand that the EU end the trade embargo against northern Cyprus at the same time. As a consequence, the Commission proposed freezing eight trade-related chapters and preventing any other chapters from being declared provisionally closed until Turkey lifted the restrictions against Cyprus. These sanctions were accepted by the member states in December 2006.

What are the conditions of political conditionality in the Turkish case? First, whereas the incentives were high – membership – the credibility of the punishment was lower than in the endgame of negotiations with Estonia, Latvia, and Croatia. Turkey had just secured the opening of accession negotiations, which were designed to last until 2014, and the sanctions did not preclude further progress in the negotiations altogether. Thus, there was no immediate pressure on Turkey to comply or lose everything. Moreover, opposition to full membership by key member states such as France and Germany reduced the credibility of the incentives. Under these conditions, short-term domestic political considerations could get in the way of compliance more easily than in endgames.

A strong identification with Europe is a core feature of modern Turkey. The Kemalist state élites have always considered themselves as Western and have regarded the West as their primary 'in-group' in international relations (Kubicek 1999: 159). The moderately Islamist Justice and Democracy Party (AKP), which came to power in 2002, had also broken with the traditional anti-Western identification of their predecessors and strove to become a democratic party with religious roots along the lines of Christian Democracy in the EU. There was equal consensus on the project of EU membership in the Kemalist élites and in the AKP. The high commitment of the élites was mirrored in Turkish society: during the run-up to the start of accession negotiations, approval rates of EU membership ranged from 60 to 80 per cent (Robins 2007: 292; Schimmelfennig et al. 2006: 100).

By contrast, the Turkish community of Cyprus was of less relevance to the new AKP government. The AKP had already advocated the reunification of the island in its 2001 party programme and regarded the issue mostly as a stumbling block to be removed from the path to EU membership (Robins 2007: 297; Schimmelfennig et al. 2006: 206). However, the rejection of the Annan peace plan by the Greek community ahead of the RoC's accession to the EU in 2004, and the attempts of the RoC to achieve a better deal for the Greek community from the position of strength as an EU member, have made concessions by the Turkish government hard to sell at home. The EU's insistence on the recognition of the RoC has contributed strongly to reducing popular support for membership in Turkey to less than 50 per cent in 2006. In the run-up to the parliamentary elections of 2007, the Erdogan government considered major concessions on the Cyprus issue too

Table 2 Conditions of compliance in Croatia, Serbia, Turkey

	Endgame	Political costs	Identification	Compliance
Estonia/Latvia	Yes	High	High	→ yes
Croatia	Yes	Low	High	→ yes
Serbia	No	Lower	Higher	→ better
Turkey	No	High	High	No

Note: Italics indicate conditions that changed and led to compliance.

risky, given that the situation did not require immediate action to secure the ultimate goal of EU membership.

In sum, these brief case studies largely confirm the conditions of compliance established in earlier studies, in which the EU demanded compliance on politically sensitive national identity issues (see Table 2). The case of Croatia closely mirrors the cases of Estonia and Latvia, in which governments that strongly identified with the European international community discounted high political costs in endgames of the opening or closing of accession negotiations. In addition, Croatian compliance was helped by the fact that the arrest of Gotovina outside Croatia reduced domestic costs. By contrast, the Turkish government was for a long time ahead of the next 'endgame' so that high political costs could not be balanced by immediate rewards. Finally, the case of Serbia shows that, in the absence of an endgame, political costs need to go down, and identification needs to increase, in order to improve compliance.

CONCLUSIONS

This article has analysed the consistency and effectiveness of EU political accession conditionality after the 2004 enlargement against the backdrop of apparent 'enlargement fatigue' among major member states and domestic obstacles in the remaining non-member countries. Starting from the proposition that political accession conditionality is based on a credible and normatively consistent commitment to rewarding the democratic consolidation of European countries with EU membership (and controlling for the ceiling effects of enlargement), the analysis found no decrease in, or negative discrimination of, eligible countries.

Rather, the recent troubles in the negotiations of the EU with Croatia, Serbia, and Turkey have been caused by EU conditions that are related to legacies of ethnic conflict and are likely to create significant political costs to the target governments because of their high relevance for national identity. It could be shown, however, that the conditions of compliance and effectiveness were the same as in earlier cases of political accession conditionality. Overall, the analysis emphasizes the relevance of credible and high EU incentives as well as political costs for the target governments, and thus confirms the core hypothesis of the external incentives model of political conditionality.

The policy conclusions are more ambivalent. The analysis certainly shows that the EU has continued its, by and large, consistent policy of political conditionality. Its effectiveness, however, is weakened by the legacy of ethnic conflict that bedevils most remaining eligible non-member countries and increases the domestic political costs of compliance with EU political conditionality. In order to maintain its impact on political reform under these conditions, the EU will need to reassure applicant governments even more convincingly of the credibility of its commitment to enlargement and move negotiations closer to the endgame. Creating uncertainty about admission even after full compliance, as in the case of the referendum on Turkish membership, destroys this credibility and will reduce the effectiveness of conditionality even further.

APPENDIX 1

	Start year	FH score of 3	Association negotiations (FH score)	Association treaty signed (FH score)	Association in force	Accession negotiations
Albania	1989	2002–	2003 (3)	2006 (3)		
Belarus	1991					
Bosnia-Herzegovina	1992		2005 (3.5)			
Bulgaria	1989	1991–	1992 (2.5)	1993 (2)	1995	2000
Croatia	1991	2000–	2000 (2.5)	2001 (2)	2005	2005
Czech Republic	1993	1993–	1993 (1.5)	1993 (1.5)	1995	1998
Czechoslovakia	1989–92	1990–	1990 (2)	1991 (2)		
Estonia	1991	1991–	1994 (2.5)	1995 (2)	1998	1998
Hungary	1989	1990–	1990 (2)	1991 (2)	1994	1998
Latvia	1991	1991–	1994 (2.5)	1995 (2)	1998	2000
Lithuania	1991	1991–	1994 (2)	1995 (1.5)	1998	2000
Macedonia	1992	1993, 1998–99, 2002–	2000 (3.5)	2001 (3.5)	2004	
Moldova	1991	1998–2001				
Montenegro	2006	2006	2006 (3)	2007		
Poland	1989	1990–	1990 (2)	1991 (2)	1994	1998
Romania	1989	1996–	1992 (4)	1993 (3.5)	1995	2000
Serbia (Yugoslavia)	1989	2001–	2005 (2.5)			
Slovakia	1993	1994–	1993 (3.5)	1993 (3.5)	1995	2000
Slovenia	1991	1991–	1995 (1.5)	1996 (1.5)	1998	1998
Turkey	1989	2004–	(1962)	(1963)	(1964)	2005
Ukraine	1991	2005–				

APPENDIX 2

	Association						Accession					
	Euro*	Elig.**	Ratio+	Neg. disc.++	Ratio	Pos. disc.†	Ratio	Euro	Elig.	Ratio	Neg. disc.	Ratio	Pos. disc.	Ratio
1990	7	3	0.43	0	0	3	0.43	8	3	0.38	0	0	0	0
1991	12	5	0.42	0	0	1	0.08	16	8	0.5	0	0	0	0
1992	14	5	0.36	0	0	2	0.14	18	8	0.44	0	0	0	0
1993	14	5	0.36	4	0.29	3	0.21	19	9	0.47	0	0	0	0
1994	12	4	0.33	1	0.08	3	0.25	19	9	0.47	0	0	0	0
1995	11	1	0.09	0	0	1	0.09	19	9	0.47	0	0	0	0
1996	8	0	0	0	0	0	0	19	10	0.53	2	0.11	0	0
1997	8	0	0	0	0	0	0	19	10	0.53	6	0.32	0	0
1998	8	2	0.25	0	0	0	0	19	12	0.63	3	0.16	2	0.11
1999	8	2	0.25	0	0	0	0	14	7	0.5	3	0.21	2	0.14
2000	8	2	0.25	1	0.13	1	0.13	14	7	0.5	0	0	0	0
2001	6	2	0.33	1	0.17	1	0.33	9	3	0.33	0	0	0	0
2002	6	2	0.33	0	0	0	0	9	3	0.33	0	0	0	0
2003	6	2	0.33	0	0	1	0.17	9	4	0.44	0	0	0	0
2004	5	1	0.2	0	0	0	0	9	5	0.56	0	0	0	0
2005	5	2	0.4	0	0	1	0.2	9	6	0.67	0	0	2	0.22
2006	4	2	0.5	0	0	2	0.5	8	5	0.63	0	0	0	0

*Number of European countries not yet associated or admitted.
**Number of European countries with Freedom House of 3 and higher, not yet associated or admitted.
+Ratio is always the value of the column to the left divided by the number of European countries not yet associated or admitted (*Euro*).
++Number of negatively discriminated countries.
†Number of positively discriminated countries.

NOTES

1 For an argument that the EU has indeed, by and large, abided by this consistency standard, see Schimmelfennig (2003).
2 The ratings can be downloaded from www.freedomhouse.org
3 See http://www.freedomhouse.org/template.cfm?page=351&ana_page]=298&year]=2006
4 See Appendix 1. I will also argue below that this threshold matches past EU enlargement policy best.
5 The raw data used for the figures in this section can be found in Appendix 2. Note that countries without association negotiations are a subset of the countries with no accession negotiations, and that the countries eligible for association are a subset of the countries eligible for membership.
6 See page 922 above for a justification for using the opening rather than the conclusion of negotiations. This specification produces 47 cases of discrimination in the period 1990–2006. Raising the threshold to 2.5 increases the number of positive discriminations and results in 55 cases overall. Reducing the time lag to one year increases the number of negative discriminations and results in 56 cases overall. Both changes at the same time (a threshold of 2.5 with a one-year lag) produce 54 cases of discrimination. The proportion of negative and positive discriminations (and between discriminations in association and in accession negotiations) remains roughly the same as for the best fit model.
7 In the case of accession negotiations, positive discrimination almost always resulted from shortening the assumed two-year waiting period after association and did not have anything to do with a lack of democratic consolidation.
8 'Western Balkans: Is There Life Outside the EU?', *RFE/RL*, 16 September 2005, available at http://www.rferl.org/featuresarticle/2005/09/0189A1B5-E9A4-469D-8AD6-1E876B5B572F.html; see also Roter and Bojinovic (2005: 451); Freyburg (2006).

REFERENCES

Commission (2006) 'Enlargement strategy and main challenges 2006–2007', COM(2006) 649 final, 8 November.
Epstein, R.A. and Sedelmeier, U. (2008) 'Beyond conditionality: international institutions in postcommunist Europe after enlargement', *Journal of European Public Policy* 15(6): 795–805.
Freyburg, T. (2006) 'Der EU mehr als dem Volk verpflichtet? Die Um- und Durchsetzung der politischen Beitrittskriterien am Beispiel Slowakei und Kroatien'. Paper, Graduate Student Conference, IR Section, German Political Science Association, Arnoldshain, May 2006.
Johnson, J. (2008) 'The remains of conditionality: the faltering enlargement of the euro zone', *Journal of European Public Policy* 15(6): 826–41.
Kelley, J. (2004) *Ethnic Politics in Europe. The Power of Norms and Size*, Princeton, NJ: Princeton University Press.
Kubicek, P. (1999) 'Turkish–European relations: at a new crossroads?', *Middle East Policy* 6(4): 157–73.
Kubicek, P. (ed.) (2003) *The European Union and Democratization*, London: Routledge.
Munck, G. and Verkuilen, J. (2002) 'Conceptualizing and measuring democracy. Evaluating alternative indices', *Comparative Political Studies* 35(1): 5–34.
Pridham, G. (2005) *Designing Democracy: EU Enlargement and Regime Change in Post-Communist Europe*, Basingstoke: Palgrave Macmillan.
Robins, P. (2007) 'Turkish foreign policy since 2002', *International Affairs* 83(2): 289–304.

Roter, P. and Bojinović, A. (2005) 'Croatia and the European Union: a troubled relationship', *Mediterranean Politics* 10(3): 447–54.

Schimmelfennig, F. (2003) *The EU, NATO and the Integration of Europe: Rules and Rhetoric*, Cambridge: Cambridge University Press.

Schimmelfennig, F. and Sedelmeier, U. (eds) (2005) *The Europeanization of Central and Eastern Europe*, Ithaca, NY: Cornell University Press.

Schimmelfennig, F., Engert, S. and Knobel, H. (2006) *International Socialization in Europe: European Organizations, Political Conditionality, and Democratic Change*, Basingstoke: Palgrave Macmillan.

Vachudova, M. (2005) *Europe Undivided. Democracy, Leverage, and Integration since 1989*, Oxford: Oxford University Press.

A governance perspective on the European neighbourhood policy: integration beyond conditionality?

Sandra Lavenex

INTRODUCTION

A few years after the launch of the European neighbourhood policy (ENP) in 2004, first analyses draw relatively bleak conclusions on its potential for promoting policy diffusion and more comprehensive political change in neighbouring countries. The main reason is that 'without the membership perspective, the NP countries may not be motivated to undertake domestic reforms' (Kelley 2006: 36, see also Schimmelfennig and Scholtz 2008; Smith 2005). Although prompted by the aim to find an alternative to European Union (EU) membership, the general set-up of the ENP has been very much influenced by the politics of eastern enlargement (Kelley 2006). Yet, it is evident that, without the prospect of membership, it lacks 'the Union's most successful foreign policy instrument' (Commission 2003: 5): accession conditionality.

What does the absence of the membership incentive mean for our assessment of the ENP and its external influence (see also Epstein and Sedelmeier 2008)? One option would be to concur that the ENP is doomed to failure, hence not very worthwhile studying. Alternatively, we propose a different way of conceiving of the ENP, its mechanisms and targets of influence. Opting for a governance perspective, this article argues that the ENP is less a traditional 'conditionality framework' or integrated foreign policy, with a clear hierarchy of goals, strategies, and instruments, but rather a roof over an expanding system of functional regional integration that moves at different speeds and with different dynamics in different policy fields. In particular, it will be shown that the emergence of more horizontal, process-oriented modes of network governance allows for hitherto under-investigated forms of flexible integration for non-member states. Shifting the focus from the ENP's 'macro-policy' to the level of sectoral 'meso-policies' (Sedelmeier 2007), EU influence is thus examined in terms of establishing sectoral governance networks as a basis for regulatory approximation and organizational inclusion of ENP countries.

In contrast to conventional approaches to EU influence that conceive of the EU as a foreign policy actor, the governance perspective takes a more structural, institutionalist view on the expansion of the boundaries of regional integration and the continuities and disruptions between internal policies and their external dimension. EU neighbourhood relations, and herewith EU influence, are viewed in terms of a process of gradual formal and informal 'horizontal institutionalization' (Schimmelfennig and Sedelmeier 2002: 503) or as the extensions of the EU's 'boundaries of order' beyond formal membership (Lavenex 2004: 684).

Combining insights from the newer governance literature with regime analytical approaches, this article argues that the opportunities for integrating ENP countries into EU regulatory structures depend on the presence of horizontal and inclusive modes of policy-making in the sector (in contrast to the hierarchical 'Community method' of integration) as well as on the issue-specific constellation of interdependence with the third country in question. In short, the theoretical model developed argues that network governance may extend to ENP countries where interests converge and enforcement problems are low. Echoing (neo)functionalist assumptions, this is most likely to be the case in technical areas of functional co-operation. Our case studies also show, however, that network governance is demanding. In particular, it presupposes a certain degree of decentralization, resources and civil society empowerment that cannot be taken for granted in ENP countries. In politicized or 'high politics', in contrast, we expect the EU to seek influence through more hierarchical means and the use of conditionality. However, in the absence of strong leverage, it may nevertheless resort to network governance by default. In both cases, when either the third country lacks governance capacity or when networks are being used to compensate for a lack of leverage, asymmetries of influence prevail, thereby contributing to a hegemonic picture of EU neighbourhood relations.

After a brief delimitation of the notion of governance and the characterization of the ENP's macro-institutional set-up, the article develops an analytical framework elucidating the conditions under which extended governance may take place in different policy sectors. The framework is then applied to three sectors representing different constellations of interdependence in terms of associated enforcement and distribution problems (air transport regulation, transboundary water management, immigration). We then conclude on the integrative potential of network governance in the ENP, its preconditions and its relationship with conditionality. The data used in this article include official documents plus agendas and minutes of relevant ENP sectoral subcommittees and other relevant policy networks, as well as 46 semi-structured interviews with EU and third-country representatives participating in these processes.

NETWORK GOVERNANCE AS AN ALTERNATIVE TO CONDITIONALITY

The notion of 'governance' has seen a fabulous spread in the social sciences; it has rapidly travelled from domestic politics to EU studies and, increasingly, EU external relations and international relations. The domestic sources of the term governance derive from its opposition to the notion of 'government' and reflect a broader transformation from the interventionist to the co-operative state (Jachtenfuchs 2001; Mayntz 2005). This transition finds its expression in the specific institutional modes through which governance is exerted, that is, its horizontal instead of hierarchical nature, its focus on process rather than output, the emphasis on voluntary instruments in contrast to legal obligations, and its inclusive character, providing open fora for the inclusion of stakeholders and, in many sectors, private actors. As pointed out by Renate Mayntz, a key characteristic of governance is the vanishing distinction between the subject and the object of political steering. In this context, the notion of network delineates the horizontal, participatory, flexible and inclusive structure of governance frameworks in contrast to the vertical, bureaucratic notion of hierarchical government.

In EU studies, this notion has been introduced to challenge the traditional 'Community model' or 'Monnet method' of integration. Whereas the latter is based on the supranational formulation of binding European Community (EC) law through the interaction between Commission, Council of Ministers and European Parliament, the governance literature underlines the importance of 'soft', weakly legalized forms of policy-making by alternative fora such as formal and informal policy networks and agencies (Héritier 2002; Tömmel 2007). The notion of the *acquis* is thus transformed: integration occurs no longer through law but rather through co-ordination.

More recently, the notion of governance has also been introduced to study EU external relations. Less than 'government', 'governance' is more than 'co-operation', as it implies a system of rules which exceeds the voluntarism implicit in the term co-operation (Lavenex 2004: 682). In extrapolating this concept from its domestic origins, however, the specificity of the notion of governance as a non-hierarchical mode of interaction *vis-à-vis* other forms of external interaction, such as the conditionality model mentioned above, has tended to be blurred.

In order to grasp this specificity this article distinguishes horizontal network governance from hierarchical policy transfer through conditionality. This distinction can be related to Michael Smith's differentiation of various boundaries of EU political order (Smith 1996), and in particular the relationship between what he calls the 'legal' and 'institutional' boundaries (see also Lavenex 2004). The legal (here: regulatory) boundary refers to the extension of the regulatory scope of EU rules or policies to non-member states, while the institutional (here: organizational) boundary refers to the inclusion of non-member states in EU policy-making organizations. Whereas it is true that under the Community model of hierarchical integration, institutional inclusion would be 'a synonym for full membership' (Filtenborg *et al.* 2002: 400), the advent of network governance and functional policy-making organizations has opened new opportunities for institutional inclusion below the level of the central legislative authorities.[1] In contrast to the conditional transfer of a predetermined legal *acquis*, which would only expand the EU's regulatory boundary, network governance, as a process-oriented mode of policy-making, amounts to a more structural mode of exerting influence since it allows in principle for the simultaneous extension of regulatory and organizational boundaries. Thereby, external governance becomes a form of extended governance or flexible horizontal integration. Table 1 summarizes the main characteristics of these two ideal-typical modes of external governance. We exclude from this typology traditional forms of loose intergovernmental co-operation and bargaining as a third mode of external reaction which, however, due to its low degree of institutionalization, does not qualify as governance.

Hierarchy describes a relationship of superiority and subordination in which one party unilaterally expands predetermined parts of its regulative boundary to the other without, however, allowing for the latter's participation in the determination of these obligations or organizational inclusion in the policy frameworks where these obligations are shaped. Although lacking the strong jurisdictional aspect inherent in national hierarchies, this constellation basically corresponds to the conditionality model that has been identified as the main mode of external governance in EU enlargement politics (e.g. Grabbe 2005; Schimmelfennig and Sedelmeier 2004). As observed by Dimitrova (2002) and Schimmelfennig and Sedelmeier (2004: 674), this model exhibits primarily characteristics associated with 'old governance' – or 'government'. It is hierarchical in the sense that it works through a vertical process of command – where the EU transfers predetermined, non-negotiable rules – and control, where the EU ensures compliance through regular monitoring mechanisms. The main actors involved are supranational ones and political, high-level representatives of the third country. Although essentially drawing on power asymmetries and the presence of incentives, this mode of interaction also presupposes high degrees of internal communitarization (that is, the existence of an *acquis* with strong supranational competences) and external institutionalization in EU–third-country relations, including monitoring mechanisms.

Table 1 Ideal-types of EU external governance

Modes of governance	Instruments	Mechanism	Actors	Boundary shift
Hierarchy	EC and EU law, precise requirements, conditionality, monitoring	Policy transfer	Supranational EU institutions and Council *vis-à-vis* 3rd country	Only regulatory boundary is shifted
Networks				
Information networks	Voluntary instruments, process-oriented: Data, information, best practices	Co-ordination	Multi-level and polycentric transgovernmental and transnational; including agencies, international organizations, public and private actors	Very moderate shift of regulatory and organizational boundary
Implementation networks	Like information networks + operational co-operation, capacity-building			Moderate shift of regulatory and organizational boundary
Regulation networks	Like information networks + adoption of benchmarks, common standards			Strong shift of regulatory and organizational boundary

A *network* constellation by contrast reflects the third basic form of societal organization beyond market and hierarchy. Theoretically, network governance beyond the EU consists in the simultaneous expansion of its regulatory and organizational boundary. The process-oriented, horizontal, voluntaristic and inclusionary attributes of network governance allow for the extension of norms and rules that goes along with participatory openness in decision-making processes and practices. The inclusiveness of governance arrangements further suggests that these will usually take on 'multi-level' structures that may involve not only national, but also subnational, supranational and international actors, as well as non-state ones (Héritier 2002: 3). The composition of networks may contribute to a depoliticization of co-operation since participating actors are experts and technocrats specialized within the issue area but not representing a country's national interests. By omitting the legislative arena and its institutions (the Council, Parliament and Commission), this mode of interaction opens the way for functionally specific forms of organization, such as agencies (e.g. the European Environmental Agency), co-ordinating bodies (e.g. Europol), or less formalized policy networks (e.g. the DABLAS Initiative, see below). Whereas the concrete competences and degree of autonomy of these various organizations vary strongly, the possibility for third countries to become members amounts to a shift of the organizational boundary of the EU system, even if only at a 'subordinate' or specialized level.

Drawing on Slaughter's work on transgovernmentalism (Slaughter 2004: 52ff.), we distinguish between three different functions of policy networks:[2]

(a) *Information networks* are set up to diffuse policy-relevant knowledge, best practices and ideas among the members.
(b) *Implementation networks* focus primarily on enhancing co-operation among national regulators to implement/enforce existing laws and rules – be they national, international, or European. These networks can complement more hierarchical modes of interaction when adding a more co-operative implementation structure to a unilateral decision-making one.
(c) *Regulatory networks* are the most powerful ones in terms of governance since they have an implicit or explicit legislative mandate and are geared at the formulation of common rules and standards in a given policy area. According to Slaughter, 'behind the facade of technical adjustments for improved coordination ... and uniformity of standards lie subtle adjustments' of national laws (Slaughter 2004: 59). In so far as they are inclusionary and voluntary, these networks represent the most advanced form of flexible sectoral integration in terms of shared governance.

From a governance perspective, 'EU influence' thus consists not primarily in leading third countries to adopt EU rules but rather in extending integration dynamics in the sense of creating joint regulatory structures. The questions that need to be answered are: (a) under what conditions network governance emerges – in contrast to hierarchical policy transfer, how this differs across sectors and countries; and (b) under what conditions policy networks really work as governance arrangements and how they relate to other modes of interaction – for example, become instrumentalized by supranational actors for more top-down forms of policy transfer. Before turning to this sectoral perspective, the next section specifies the ENP's macro-institutional set-up by contrasting it with enlargement policy. This will allow us to better identify both the commonalities and differences with the conditionality model.

THE ENP'S MACRO-INSTITUTIONAL SET-UP

Launched as a policy to avoid new dividing lines in Europe after the 2004 accessions, the ENP is usually compared with EU enlargement policy. The ENP's macro-policy contains both hierarchical elements, which are reminiscent of the enlargement approach, and more governance-oriented ones. In hierarchical terms, it requires legislative approximation, yet omits the terms 'harmonizatization' or 'adoption' of the EU *acquis*. It also includes monitoring mechanisms, yet political (the Commission's reporting and evaluation in the joint Association Councils) rather than juridical ones. Like enlargement, the ENP applies the notion of a conditional deepening of relations. This progressive approach is sustained by accompanying mechanisms first introduced in the accession process, Twinnings and the Commission's Technical Assistance Information Exchange Office (TAIEX). In contrast to enlargement, however, the application of conditionality is much less straightforward (Kelley 2006). Commitments anchored in the so-called Action Plans are jointly agreed rather than unilaterally imposed, reflecting the ENP countries' different degrees of interest in deeper association. The weaker regulatory scope of association and the ambiguous relationship to hierarchy and conditionality is complemented by the perspective for organizational participation in sectoral governance structures, including also Community Programmes and Agencies. While it is true that such participation is part of the conditional incentives offered in the ENP Action Plans, 'prerequisites for participating in activities of Community agencies' need not necessarily be 'approximation with the Community' but instead 'the establishment of relevant national institutions with sufficient capacities' (Commission 2006d: 3). Discussions within ENP subcommittees document a gradual approach towards co-operation with EU agencies and bodies which may start with individual projects and later lead to more formal co-operation agreements.[3] One can therefore conclude that as a macro-policy, the ENP is in principle more open to more horizontal, co-owned governance structures. How far this plays out in practice, however, must be analysed at the sectoral level within individual policy fields.

SECTORAL GOVERNANCE PATTERNS IN THE ENP

Since the ENP is a roof over a dense web of functional co-operation arrangements that have developed partly prior to, and only in loose co-ordination with, the macro-policy, the forms of interaction vary from sector to sector, with different inclusionary potentials. Under what conditions does network governance take place in the ENP within individual sectors? And to what extent does it allow for horizontal forms of flexible integration? Combining insights from the governance literature with regime theories of institutional design, this section presents an analytical approach to explaining the emergence and prevalence of different modes of external governance at the sectoral level, before we substantiate this framework in three policy fields.

Explaining external patterns of interaction

At the sectoral level, the ENP can be conceptualized as the external dimension of internal EU policies or as extended sectoral policy regimes. The external dimension will normally reflect the modes of interaction that dominate internal policy-making in this area; the extension of network governance presupposes the existence of such networks internally. Nevertheless, in the external dimension, problem constellations may take very different forms from within the EU and interaction is much less pre-structured by institutional norms, rules and routines. Approaches on institutional design and international regimes can give us some indications of the interplay between the constellation of collective action problems at the sectoral level and the functional requirements for problem-solving structures (Hasenclever *et al.* 1997; Koremenos *et al.* 2001; Zürn *et al.* 1990). According to this literature, two dimensions of given problem constellations influence the institutional choice of co-operative arrangements: enforcement and distribution problems. Enforcement problems refer to the strength of incentives to cheat on a given institutional arrangement. The greater the enforcement problems associated with a given solution, the 'stricter', that is more hierarchical and formal, the governance mode should be (Koremenos *et al.* 2001: 773ff.). Enforcement problems result from the partners' disagreement on the desirability of common rules because of conflicts of interests; this is typically the case for common pool resources, such as transboundary waters where the incentives to free-ride are strong. Such situations require clear rules and monitoring as well as enforcement mechanisms in order to secure compliance. There are, however, situations where the participating actors agree on the need for common arrangements, but favour different solutions. Such co-ordination problems usually need a lesser degree of formal institutionalization and may be governed by more informal, legally non-binding arrangements such as those described in the model of network governance.

A second, analytically distinct dimension of problem constellations is the distributive effects of co-operative arrangements (Martin and Simmons 1998: 745). A common source of such distributive effects are geographic factors, such as in the case of international rivers, the unequal benefits from co-operation covered by upstream and downstream countries, or in migration the relationship between sending, transit and receiving countries. In such situations, the institutional framework is demanding as it is difficult to find a commonly accepted solution. According to Koremenos *et al.* (2001: 775), distribution problems should have the opposite effect on governance arrangements: whereas difficult enforcement problems require strong institutions, difficult distribution problems should be easier to tackle with soft and more decentralized, process-oriented modes of governance that do not demand that the participants agree on specific substantive rules from the start.

While these approaches allow us to specify the intended mode of interaction owing to functional prerogatives, they do not account for a range of contextual institutional factors that are likely to intervene between the intended and actual form of co-operation. In particular, our study has identified two variables that may modify either hierarchical or network models of interaction. First, hierarchical arrangements require a strong degree of EU competence in the relevant policy area: they are based on the transfer of formal rules and require strict monitoring mechanisms as well as, in the absence of means for sanction, the possibility to entice compliance through positive incentives, that is, conditional rewards. This means that even in problem constellations in which enforcement and distributive issues motivate a stricter mode of hierarchical policy transfer, we may find the emergence of other forms of interaction by default. The EU might simply lack the necessary degree of competence, including a precise *acquis*, and resources, and hence turn to network governance because of a lack of alternatives. Our second set of intervening variables affects the network governance model of interaction. This mode of interaction requires a compatible 'governance capacity' on the part of the participating actors which falls in two dimensions. The active participation from stakeholders representing either specialized levels of public administration or relevant private actors presupposes a certain decentralization of decision-making structures and civil society empowerment that do not necessarily exist in ENP countries. Their participation involves also financial costs that can be prohibitive, either as contributions to the respective programmes/organizations or just for travel to the respective meetings. In addition, such policy networks are very much based on non-legal instruments such as processes of mutual learning and exchange of best practices, where influence relies on knowledge and expertise. Qualified personnel and compatible expertise are thus key to the principle of 'co-ownership'. In both cases, that is, when EU actors exploit or instrumentalize networks to compensate for lack of leverage, and when third countries lack the capacity to participate on equal footing, network governance becomes asymmetric, giving the EU a dominant position. Figure 1 summarizes this analytical model before we turn to the four sectoral case studies.

Summing up the main expectations of this model, network governance as a horizontal mode of partnership-oriented association should prevail in particular where enforcement problems are low. Echoing (neo)functionalist assumptions, this is most likely to be the case in technical areas of functional co-operation, such as transport policy. In contrast, in politicized and even securitized 'high politics' such as Justice and Home Affairs (JHA) we expect the EU to seek hierarchical means, and to rely on network governance 'by default' if it lacks the necessary means.

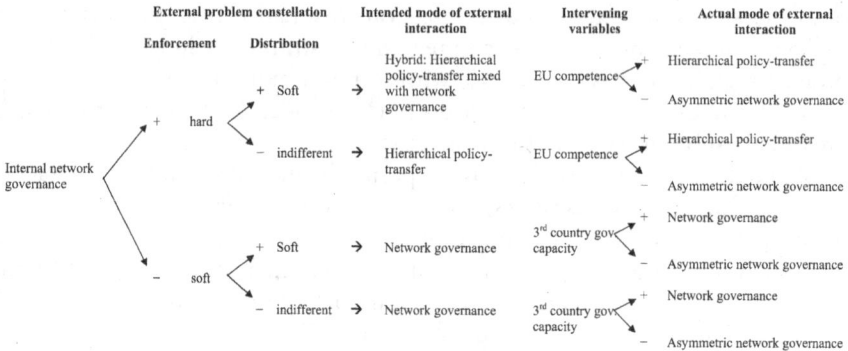

Figure 1 Analytical model of sectoral interaction frameworks

Policy networks in selected policy fields: participatory governance or policy transfer in disguise?

In this section, we review the advent and the operation of extended policy networks in three policy areas reflecting different internal modes of governance and different problem constellations. We start with two 'low politics' areas, where our theoretical model predicts higher chances of network governance, air transport regulation and transboundary waters management; and end with a politicized matter of 'high politics', immigration control.

Air transport regulation

In its White Paper on the European Transport Policy of 2001, the European Commission (2001: 98) announced the 'urgent need' for an external dimension to European air transport policy. In March 2005, it presented a Communication on external aviation relations, followed by the Conclusions of the Council of Transport Ministers. These texts set out an ambitious roadmap including developing the wider European Common Aviation Area by 2010 which will cover all neighbourhood countries of the EU. As a 'sectoral contribution to the Union's neighbourhood policy' this shall provide for 'the same market operation rules, not only from an economic point of view but also with regard to air traffic, security or air safety' in the EU and ENP countries (Commission 2005a: 8).

The regulatory landscape of European air transport consists of a complex web of bilateral agreements, the *acquis* and other pan-European regulatory organizations such as the European Civil Aviation Conference (ECAC), its associated Joint Aviation Authorities (JAA) and Eurocontrol which, since the so-called European Single Sky Initiative of 1999, are increasingly tied to the EU's aviation policy and its recently created European Aviation Safety Agency (EASA). These organizations operate mainly as networks of national civil aviation regulators; they may produce binding regulations (air transport control standards in the case of Eurocontrol, certification standards in the case of the JAA), but focus also very much on 'soft' information instruments such as the exchange of best practices and training.

Armenia, Moldova and Ukraine are members of all three organizations, including Eurocontrol. All other eastern ENP countries are candidates for the JAA and members of ECAC. Since Eurocontrol is a member of the EU's agency EASA, some of these countries already have a sort of indirect membership there. Furthermore, since EASA took over JAA functions in January 2007, those JAA members which are not EASA members have established liaison offices with the EU agency.[4] Thus, with the launch of the Single European Sky initiative, these pan-European organizations have come to play a central role in the realization and implementation of the wider European Common Aviation Area – and so also of central parts of the EU's *acquis* on market rules and aviation security. A key implementation instrument is the Single European Sky ATM Research (SESAR) project in which Eurocontrol has the lead and which proceeds in direct consultation with stakeholders, including industry and other civil society actors. To the South, the expansion of the EU's system of air traffic regulation operates through the conclusion of a new generation of Euro-Mediterranean air transport agreements such as the 'pilot' agreement concluded with Morocco at the end of 2006. Without offering the same organizational openings as to the European non-member states, this agreement provides for a significant extension of the EU's air transport *acquis*. It includes an extensive alignment of aviation legislation with key parts of the Community rules and regulations, including safety, economic regulation and in particular competition laws, air traffic management and consumer protection. A similar agreement is currently being negotiated with Ukraine.

To sum up, aviation transport regulation is a good case of technocratic, functionally oriented low politics expanding beyond the EU's borders. The extension of network governance is stronger to the East than to the South, given the possibility of involving pre-existing pan-European aviation organizations, while the regulatory extension moves in both directions. A first evaluation of the actual operation of governance shows that the 'public good' of aviation security bears more participatory, inclusive and horizontal co-operation structures than the aspects linked to market liberalization, where distributive questions come in. In this field, the EU *acquis* is more determinate and less open to joint co-ordination and hence extended governance carries more hierarchical traits. In both areas, the Commission states good progress on meeting the ENP's goals: 'Stricter security standards have been introduced, groundhandling services have been liberalized and most countries have established civil aviation authorities' (Commission 2006a: 5).

Transboundary water management
Transboundary water management is another area where the EU is actively promoting functional rather than territorial regulatory structures. This idea is embedded in the Water Framework Directive (WFD) of 2000. This is the first instrument of Community legislation to implement the principle that

regulations should not be organized along jurisdictions but along functional lines. The basis for this is the notion of integrated river basin management that creates functional 'competent authorities' charged with the implementation of the directive. The WFD also compels the member states to bind their neighbouring countries into these co-operative frameworks. The same principle was taken over for the EU's Marine Strategy, currently under consultation. The WFD is a good example of the connection between 'old' and 'new' modes in environmental governance. It combines legally binding standards with a special co-operative structure for their implementation that functions according to the pattern of network governance.

Inspired by the workings of the International Commission for the Protection of the Rhine, the European Commission has set up parallel structures first for the Danube and then for the Black Sea region (the so-called DABLAS process; see Lavenex and Stulberg 2007). With the Marine Strategy, the same model will be realized with the Mediterranean countries. In these Commissions, DG Environment often occupies a central position by providing the secretariat. The focus of activity is the implementation of the WFD, although the Black Sea Commission, for instance, did not include any EU member states until Romania's and Bulgaria's accession.[5] As laid down by the Commission in an ENP subcommittee meeting with Ukraine in 2006, the Marine Strategy will require each member state and third country within a marine region to develop marine strategies with a view to enhancing work within existing regional seas conventions. As in the DABLAS process, this will imply mechanisms of open co-ordination such as a detailed assessment of the state of the environment, a definition of what constitutes 'good environmental status' at regional level, and the establishment of clear environmental targets and monitoring programmes.[6]

In terms of regulatory and organizational boundaries, the institutional framework of the European Water Policy combines relatively open legal obligations with participatory, horizontal, inclusive regulatory networks involving competent authorities at different levels of government as well as non-governmental organizations (NGOs) and other private actors in the specification and implementation of these general obligations (see also Lenschow 2005). According to our analytical model, transboundary water management is characterized by strong enforcement problems given the character of rivers or common seas as 'common pool resources'. Whereas the model would hence suggest the recourse to more hierarchical instruments, the distributive aspects involved mitigate their effectiveness. In particular in countries with lower levels of ecological standards where adoption of the EU *acquis* would be prohibitively costly, the extension of EU governance is thus more effectively served through less strict, more process- and learning-oriented arrangements. Nevertheless, our interviews with participants in the DABLAS initiative show that a third country's capacity to shape the policy depends strongly on its level of expertise and resources to make innovative propositions. Whereas the Commission's ENP Progress Report states that Ukraine 'participates actively' in these networks (Commission 2006b: 15), other sources argue that Ukraine's influence is limited by the fact that these forms of co-operation require strong input from local staff, who lack funding and 'the necessary planning skills' (Economic Commission for Europe 2007: 61). For Moldova too, the Commission identifies the need to 'strengthen administrative implementation capacity' as a 'major challenge' (Commission 2006c: 13). Given the EU's leadership on these issues, and ENP countries' limited governance capacities, these networks thus develop asymmetric structures as fora for learning and capacity-building where the EU takes the lead.

Immigration control
The fight against irregular immigration has early on developed an external dimension and is characterized by a dominance of networking through intensive transgovernmentalism and operational co-operation (Lavenex and Wichmann 2009). Nevertheless, the strong asymmetry of interests between the EU's receiving countries and the would-be 'gate-keepers' at their borders entails strong enforcement and distribution problems that provoke the EU's attempt to use more hierarchical instruments. The most important hierarchical instrument has been the inclusion of conditional readmission clauses in the newer generation of Association Agreements. The conclusion of more comprehensive and binding readmission agreements has, however, met strong resistance. Whereas with Ukraine and Moldova, agreements could be negotiated in exchange for visa facilitations, the Mediterranean ENP countries have hitherto rejected any binding commitments, thereby forcing the EU to resort to alternative modes of interaction. In particular, EU member states have engaged in an 'informalization' strategy that focuses on a broader framework of co-operation based on administrative arrangements, bilateral deals and exchanges of letters and memoranda of understanding including operational co-operation (e.g. police co-operation, joint border operations) (Cassarino 2007).

In order to intensify contacts with ENP countries, the Commission has started to focus more strongly on established transgovernmental networks. To the East, this is the so-called Söderköping process that was launched in 2001 on a Swedish initiative and involves immigration officials from the would-be new member states and the Western newly independent states (NIS). Since 2004, the network has focused on transferring the experience of the newly acceded EU member states to the Western NIS 'in aligning their migration and asylum related legislation, policies and practices with the EU *acquis* standards' (Söderköping 2005: 1). In terms of our network typology, the Söderköping process can be seen as an information and implementation network implying also capacity-building. However, as the quotation and documents from ENP subcommittee meetings[7] show, the transfer of EU policies and practices is at the core. Other informal fora being increasingly mobilized are the Budapest process in eastern Europe and the informal 5 + 5 Ministerial western Mediterranean dialogue to the South. Recognizing the potential of such bottom-up, horizontal transgovernmental networks, Commission documents declare the aim of linking them more closely to ENP activities and, in particular, discussions in technical subcommittees (Commission 2005b).

Finally, operational network governance also occurs through 'projects' financed by the EU budget (e.g. the AENEAS and AGIS programmes in JHA) where member states, third countries or international organizations compete for tender. Such project-based networks often also involve, apart from member and non-member states, NGOs and international organizations. A closer look at their description shows that such projects are not void of policy transfer. For instance, with regard to trafficking in eastern Europe, Project JAI/2004/AGIS/031(15) foresees, next to the identification and exchange of best practices, the aim of 'uniform application of international/EU law and practices'. Networking has also started to figure more prominently in operational border politics, such as joint operations started under the co-ordination of the new European Border Agency Frontex. The Agency has concluded working arrangements with Russia and Ukraine, and informal contacts have been established with Morocco, Algeria, Egypt and Lebanon (Carrera 2007). Co-operation agreements with the EU's police office Europol have been envisaged with Israel, Moldova, Morocco and Ukraine.

Although immigration is one of the most politicized and controversial themes in the ENP, analysis of subcommittee documents and interviews with Commission officials show that influence exerted through deliberative networks need not be purely unidirectional. This is the case for the (hitherto mainly rhetorical) 'global approach' to immigration launched in 2005 that takes over some ideas first developed by Morocco and proclaims a pan-African strategy of immigration management (Kunz and Lavenex 2008).[8]

In sum, in JHA, transgovernmental networks play a crucial role. Whereas to the South, co-operation with Morocco has to some degree allowed for the development of a common initiative, the overarching tendency is to replicate EU policy transfer by 'softer', non-hierarchical means. Networks are promoted by default, because the EU lacks the competence and resources to act hierarchically and because of the strong enforcement and distribution problems involved. The hierarchy in networks is further facilitated by the lack of prior domestic legislation in these countries that could counter unilateral policy export. This turns an organizationally horizontal mode of governance into an instrument of policy transfer through the one-sided exchange of 'best practices', equipment and 'training'.

CONCLUSION

This article has argued that traditional rationalist, actor-based foreign policy approaches to the ENP that stress its weakness owing to the absence of accession conditionality may miss an essential part of EU external influence. Rather than a unified foreign policy with a clear hierarchy of goals, actors, strategies and instruments, the ENP may be conceptualized as a (loosely coupled) roof over expanding structures of sectoral, functional co-operation in Europe. This expansion of a sectoral co-operation structure has been made possible through a double flexibilization of the EU since the 1990s: an internal flexibilization of modes of governance, implying a shift away from the hierarchical Community Method of integration towards co-ordinative network governance; and an external flexibilization involving different forms of deep association towards neighbouring non-member states.

Combining insights from regime theory with a governance approach, this article's main interest was to see how far network governance opens opportunities for the horizontal inclusion of third countries into common regulatory frameworks, and how this relates to more hierarchical modes of governance by conditionality. We scrutinized this question on the basis of three case studies in policy fields posing different problem constellations to co-operation.

While keeping in mind the limited generalizability of three case studies, the expectation that we would find an extension of network governance especially in more technocratic and unpoliticized policy areas can be confirmed. Both in the areas of air transport and transboundary water management, ENP countries have been included in network models of governance which gives them a certain access to decision-making in the respective policy fields. In these cases, the shift of the EU's regulatory boundary implied in the ENP is accompanied by an opening of its organizational boundary; that is, the structures through which the regulations are produced. Our study, however, also identified structural limits to the extension of network governance to heterogeneous contexts. Third countries' ability to participate as equal partners depends very much on their governance capacity; that is, in particular the availability of competent personnel with a certain degree of independence from central government and the expertise to be proactive in the exchange of best practices and definition of benchmarks.[9] Furthermore, the extension of EU network governance works particularly well when it can be linked to ongoing co-operation within pre-existing intergovernmental organizations, such as Eurocontrol or JAA in aviation, the Black Sea Commission in environmental matters, or the Budapest and Söderköping processes in JHA. The fact that we find more common pan-European organizations including eastern neighbours than with southern Mediterranean states is one of the reasons why extended network governance is more pronounced to the East than to the South.

Apart from the question of governance capacity, more strategic sources of asymmetry were identified in JHA. In the case of immigration control, we could show that network governance has developed as a default option because of the inherent limits on the EU's capacity to act hierarchically. These limits stem from the partly intergovernmental structure of internal governance and the lack of resources to compensate for the distribution problems implied. In these cases, policy networks become alternative fora to seek unilateral policy transfer through 'softer' means. Nevertheless, the case of Morocco and the launch of the 'global approach' also show that, even in the case of strong EU pressure, influence must not remain unidirectional.

To conclude, extended network governance represents a hitherto neglected structural dimension of the ENP. Despite their theoretically integrative potential, the opening-up of policy networks to third countries does not necessarily mean the absence of hegemony. On the one hand, networks can be mobilized as alternative instruments of policy transfer, thus compensating for weaknesses of strategic conditionality. On the other hand, their participatory potential is currently hampered by heterogeneous political structures, unequal expertise and policy traditions in ENP countries. Nevertheless, these emerging webs of institutionalization indicate a revival of functional, sector-specific forms of organization in and around Europe, thereby pointing to the advent of flexible integration beyond formal EU membership.

NOTES

1 Although presenting his first neighbourhood initiative as 'everything but institutions', Romano Prodi had already argued in 2002 that this 'does not exclude the possibility of developing new structures with our neighbours at a later stage, if necessary. I am thinking of innovative concepts such as institutions co-owned by the partners' (Prodi 2002).
2 In order to avoid conceptual confusion with EU jargon, we slightly modify Slaughter's terminology and speak of implementation instead of enforcement networks and regulatory instead of harmonization networks.
3 See, e.g., minutes of the EU-Ukraine Subcommittee no. 4 'Energy, Transport, Environment and Nuclear Safety', 2006 and 2007.
4 Minutes of the first meeting of the EU-Ukraine Subcommittee no. 4 'Energy, Transport, Environment and Nuclear Safety', Kyiv, 31 May and 1 June 2006.
5 The members of the Black Sea Commission are Bulgaria, Georgia, Romania, Russia, Turkey and Ukraine.
6 See note 5, pages not numbered.
7 See, e.g., minutes of the fifth meeting of the EU-Moldova Subcommittee no. 3 'Customs, Cross-Border Cooperation, Money Laundering, Drugs, Illegal Immigration', Brussels, 21 October 2005, p. 5.
8 Morocco's input on this strategy can be retraced in the documents of the subcommittee meetings on 'social affairs and migration' as well as the recent 'JHA

subcommittee', and was confirmed in interviews with Commission officials, such as with Directorate General for Justice, Liberty and Security representatives on 17 April 2007 and 3 May 2007.
9 This finding echoes Kal Raustiala's critique of Anne-Marie Slaughter's praise of transgovernmentalism according to which, in asymmetric relations between 'Western' and 'non-Western' countries, horizontal networks quickly develop hierarchical traits (Raustiala 2002).

REFERENCES

Carrera, S. (2007) 'The EU border management strategy – FRONTEX and the challenge of irregular immigration to the Canary Islands', *CEPS Working Document* 261.
Cassarino, J.-P. (2007) 'Informalising readmission agreements in the EU neighbourhood', *International Spectator* 42(2): 179–96.
Dimitrova, A. (2002) 'Enlargement, institution-building and the EU's administrative capacity requirement', *West European Politics* 25(4): 171–90.
Economic Commission for Europe (2007) *Environmental Performance Reviews Ukraine*, second review, New York and Geneva: United Nations.
Epstein, R.A. and Sedelmeier, U. (2008) 'Beyond conditionality: international institutions in postcommunist Europe after enlargement', *Journal of European Public Policy* 15(6): 795–805.
European Commission (2001) White Paper, 'European Transport Policy for 2010: Time to Decide', COM(2001)370, 12 September 2001.
European Commission (2003) Wider Europe – Neighbourhood: A New Framework for Relations with our Eastern and Southern Neighbours, COM(2003)104, 13 March 2003.
European Commission (2005a) Developing the agenda for the Community's External Aviation Policy, COM(2005)79, 11 March 2005.
European Commission (2005b) Communication on Priority Actions for Responding to the Challenges of Migration: First Follow-up to Hampton Court, COM(2005)621, 30 November 2005.
European Commission (2006a) ENP Sectoral Progress Report, SEC(2006)1512/2, 4 December 2006.
European Commission (2006b) ENP Progress Report Ukraine, SEC(2006)1505/2, 4 December 2006.
European Commission (2006c) ENP Progress Report Moldova, SEC(2006)1506/2, 4 December 2006.
European Commission (2006d) Communication on the General Approach to Enable ENP Partner Countries to Participate in Community Agencies and Community Programmes, COM(2006)724, 4 December 2006.
Filtenborg, M.S., Gänzle, S. and Johansson, E. (2002) 'An alternative theoretical approach to EU foreign policy. "Network governance" and the case of the Northern Dimension Initiative', *Cooperation and Conflict* 37(4): 387–407.
Grabbe, H. (2005) *The EU's Transformative Power: Europeanization Through Conditionality in Central and Eastern Europe*, Basingstoke and New York: Palgrave Macmillan.
Hasenclever, A., Mayer, P. and Rittberger, V. (1997) *Theories of International Regimes*, Cambridge: Cambridge University Press.
Héritier, A. (2002) 'New modes of governance in Europe: policy-making without legislating?', in A. Héritier, (ed.), *Common Goods: Reinventing European and International Governance*, Lanham, MD.: Rowman & Littlefield. pp. 185–206.
Jachtenfuchs, M. (2001) 'The governance approach to European integration', *Journal of Common Market Studies* 39: 221–40.

Kelley, J. (2006) 'New wine in old wine skins: policy adaptation in the European neighbourhood policy', *Journal of Common Market Studies* 44(1): 29–55.

Koremenos, B. et al. (2001) 'The rational design of international institutions', *International Organization* 55(4): 761–99.

Kunz, R. and Lavenex, S. (2008) 'The migration–development nexus in EU external relations', *Journal of European Integration* 30(3): 439–57.

Lavenex, S. (2004) 'EU external governance in "Wider Europe"', *Journal of European Public Policy* 11(4): 680–700.

Lavenex, S. and Wichmann, N. (2009) 'The external governance of EU internal security', *Journal of European Integration*.

Lavenex, S., Lehmkuhl, D. and Wichmann, N. (2007) 'Die Nachbarschaftspolitiken der Europäischen Union: zwischen Hegemonie und erweiterter Governance', in I. Tömmel, (ed.), Die Europäische Union. Governance und Policy-Making, *PVS-Sonderheft* 40/2007: 367–88.

Lenschow, A. (2005) 'Environmental policy: contending dynamics of policy change', in H. Wallace, W. Wallace, and M. Pollack (eds), *Policy-Making in the European Union*, Oxford: Oxford University Press, pp. 305–27.

Martin, L.L. and Simmons, B.A. (1998) 'Theories and empirical studies of international institutions', *International Organization* 52(4): 729–57.

Mayntz, R. (2005) 'Governance Theory als fortentwickelte Steuerungstheorie?', in G. F. Schuppert, (ed.), *Governance-Forschung, Vergewisserung über Stand und Entwicklungslinien*, Baden-Baden: Nomos.

Prodi, R. (2002) 'A wider Europe – a proximity policy as the key to stability'. Speech at the Sixth ECSA World Conference in Brussels.

Raustiala, K. (2002) 'The architecture of international cooperation: transgovernmental networks and the future of international law', *Virginia Journal of International Law* 43(1): 1–92.

Schimmelfennig, F. and Scholtz, H. (2008) 'EU democracy promotion in the European neighborhood. Political conditionality, economic development and transnational exchange', *European Union Politics* 9(2): 187–215.

Schimmelfennig, F. and Sedelmeier, U. (2002) 'Theorizing EU enlargement: research focus, hypotheses, and the state of research', *Journal of European Public Policy* 9(4): 500–28.

Schimmelfennig, F. and Sedelmeier, U. (2004) 'Governance by conditionality: EU rule transfer to the candidate countries of Central and Eastern Europe', *Journal of European Public Policy* 11(4): 661–79.

Sedelmeier, U. (2007) 'The European neighbourhood policy: a comment on theory and policy', in K. Weber, M. Smith and M. Baun (eds), *Governing Europe's Neighbourhood*, Manchester: Manchester University Press, pp. 195–208.

Slaughter, A.-M. (2004) *A New World Order*, Princeton: Princeton University Press.

Smith, K.E. (2005) 'The outsiders: the European neighbourhood policy', *International Affairs* 81: 757–73.

Smith, M. (1996) 'The European Union and a changing Europe: establishing the boundaries of order', *Journal of Common Market Studies* 34(1): 5–28.

Söderköping process (2005) 'Roadmap of the Söderköping process'.

Tömmel, I. (ed.) (2007) Die Europäische Union. Governance und Policy-Making, *PVS-Sonderheft* 40/2007.

Zürn, M., Wolf, K. and Efinger, M. (1990) 'Problemfelder und Situationsstrukturen in der Analyse internationaler Politik. Eine Brücke zwischen den Polen', in V. Rittberger, (ed.), Theorien der internationalen Beziehungen, *PVS-Sonderheft* 21: 151–74.

Index

Page numbers in *Italics* represent tables. Page numbers in **Bold** represent figures.

accession: close to 76-80; conditionality 143; eligibility ratio 128-9; progress towards 52
acquis communautaire: EU's 2-3, 32
acquis legislation: imposition of 119
active leverage 32
adapting: key mechanism of 69-70
Additional Protocol 136; in (2005) 132
adjustment costs 13-14
administrative capacity limitations 14-15
air transport regulation 152-3
analytical model of sectoral interaction frameworks **152**
Attack party: Bulgarian 79

Baltic states: commitment to the Euro 42-3
bank privatization 95; conflicts over 97; foreign participation in 89
banking: domestic ownership in 88; protection of domestic ownership in 95
banking reform 92
banking sectors: protection from foreign control 85-6
Barr, N. 112
baseline model of: discrimination 129-30
behaviour values: socialization of new 60
beyond conditionality 1-10, 100, 108
Birdsall, N. 111
Bockman, J. 89
breaching the: Stability and Growth Pact 43
Bretton Woods conditionality 91
Brooks, S. 110
Bruncko, M. 114
Budapest process 155
Bulgaria: Socialist Party 75
Bulgaria and Romania: communist parties 75
Bulgarian: Attack party 79

campaigns of: persuasion 118
candidate countries: EU 4-5
capacity-building: legislative 25-6
case of: Czech Republic 74
CEE investment openness: influences on 87
Central and Eastern Europe (CEE) 85; pension privatization in 105-22

centrist-gal ex-communist party 73
changes in: party positions 71
changing to a funded pension system 109
Chapel Hill: dataset on party positions 80
Chile: pension privatization 105-6
civil aviation authorities 153
co-operative arrangements: distributive effects of 150-1
co-ordination problems 150
Cohen, B. 43
commission infringement decisions (2005-07) **19**
commitment to the Euro: Baltic States 42-3
communism: legacies of 14; opposition to 72-3
communist parties: Bulgaria and Romania 75; reform of 73
Communist Party of Bohemia and Moravia (KSČM) and Czech Civic Democratic Party (ODS) 74
compatible 'governance capacity' 151
competitiveness pressures 118
complaints of: Infringements 23-4
compliance: conditions of 137; domestic costs of 2
compliance research: EU 13
compliance with EU law 2
components of 'democratic conditionality' 50
concept of conditionality 50
conceptual challenges in conditionality 49-51
conditional membership incentive: dominance of 16
conditionality: accession 143; after the 2004 enlargement 124-42; as a construct 50; beyond 100, 108; concept of 50; conceptual challenges in 49-51; Europeanization 107-8; hierarchical policy transfer through 146; Maastricht conditions 32; network governance an alternative to 145-9; pre-accession 1-9; socialization effects of 61; straightforward 68-9; the laggards 38-42
conditionality hypothesis: expectations of 3-9; incentive-based 2

conditions of compliance in Croatia: Serbia; Turkey 137
conflicts over: Bank privatization 97
construction of the EU's minority condition 51-3
continuation of conditionality 3-4
Copenhagen criterion 32, 48, 50-1, 51-2
Council of Europe 61
credibility hypothesis 95, 96
credibility and status: discontinuity 91-7
credible commitment mechanism 69
Croatia 133-4
currencies, fixed 37
Curtin, D. 14-15
Cyprus 135-6
Czech Civic Democratic Party (ODS) 71, 74, 79: and Communist Party of Bohemia and Moravia (KSCM) 74
Czech Republic 35; case of 74

DABLAS process 154
data: early stages of 22-3; effect of transition periods 23; short observation period of 22; time lag of 22
democracy measurement of Freedom House 127
democratic conditionality: components of 50; study of 48
demographic aging 109
demographic crisis: pension privatization and 109
demographic and economic factors 108
difference between Poland and Romania 98
discontinuity: hypothesis 91-3; status and credibility 91-7
discontinuity in Ukraine 99
discontinuity of sectors and regimes 88
discrimination: baseline model of 129-30; negative 131; positive 131
discrimination in EU enlargement policy 130
discrimination in EU political accession conditionality 129-32
distributive effects of co-operative arrangements 150-1
Dlouhy, V. 117
domestic political factors 109
domestic adjustment costs 5
domestic compliance mechanism in the EU8 23-4
domestic costs of compliance 2
domestic ownership in banking 88
domestic politics: measuring the EU's effect against 58-60

domestic susceptibility 87
dominance of conditional membership incentive 16
dynamics of pension privatization 117-19
Dyson, K. 35, 40

eastern problem: new members 13-16; unfounded 27
echoing (neo)functionalist assumptions 151-2
economic and demographic factors 108-9
eligibility of non-member countries 126-9
eligibility ratios in EU enlargement 129
eligible countries in EU enlargement 128
enforcement approach 13
enforcement problems 150
enlargement: EU 7; mechanisms of influence after 7-8
enlargement of the euro zone 31-46
ERM II 37-8, 42-3; opposition to 38-9
ERM II entry 33
Estonia: Language Law 58; Latvia 49
Estonia and Latvia: OSCE missions in 58; reports on 53-4
ethnic divide 59
EU: candidate countries 4-5; commitment to enlargement 138; compliance research 13; eastern enlargement of 11; enlargement 7; incentives of the 9; out-liberalizing 115-17; political leverage of 61
EU accession and pension privatization 115-16
EU compatible agenda: adoption of 67
EU conditionality: politics of 47-65
EU conditionality criticism of 11
EU effect 50
EU enlargement decisions and democracy in the applicant countries *131*
EU enlargement policy 124-5
EU enlargement politics 146
EU impact on party positions 74
EU influence 144
EU law: breaching 12; compliance with 2; post-accession compliance with 11
EU legislation: transposition of 16-17
EU leverage 73; effects of 77; impact on political parties 73; influence of 75
EU neighbourhood relations 144
EU support 113-15
EU8: domestic compliance mechanism 23-4; performance of 18-19
euro: adoption of 37; public attitude towards 36; staggering towards the 42-3

euro zone 31; enlargement of the 31-46; membership of 32; negative economic effects of 38; states problems 42
euro-philes and euro-skeptics 33-8
euro-skepticism 32, 41
Eurocontrol 153
European air transport: regulatory landscape of 152-3
European Border Agency Frontex 156
European Central Bank (ECB) 39-40, 41
European Common Aviation Area 153
European Court of Justice (ECJ) 3
European monetary system (ERM II) 32
European neighbourhood policy 5, 143-60
European Union's (EU's): membership conditionality 1
Europeanization and conditionality 107-8
Euroskeptic: left-tan quadrant 73; parties 73
EU's: *'acquis communautaire'* 2; acquis communitaire 32; minority condition 47-8
EU's effects against its benchmarks 54-8
EU's pre-accession process: stabilization effect of 76
exchange rate: policies 37; regimes 36
expectations of conditionality hypothesis 3-9
explanations for: pension privatization 105; post-accession compliance 25-7
Extended Fund Facility (1993) 96
external patterns of interaction 150-2
extradition of Milosevic 135
extremist parties, exclusion of 73-4
Eyal, G. 89

F.A. Hayek Foundation 111
FCNM 56-60; monitoring under 57, *see also* Framework Convention
Ferge, Z. 112
Fico, R. 37-8
finance: internationalization of 87; outcomes 97
financial crisis 43; effects of 89-90
financial market: fully integrated 85
Financial Services Action Plan 90
fixed currencies 37
foreign investors: seeking 89
foreign participation in bank privatization 89
foreign and state ownership in selected industrialized and postcomunist banking sectors (2002) *86*
Framework Convention: Latvia ratification of 56; for the Protection of National Minorities (FCNM) 49

Freedom House rating 130
Frunda, G. 57
fully integrated financial market 85
functionalist assumptions: echoing 151-2
fund management 106
fundamental political principles 125-6
funded pension system 109

General Gotovina 134
generals, indictment of 133
Gonzalez-Paramo, J.M. 40
governance: network models of 157
'governance capacity', compatible 151
governance patterns: sectoral 149-56
Groetz, K. 13

hierarchical arrangements, requirements of 151
hierarchical policy transfer through conditionality 146
hierarchy 146
horizontal network governance 146
Hungarian: banks investment in 96; Democratic Forum (HDF) 73
Hungary 35
Hungary and Poland: party shifts in 77; status hypothesis 94
HZDS party (Vladamír Mečiar's Movement for a Democratic Slovakia) 75, 76, 77, 79

ideal-types of EU external governance 147
illiberal: democracies; EU requirements in 69; pattern states 70; rule implications of 75; to liberal party systems 75-6
IMF Standby Agreements (1995) 96
immigration control 155
impact of EU leverage: on political parties 73
imposition of: *acquis legislation* 119
incentive structure: mechanism of pre-accession rule transfer 15-16
incentive-based conditionality hypothesis 2
incentive-driven rule transfer 15-16
incentive-induced pre-accession compliance 27
incentives of the EU 9
inflation rates 40
influence of international institutions 6
infringement data: resulting research question 24; value of 21-2
infringements: complaints of 23-4; settlement of 19-21
infringements of directives after 1 May (2004) *20*

infringements in the EU8 compared to earlier enlargements 22
infringements of EU legislation 16-19
integration capacity 124
integration threshold 127
interaction, external patterns of 150-2
interest rates 32
International Criminal Tribunal for the former Yugoslavia (ICTY) 124
international institutions: influence of 6; postcommunist Europe 1-10
International Monetary Fund (IMF) 1, 35, 42, 87, 94, 95, 113; Polish bank bail-out 91; Standby Agreements (1995, 1996) 96
internationalization of bank ownership 100-1; finance 87
internationalizing pressure 87
investment in Hungarian banks 96
Islamist: Justice and Democracy Party 136

Jacoby, W. 13-14
James, E. 111
joint regulatory structures, creation of 148-9
Juhasz, G. 112
Justice and Democracy Party, Islamist 136

Kelley, J. 51, 108, 126
key mechanism of adapting 69-70
Koremenos, B. 150-1
Kovalcik, B. 109
KSČM, *see* Communist Party of Bohemia and Moravia

labour mobility 55
Language Law: Estonia 58; Latvia 55-6
Latvia 54-8; Estonia 49; Language Law 55-6; minority-oriented deputies 59
Latvia ratification of Framework Convention 56
legacies of: communism 14; pre-accession conditionality 12-13
legacy of conditionality: legislative capacity and socialization 25-7
legal codes, restructuring 32
legislation, minority-sensitive 50
legislative capacity-building 25-6
legislative capacity and socialization, legacy of conditionality 25-7
liberal trajectory, party systems on a 71-4
limits of Europe 126
Lithuania 26
long-term perspective of post-accession phase 9

Maastricht: conditions; interpretation of 43; criteria 31-3, 35
Maastricht Treaty 32; opt-outs from 41
macro-institutional set-up 149
Mayntz, R. 145
measuring the EU's effect against domestic politics 58-60
mechanism of pre-accession rule transfer 15-16
mechanisms of influence after enlargement 7-8
mechanisms that shape party positions 68-71
membership conditionality, European Union's (EU's) 1
Milosevic, extradition of 135
Ministerial western Mediterranean dialogue 155
minorities of Russophones 53
minority condition: construction of 51-3; EU's 47-8; politics of 53-60; regular reports 52
minority protection, norm of 50-1
minority-sensitive legislation 50
mixed reforms 106-7
Mladic 132, 135
mobilization, post-communist societal 14
modification of restrictive citizenship laws 53
monitoring under FCNM 57
monitory progress towards accession 52
Monnet method of integration 145
Moravcsik, A. 108
MSZP (Hungarian Socialists) 73, 94: Orban, V. 77
multi-pillar pension model 112

national identity and statehood 5
national minorities: politicized definition of 57; protection of 47-65
national minority, definition of 56
nationalist discourse of radical *tan* parties 79
negative Discrimination 131
network constellation 148
network governance 144; an alternative to conditionality 145-9
network models of governance 157
new EU Members' convergence status *34*
new member states: post-conditionality compliance 3-4
new members: eastern problem 13-16; pre-accession alignment compliance conditions 13-16

Index

Nokia 116
non-member countries, eligibility of 126-9
normative consistency 95

ODS, *see* Czech Civic Democratic Party
O'Dwyer, C. 109
Ooik, R. 14-15
operational network governance 155-6
opposition to communism 72-3
opt-outs from Maastricht Treaty 41
Orange Revolution: Ukraine 99
Orban, V.: MSZP (Hungarian Socialists) 77
Orenstein, M. 118
Organization for Security and Co-operation in Europe (OSCE) 48, 49, 52, 53, 54, 57, 58, 117
OSCE missions in Estonia and Latvia 58
out-liberalization 105
out-liberalizing the EU 115-17

parallel reforms 106-7
party positions: changes in 71; mechanisms that shape 68-71
party systems: evolution of 67; illiberal to liberal 75-6
party systems on a liberal trajectory 71-4
party turnover 93
party turnover in Romania and Slovenia 94
pension model multi-pillar 112
pension privatization 105-7; adoption of 106; Central and Eastern Europe 105-22; Chile 105-6; demographic crisis 109; dynamics of 117-19; EU accession and 115-16; explanation of 107-15; explanations for 105
Pinera, J. 111
Poland 35; bank privatization in 91
Poland and Hungary: party shifts in 77; status hypothesis 94
Poland and Romania, difference between 98
policies, exchange rates 37
policy competition 118
policy networks 152-6
Polish Law and Justice Party (PiS) 77, 79, 80
political accession conditionality: discrimination in 129-32
political conditionality: conditions of success 125-6; rules of 4
political factors, domestic 109
political leverage of: EU 61
political parties: agendas of 67-8; changing positions of 71; effect of EU

conditionality on 80; impact of EU leverage 73; positional shift of 80-1
political parties before and after accession 67-84
political principles, fundamental 125-6
politicized: civil service 14
politicized definition of: national minorities 57
Politics of: EU conditionality 47-65; minority condition 53-60
polarization of ethnic divide 59
positive discrimination 131
post-accession compliance, explanations for 25-7
post-accession compliance with EU law 11
post-accession phase, long-term perspective of 9
post-accession sanctions, threat of 25
post-communist societal mobilization 14
post-conditionality compliance, new member states 3-4
postcommunist Europe, international institutions in 1-10
pre-accession alignment compliance conditions, new members 13-16
pre-accession compliance, incentive-induced 27
pre-accession conditionality: legacies of 12-13; success factors of 126; success of 12
pre-accession rule transfer, mechanism of 15-16
privatization as condition of World Bank and IMF support 98
problematic cases: Croatia; Serbia; Turkey 132-7
problems of West European pension systems 114
process-tracing 50-1
protection of domestic ownership in banking 95
protection of national minorities' 47-65
public attitude towards Euro 36

radical *tan* parties, nationalist discourse of 79
readmission agreements 155
Reasoned Opinions and ECJ referrals 18-20
Regime, and sectoral discontinuity 99
regional approach 132
regular reports 52; minority condition 52
regulatory landscape of European air transport 152-3

regulatory networks 154
reliability of data and findings 21-4
reports on Estonia and Latvia 53-4
restrictive citizenship laws, modification of 53
restructuring legal codes 32
Romania, bank privatization in 92
Romania and Bulgaria: Communist parties 75
Romania and Poland, difference between 98
Romania and Slovenia, party turnover 94
Romanian Party of Social Democracy 75
Romanian price liberalization 92
rule transfer, incentive-driven 15-16
rules not subject to EU conditionality 4
rules of political conditionality 4
Russophones 59; minorities of 53, 55-8
Rutkowski, M. 112

Sanader, I. 134
Sanction, instruments of 15
saturation effect 127
Schengen rules 3
Schimmelfennig, F. 51, 126
sectoral governance patterns 149-56
sectoral and regime discontinuity, Hungary 99
sectors and regimes, discontinuity of 88
Sedelmeier, U. 51
seeking foreign investors 89
Serbia 134-5
settlement of infringements 19-21
shaming strategies 27
Single European Sky initiative 153
Slaughter, A. 148
Slovakia: EU membership of 37-8; nationalist-populist party 75; Slovenia 35; World Bank support for 115
Slovenia 36; banking sector in 99-100; Slovakia 35; transition of 92-3
Slovenia and Romania, party turnover 94
social context in conditionality: finance in postcommunist Europe 85-103
social learning 110
socialization 26-7; effects of conditionality 61; new behaviour values 60
Söderköping process 155
source of detected infringements 24
sources of asymmetry 157
Stability and Growth Pact, breaching the 43
statehood, national identity and 5
status and credibility, discontinuity 91-7
status hypothesis 93-5; Poland and Hungary 94; Ukraine 95

straightforward conditionality 68-9
structure of party competition and support for European integration: nine post-communist EU candidate states (2002) **68**
structure of party competition and support for European integration (2002) **72**, **78**
study of democratic conditionality 48
subordinated status of normative consistency, domestic actors' 88
subsequent actions after receiving a Reasoned Opinion **20**
substitutive reforms 106-7
success factors of political conditionality 126
success of pre-accession conditionality 12
Summers, L. 111
support: USAID 112-13; World Bank 112-13

threat of post-accession sanctions 25
towards the Euro 42-3
transboundary water management 153-5
transnational policy campaign 110
transposition of EU legislation 16-17
transposition rates in the enlarged EU EU25 17
Trichet, J. 39
Tuma, Z. 38-9
Turkey 135-7
Twinning Arrangements 91
types of pension privatization worldwide *107*

Ukraine: discontinuity in 99; Orange Revolution 99; status hypothesis 95
United States Agency for International Development (USAID) 105, 111; support 112

Vachudova, M. 108, 117

war criminals 132
war criminals 2005: additional protocol 132
Water Framework Directive 153-4
water management, transboundary 153-5
West European pension systems, problems of 114
Weyland, K. 110
window system 54
World Bank 87, 105; and IMF support privatization as condition of 98; report *Averting the Old Age Crisis* 111-12; support 112-13; support for Slovakia 115

ZUS 112